Immigrant-Survivors

Immigrant-Survivors

Post-Holocaust Consciousness in Recent Jewish American Fiction

by Dorothy Seidman Bilik

Wesleyan University Press
Middletown, Connecticut

Library of Congress Cataloging in Publication Data

Bilik, Dorothy.
  Immigrant-survivors.

  Bibliography: p.
  Includes index.
  1. American fiction—Jewish authors—History and
criticism.   2. American fiction—20th century—History
and criticism.   3. Jews in literature.   4. Immigrants
in literature.   5. Holocaust, Jewish (1939–1945) in
literature.   I. Title.
PS374.J48B5   813'.54'09352296   80-15326
ISBN 0-8195-5046-3

Distributed for Wesleyan University Press by Columbia
University Press
136 South Broadway, Irvington, NY 10533

Manufactured in the United States of America
First edition

Contents

Acknowledgments

A **number** of friends and colleagues offered valuable suggestions during the course of this work. Especially important was the support of my articulate family. I particularly want to thank Clare Herzog for her editorial acumen and sisterly empathy. Above all I am grateful to Al Bilik for his critical insight, understanding, and encouragement.

Note on Yiddish and Hebrew Words

Some Hebrew and Yiddish words are cited in widely used accepted spellings as found in American Judaistic publications (aggada, shlemiel). Other Yiddish words are transcribed according to the system of the YIVO Institute for Jewish Research and appear in italics (*luftmentsh, tsadik*). Inconsistencies in orthography occur when the author cited does not follow the same transcription system.

Part I

Introduction

One

The New Immigrant Novel

Jewish American fiction written in the 1950s and sixties is primarily about second- and third-generation American Jews. The novels usually focus on affluent Jewish Americans in suburbia; symbiotic relationships between Jews and anti-Semites (Bruce Jay Friedman's *Stern* [1962]; Saul Bellow's *The Victim* [1947]); or Jewish variants of Huckleberry Finn (Bellow's *The Adventures of Augie March* [1953]; Bernard Malamud's *A New Life* [1963]). At the same time another kind of Jewish American literature was being written that is not concerned with second- and third-generation American Jews. As early as 1957, the Jewish immigrant, missing from American fiction since the 1930s, reappears as a major fictional character. The new immigrant novel differs from prevailing Jewish American novels and from earlier immigrant novels as well.

In essence the new immigrant novel is not a literature of assimilation. Instead, deeply concerned with the continuing importance of the Jewish experience, it can be thought of as a manifestation by Jewish American writers of a delayed post-Holocaust consciousness. Because it has not been seen as such in the major criticism of the 1960s and seventies, it is the purpose of this study to further delineate and distinguish the new immigrant novel and its pervading post-Holocaust sensibility.

Critics writing in the 1960s and early seventies made predictions about the future of Jewish American literature based largely on their reading of second- and third-generation Jewish American novels. Robert Alter in 1969 wrote that "the vogue of Jewish writing, quickly exhausting its artistic possibilities, offers many indications that it may be falling into a declining phase of unwitting self-parody."[1] For Leslie Fiedler, in 1964,

> the very notion of a Jewish-American literature represents a dream of assimilation, and the process it envisages is bound to move toward a triumph (in terms of personal success) which is also a defeat (in terms of meaningful Jewish survival).[2]

Alan Guttmann in 1971 repeated his 1964 prediction that "the Renaissance of Jewish writers had very nearly run its course."[3] Guttmann also, with some qualification, agreed with Fiedler that Jewish American literature by and large is about "the process of assimilation and the resultant crisis of identity." Assimilation in America, according to Guttmann, has taken the form of "voluntary conversions" from orthodoxy to Protestantized Judaism, from religious commitment to political or social commitment (socialism, Zionism), but above all to some form of "Americanism."[4] Assimilation to American ways also meant to Guttmann that "the survival in America of a significant and identifiably Jewish literature depends upon the unlikely conversion to Judaism . . . of a generation [of Jews] that no longer chooses to be chosen."[5]

The future of Jewish American literature is most uncertain, these critics warned. How can literature be "Jewish" if its subject matter is "if not terminal Jews, at least penultimate ones: the fathers and grandfathers of America's last Jews."[6] Leslie Fiedler points to Philip Roth's *Goodbye Columbus* (1960) as an exemplary "comedy of Jewish dissolution in the midst of prosperity" and to *Portnoy's Complaint* (1969) as the final example of such comic satire.[7] Yet the case for a terminal Jewish American literature is not persuasive. While themes of assimilation and the dissolution of Jewish identity among second- and third-generation Jews seemed to dominate the fiction of the period, there could be discerned at the same time an undercurrent, a backwards movement toward an earlier time when the Jewish immigrant figured as a major fictional character.

Twenty years ago Malamud wrote and today writes about

the remnant of the earlier generation of Jewish immigrants. So do more recent writers, such as Cynthia Ozick, Hugh Nissenson, and Jay Neugeboren. In the 1970s, moreover, Isaac Bashevis Singer, Arthur Cohen, and Susan Fromberg Schaeffer began writing a new kind of immigrant fiction, in which Jewish survivors of the Holocaust (the destruction of European Jewry by the Nazis during World War II) were the central figures. In this fiction attention focuses upon orthodox and traditional Jews and their Eastern European backgrounds, not upon the assimilated characters and American suburban settings that dominated the Jewish American literature of the fifties. Rather than that diminution of interest in Jewish subject matter predicted by Alter, Guttmann, and Fiedler, there is here a resurgence of interest in the European and American Jewish past. This renewed concern for the Jewish immigrant and immigrant-survivor as central fictional characters reflects the delayed expression by Jewish American writers of a post-Holocaust consciousness.

The immigrant, whether or not he is a survivor, can be seen as the embodiment of the history and tradition of European Jews. The immigrant-survivor of the Holocaust is further imbued with the moral power and the will to preserve and transmit in the American Diaspora that Jewish heritage that was tragically destroyed in Europe. Recent fictional immigrants, especially immigrant-survivors, are thus often modern, secular versions of the *tsadik* (pious, saintly man) of traditional Yiddish and Hebrew literature, who acts as teacher and moral example to others. Even when the central characters in these novels are not exemplary *tsadikim*, their fictional world is certain to contain a character who functions as preserver and transmitter of the past. For the writer, the immigrant-survivor and the *tsadik* are rhetorically effective personae and aesthetically economical determiners of distance. Remnants of a vanished European Jewish culture, the immigrant-survivors in America bridge the historical and psychological distance between the modern Jewish American writer and the somber events that the writer confronts through the fictive imagination.

It follows then that those works directly employing a Holocaust survivor as center of consciousness are particularly important to this study. They include Edward Wallant's *The Pawnbroker* (1961); Isaac Bashevis Singer's *Enemies* (1972); Saul Bellow's *Mr. Sammler's Planet* (1970); Susan Fromberg Schaeffer's *Anya* (1974). Of equal importance is Arthur Cohen's *In the Days of Simon Stern* (1973). Although the protagonist of Cohen's novel is not an immigrant, he is representative of the immigrant milieu; the narrator and all the major characters are Holocaust survivors. Both Cohen and Singer have extensive theological and traditional knowledge and their novels are particularly appropriate examples of post-Holocaust sensibility. Bernard Malamud is also of importance. Although he peoples his fictional world with immigrants rather than survivors, his Yiddish-accented *tsadikim* in *The Assistant* (1957), *The Magic Barrel* (1958), and other works are indirect embodiments of post-Holocaust consciousness. In *The Fixer* Malamud specifically uses the persecuted Jew Mendl Beilis as synecdoche, indeed as "one man to stand for six million."[8]

The individual novels of Wallant, Bellow, Singer, Cohen, and Schaeffer, and a number of works by Malamud, therefore, are the major focus of this study. Although not subject to detailed analysis, a little-known novel by Isaac Rosenfeld, *Passage from Home* (1946), is also discussed. It is important as a transitional novel for its presentation of the *tsadik* figure and as an example, in Daniel Bell's formulation, of a "parable of alienation." Also discussed briefly for background purposes are two important novels of earlier immigrant life: Abraham Cahan's *The Rise of David Levinsky* (1917) and Henry Roth's *Call It Sleep* (1934). Since this study concentrates on the immigrant in America, those works set primarily in Europe or Israel are excluded from detailed analysis as are works with essentially second-generation protagonists.

For comparative purposes some attention is given to European survivor literature, examples of which were being written as early as in the late 1940s. An examination of criticism of this literature by Lawrence Langer and Terrence Des

Pres is useful to show similarities and differences between European and American approaches to related themes. Of similar comparative value is the exile literature written in America in languages other than English. With the exception of Isaac Bashevis Singer, whose novels are written originally in Yiddish, the works analyzed here are by American writers who write in English.

Historical and philosophical material relating to the immigrant experience is also significant as background. For example, there are a number of important concepts that are associated with the Jewish fictional persona in twentieth-century literature. The Jew is conventionally presented as the representative twentieth-century man embodying homelessness, exile, and alienation. The general sense of these concepts does not always correspond to what they signify in Jewish thought. I found that some of the differences between the idea as generally held and its Jewish interpretation illuminated aspects of the new immigrant literature.

Those novels analyzed in detail required summary, paraphrase, and explication in varying proportion. My methodological goal was to suit the analytical tool to the particular book rather than to make the work fit the tool. For example, Malamud requires explicit discussion of language since his use of Yiddish idioms, rhythms, and sentence structure is extensive and his method is indicative of a post-Holocaust sensibility at work. Analysis of language was also occasioned by a reading of the original Yiddish version of Singer's *Enemies*, which resulted in the discovery of interesting stylistic differences between the Yiddish and English versions. On another level of explication, since biblical archetypes and allusions to traditional Jewish sources occur more frequently in Singer and Cohen than, for example, in Wallant, the novels of Singer and Cohen require more exegesis and reference to secondary sources. Schaeffer's *Anya*, a historical novel of the Holocaust, requires less structural analysis and explication than does Bellow's complex narrative.

Most helpful in distinguishing among immigrant-survivor novels are the genre distinctions explored by Northrop Frye.[9]

Striking and not accidental is the fact that four of the protagonists in the novels discussed are conceived as philosophers, three even possessing academic credentials. In addition, Malamud's synecdochic fixer develops as a thinker during his ordeal. The central characters of immigrant-survivor novels are often concerned with metaphysical, ethical, and theological questions and are fitting personae for what Frye defines as the anatomy, a form that allows for metaphysical digressions, historical references, and moral commentary. The aggada is a corresponding Jewish form that uses imaginative literature to illustrate "the foundations of a system of ethics and faith."[10]

Enemies and *Mr. Sammler's Planet* with their variety of subject matter and strong and explicit interest in ideas can be described as anatomical novels, whereas *In the Days of Simon Stern* is unabashedly didactic and more pure anatomy. In contrast, Wallant's *The Pawnbroker,* despite its supposed philosopher protagonist, is a naturalistic novel with little or no commentary and little overt interest in ideas. Schaeffer's *Anya* is a physician *manqué* rather than a philosopher and the work is centered on physical survival rather than metaphysical speculation. Neither *The Pawnbroker* nor *Anya* includes much reflection or commentary on the harrowing experiences depicted in both novels. The protagonists are therefore less comprehensive embodiments of post-Holocaust consciousness than are Singer's and Bellow's wiser heroes. The novel *In the Days of Simon Stern* with its coterie of wise men and its philosophical, historical, and theological digressions appears to sink with the weight of its comprehensiveness. Admittedly, Cohen, Wallant, and Schaeffer are not master novelists as are Malamud, Bellow, and Singer. Nevertheless, *The Pawnbroker,* *Anya*, and *In the Days of Simon Stern* are serious attempts to present unprecedented subject matter and are worthy of attention and commentary.

In summary, my exploration of the new immigrant novel reveals that it differs from other contemporary Jewish American literature in that it is more concerned with the tragedy of the Jewish historical past than with the comic sociology of the American Jewish present. The best of the new immigrant novels are inclined to be philosophical, even theological, rather than sociological or psychological. The archetypes, metaphors, and images tend to come from the Bible and other Jewish sources rather than from Jungian psychology or Greek mythology. The Yiddish language in the novels of Malamud, Singer, Bellow, Ozick, and Cohen is used carefully and sympathetically rather than comically, vulgarly, and incorrectly as in Philip Roth, Bruce Jay Friedman, and Wallace Markfield. The new immigrant novels differ from earlier works in that they focus on the preservation of cultural identity that is implicit in the retention of fragments of Yiddish and Hebrew; they do not chronicle the inevitable loss of language and the acculturation that it prefigures. The questions raised by post-Holocaust immigrant fiction have little to do with what made David Levinsky rise or Sammy run or the nature of Portnoy's complaint. Rather the novels center on the survival of individuals, and of Jewish traditions, language, history, and morality. The solipsism of sensitive Jewish sons and their problematic mothers (from Henry Roth's David Schearl to Philip Roth's Alex Portnoy) did not offer sufficient sustenance to those Jewish American writers who wished to give form to their post-Holocaust consciousness. Instead they turned to the painfully acquired wisdom of immigrant-survivor fathers and mothers as the embodiment of that consciousness.

Two

Backgrounds:
Literary
and Nonliterary

Philip Roth has not as yet portrayed an immigrant-survivor as protagonist in his fiction. But as novelist and critic Roth has demonstrated a developing interest in the European Jewish past, which is representative of a general increase in post-Holocaust consciousness. Roth's evolving interest is in sharp contrast to the attitude he expressed in 1961. He wrote at that time:

> I cannot find a true and honest place in the history of believers that begins with Abraham, Isaac, and Jacob on the basis of the heroism of these believers, or of their humiliations and anguish. I can only connect with them . . . as I apprehend their God. And until such time as I do apprehend him, there will continue to exist between myself and those others who seek his presence, a question . . . which for all the pain and longing it may engender, for all the disappointment and bewilderment it may produce, cannot be swept away by nostalgia or sentimentality or even by blind and valiant effort of the will: How are you connected to me as another man is not?[1]

On a visit to Prague some fifteen years later, Roth seems to have found the connection:

> Within the first few hours of walking in these streets between the river and the Old Town Square, I understood that a connection of sorts existed between myself and this place: here was one of those dense corners of Jewish Europe which Hitler had emptied of Jews, a place which in earlier days

must have been not too unlike those neighborhoods in Austro-Hungarian Lemberg and Czarist Kiev where the two branches of my own family had lived before their emigration to America at the beginning of the century. Looking for Kafka's landmarks, I had, to my surprise, come upon some that felt to me like my own.[2]

The results of Roth's encounter and identification with the European Jewish past can be discerned in his most recent novel, The Ghost Writer (1979). The work includes an attractive young woman with a slight foreign accent and an unknown past. The central character, a writer much like the younger Roth, creates a fictional past for the enigmatic young woman. She is Anne Frank, resurrected in the writer's imagination as having miraculously survived the gas chamber. Roth's imaginary ghost of the historic Anne Frank is placed in a fictional world that contains the ghost of his former self and other literary ghosts. Through these personae Roth acknowledges his relationship to older Jewish American writers and to the Jewish past. It is made clear, however, that unlike the literary ghosts whose fictional lives are probable and indeed recognizable, the Anne Frank episode is a poignant impossibility, a product of the surrogate author's wishful imagination. The tribute to the memory of Anne Frank is counterposed to those early stories of Roth's ("Epstein" [1959], "Defender of the Faith" [1959]) that caused discomfort in the Jewish community. With considerable distance The Ghost Writer commemorates the Holocaust and with some irony offers an apologia, thereby enabling Roth to lay a number of his own ghosts to rest.

As general editor of the Penguin series Writers from the Other Europe, Roth has helped to make important European Holocaust literature available to a wide public. The series has published an outstanding collection of stories by Tadeusz Borowski, This Way for the Gas, Ladies and Gentlemen (1976), and the works of Holocaust victim Bruno Schulz, as well as other related works. Roth's Jewish and Eastern European connections may prove even more fruitful for him as novelist and editor in the future. His is clearly an example of a growing post-Holocaust sensibility.

Some of the historic factors that may have contributed to the change in Roth and others from 1961 to 1976 are noted by Dorothy Rabinowitz in a study of actual Holocaust survivors. Rabinowitz states that "in 1961, the subject of the holocaust had not achieved the status that it was to have years later, after the histories had been written, the studies compiled."[3] Further, Rabinowitz designates the Eichmann trial as the "first in the series of shocks that would periodically, but with ever-deepening effect, close the distance between American Jews and their awareness of the holocaust, the others being Israel's wars of survival." Later, Holocaust consciousness was greatly extended by the antiwar movement of the late sixties when "the destruction of the European Jews by the Germans was widely, if erroneously, utilized as a parallel for U.S. involvement in the Vietnam war."[4] Information about the tragic recent past and deeply disturbing current events drew the attention of social scientists, historians, and novelists to the subject of the Holocaust.

Another expression of post-Holocaust sensibility was the renewed interest in the Jewish American immigrant past, a phenomenon of the late sixties and seventies. Philip Roth's desire to show the connection between the earlier immigrant and the destroyed Eastern European world is reflected in his 1976 statement. But in emphasizing the continuity between pre- and post-Holocaust immigrants, important differences in number, background, and motivation for immigration should not be ignored.

A look at the quantitative differences shows striking contrasts. In the fifteen years between 1900 and 1914, approximately 1,500,000 Jews from Eastern Europe came to the United States. In fifteen comparable postwar years, from 1944 to 1959, approximately 192,000 Jews immigrated. The restrictive quota system initiated by the Johnson Act of 1924 severely limited immigration from Eastern and Southern Europe and this accounted for the smaller figure. In the period from

1933 to 1937 only 33,000 Jews entered the United States. The extremely critical situation in Germany and German-occupied countries (Austria, Czechoslovakia, Poland, and others) boosted immigration so that in the four years between 1938 and 1941, 124,000 Jews arrived from Europe. In 1941 the United States entered the war and emigration from Europe virtually ceased. Despite the desperate plight of European Jewry and other groups, American immigration policies remained restrictive. Although the Displaced Persons Act of 1949 allowed 73,000 Jewish survivors to enter the United States, the quota system of the 1920s was buttressed by the restrictive McCarran-Walter Act of 1952. Not until 1965 was the law liberalized to allow individual immigration on a first-come first-served basis.[5]

The early immigrant differed in substantive ways from the later immigrant. The Eastern Europeans of the early decades of the century were largely workers from small towns. The majority of the men were only able to read the Hebrew prayerbook and had a smattering of Russian or Polish in addition to their mother tongue, Yiddish.[6] The refugees who began arriving in the mid-thirties had middle-class social values, were richer and better educated. But by far the most significant difference for literature and history is that the earlier immigration was voluntary. Despite extreme poverty, discrimination, and pogroms, it was possible for an East European Jew to stay in Russia or Poland and survive—until 1942. Such a choice was not available to the wartime refugee and it was at least problematic for the Jewish postwar survivor. Some earlier immigrants came because of a desire to escape a twenty-five year term of military service, some to escape political persecution, but most emigrated to escape poverty and religious persecution. Even so, in the period from 1880 to 1914, two-thirds of the Eastern European Jewish population remained in Europe.[7] Quite different were the circumstances of German and other European Jews in the period from the mid-thirties till the end of the war. These were modern, bourgeois people for the most part, shocked out of a formerly comfortable existence by unprecedented events.

The earlier Eastern European immigrant left a society in which he had little or no part; he was an eager immigrant. The German professional and intellectual represented a different social class, and, until 1933, could believe himself part of a modern, liberal society where he had attained enviable status. Even the Eastern European refugees of World War II had lived under less oppressive regimes and had made economic and educational progress in comparison with their forebears. Many German refugees of the thirties and early forties felt that they had been exiled from a beloved European homeland to a materialistic and rather vulgar America. The attitude of the German refugee was satirized in Israel Joshua Singer's Yiddish novel of German Jewish life *Di mishpokhe Karnofski* (1946; "The family Carnovsky").[8] Much later, in the sixties and seventies, American writers would record a different set of attitudes toward the European past and the American present, as embodied in post-Holocaust immigrants. But time would have to elapse before such a body of fiction could be created.

By the fifties, however, a sizable body of exile literature had already been written, primarily in German, which expressed longing for the homeland and commitment to the preservation of the German language as well as other concerns not germane to the immigrant-survivor fiction later produced by American writers.[9] Holocaust literature in Yiddish began appearing as early as in the 1940s.[10]

American writers were not yet ready to use the particulars of refugee experience as material for fiction. Instead, during the most tragic decade in Jewish experience, the Jew was universalized and mythologized as a symbol of twentieth-century man, a homeless victim in an indifferent universe.

"It was fit and proper that Kafka should have been a Jew, for the Jews have for a long time been placed in the position in which we are now all to be of having no home."[11] The British immigrant to the United States W. H. Auden, writing just before America's entry into World War II, sees the Jew as the symbol of universal homelessness. The Jew and the non-Jew, both made homeless by historical and political forces, now share the condition of rootlessness and exile. Implicit in Auden's evaluation of Kafka is recognition of the importance of the Jew as ontological and psychological outsider.

The story of the Jew, then, according to Daniel Bell, is "a parable of alienation . . . a paradigm for the condition of modern man."[12] It should be noted that the universalism expressed by Auden and Bell is considerably modified by the particularity of Jewish history and theology. From the time of the Babylonian captivity, Jewish thought has been concerned with Jewish exile and return. Modern readers may relate concepts of exile, Diaspora, and return to Mircea Eliade's myth of the eternal return, but in Jewish thought these are more historical and theological than metaphorical and mythological.

A striking and grim illustration of the particularity of the Jewish experience can be seen in the accounts of Holocaust survivors who literally crawled out of mass graves.[13] Unlike the epic hero's archetypal descent into hell, the survivor's "death-rebirth" experience is bitterly qualified, hauntingly ambiguous, and hardly metaphoric. How the literary artist attempts to meet the challenge of such unprecedented subject matter is of central importance to this study. It can readily be seen that supposedly universal experiences like exile, Diaspora, and return have additional, crucial, particular meaning in Jewish history and thought.

This implies no denial of the universal and symbolic aspects of exile, Diaspora, and return but rather a recognition that most commentators have stressed the universal rather than the particular. An extensive examination of the concepts of exile and Diaspora in Jewish thought by Raphael Patai illustrates the centrality of the sacred, the spiritual, and the moral. Of generative importance to the historic concept of Diaspora is the basic myth of the Fall of Man and the Expulsion from the Garden of Eden. The Hebrew equivalent of the Greek *diaspora* derives from the verb *l'hafitz*, 'to scatter.' According to Patai, the scattering of Israel among the nations "is in most Biblical passages attributed directly to God . . . a divinely meted out punishment, the result of a fall from grace."[14]

'Exile' was more commonly interpreted in Jewish thought

as a condition brought about by military defeat, the "condition of a Jewish community in a country in which its sojourn is involuntary." In time, and with historical experience, the idea of a God-ordained punishment receded and dispersion was understood to be "more and more emphatically due to the wickedness of the gentiles." The generic term 'exile,' especially in its Yiddish form, *goles*, refers "to a state of misery, of persecution, of homelessness, of sojourning as a stranger among strangers."[15] Since 70 C.E., the most frequently expressed Jewish prayer was for the return to Zion and the restoration of Jerusalem, events dependent upon the coming of the Messiah and the redemption of the world. Physical return and spiritual redemption were intertwined and interdependent.

In traditional thought Jews are in exile, no matter where they live, until the coming of the Messiah. With the coming of the Enlightenment and Jewish emancipation, this concept of exile with its burden of misery and its attribution of wickedness to gentile society became untenable to modernist Jews who were beginning to find life comfortable in the Western Diaspora. Reform Judaism developed the concept that God's dispersion of the Jews was a manifestation of chosenness rather than punishment. Scattered among the nations of the world, Israel had a mission "to spread the knowledge of God among the nations and to teach them the lofty ethical ideas that He had revealed to the Hebrews, through their great prophets and teachers."[16]

This accommodating and high-minded vision was by no means universally acknowledged, especially by traditionalist Jews (and surely not by non-Jews). Yet it did gain wide acceptance among modernist Jews and was believed by some traditionalists. Many Jews still felt exiled even when conditions of exile improved. The historian Haim Ben Sasson states that "the sense of exile was expressed by the feeling of alienation in the countries of the Diaspora, the yearning for the national and political past, and persistent questionings of the causes, meaning and purpose of the exile." A familar feeling of unease is expressed by Jewish mystics, ancient and modern, who perceive "a defectiveness in the Divine Order which they con-

nect with alienation in this world."[17] For them, according to
Gershom Scholem, "the redemption of Israel is one with the
redemption of God himself from his mystic exile."[18]

The Jewish sense of Diaspora projects both the image of
alienated man in a fallen universe and the possibility of moral
redemption and mission. Human powerlessness and the pervasiveness of evil do not preclude the possibility of the realization of good. Secular Jewish writers in the latter half of the
twentieth century, with or without knowledge of this background, have created exiled pariahs and prophets, shlemiels
and tsadikim, albeit sometimes with considerable irony. Nevertheless their fiction frequently includes an immigrant who,
despite his own powerlessness, and because of his relationship to the historic Jewish past or to past experience, ful-
fills an ancient Diasporal function by bringing about a moral
or perceptual change in another or in himself. In this the immigrant is related to the tsadik who teaches and renders moral
and spiritual aid to his followers.

The immigrant-tsadik, in the context of Jewish mythology, is akin to the wandering prophet Elijah, who

> wanders over the earth in many and varied guises. . . . He
> acts as a celestial messenger, a warner, and an adviser. He
> appears in times of distress and danger and befriends mys-
> tics and scholars. He brings consolation to the afflicted and
> chides the arrogant and the proud. Expectation and hope are
> associated with the prophet, for Elijah is regarded as the
> precursor of the Messiah.[19]

This Jewish wanderer with his positive attributes is quite different from the Christian conception of Ahasuerus, the Wandering Jew, with his burden of woe.[20] It is a fruitful difference, for it underscores the possibilities of a meaningful,
moral Jewish life in a fragmented, unredeemed world. Central
to the fulfillment of these possibilities is the preservation and
transmission of the historic Jewish past. The fictional immigrant-tsadik is the natural embodiment of that past.

The success story of the Jewish immigrant in America has
a biblical parallel in the story of Joseph, the protoimmigrant.

Joseph first undergoes hardship but, because of his superior gifts, his industry, and his ability to become assimilated to an alien society, he soon achieves extraordinary success in his adopted country. The patriarch Joseph does not forget his responsibility to his people and makes provision for their deliverance and survival. While not all fictional (or real) immigrants are actively and consciously committed to Jewish survival, recent immigrant literature includes not a few characters who play the role of Joseph. The immigrant protagonist projects a cluster of associations from Jewish history enriched by the biblical mythopoeia of the Fall, Exile, and Dispersion, renewal and survival. In recent Jewish American fiction the immigrant figure is frequently used as a rhetorically effective and economical symbol of Jewish life in the Diaspora. One aspect of Diasporal life frequently depicted in immigrant literature is the linguistic dislocation involved in the loss of mother tongue and the need to learn other tongues. Loss of linguistic unity is prefigured in the biblical myth of the Tower of Babel with its movement from a universal language to a multiplicity of languages. On a more homely level, Jewish American writers use vestiges of Yiddish to emphasize the unassimilated character of their immigrant protagonists and to differentiate them from those around them.

The myths of the Diaspora experience and of language dislocation are common to early and recent immigrant fiction. Another Jewish biblical myth more specifically projects post-Holocaust consciousness. The story of Job is frequently retold in the new immigrant novel. The persecution of the upright Job and his gratuitous suffering is, in microcosm, the history of the Jew in the twentieth century. In the light of the unprecedented particulars of Jewish history in this century, the supposed universality of the symbolic Jew is invalidated. The story of Job can be seen as analogous. Job's eventual restoration to his previous state is anticlimactic and disproportionately trivial when compared to what he has experienced. The sense of an unjust universe that is conveyed in Job is what makes the story so appealing to Jewish American writers in their effort to penetrate the meaning of the Holocaust.

Ancient and recent history, events of considerable magnitude, universal and particular interpretations of philosophical concepts, and a special use of biblical and other myths such as the death-rebirth tropes form the nonliterary background for much postwar immigrant fiction. To explore that fiction and its manifestations of post-Holocaust consciousness in a literary context, a brief discussion of pre-Holocaust immigrant fiction is necessary.

The immediate postwar period of the late forties and fifties is characterized by general interest in Jewish subjects and a flowering of literature that depicted contemporary Jewish life in America. In 1960 an emerging historical consciousness could be discerned in the reissuing of two outstanding novels of the older immigrant past, Abraham Cahan's *The Rise of David Levinsky* (1917) and Henry Roth's *Call It Sleep* (1934). Interest in these previously neglected novels and hence in the Jewish American immigrant past is also a part of developing post-Holocaust consciousness. These two works are particularly significant in the manner in which they both exemplify and transcend the limitations of the early immigrant novel.

Most early immigrant novels depict successful Americanization, which involves some form of assimilation. Early immigrant novels are therefore much alike in setting, in the kinds of stereotypes employed, and in theme. Typically, early immigrant novels are set in New York's lower East Side where most Jewish immigrant writers and many Jewish immigrants spent part of their lives. They are, in Irving Howe's words, "full of sentimental stereotypes" and "pander to the public conception of the East Side as an exotic curiosity" where even poverty becomes "a piece of local color to be waved before American readers."[21]

Typically also, they present the "rise" of a Jewish immigrant from piety and poverty to secularization or some other form of assimilation. Frequently, assimilation takes the form of a radical and secular conversion in which, as Walter Rideout points out, Jewish Messianic hopes are translated into faith in a socialist society.[22] Considerably less formulaic are those protagonists who yearn for something undefined, something that transcends the minimal satisfactions for which they have settled.[23] This hunger for something more is a central theme in the most important of the early novels of immigrant life, Cahan's The Rise of David Levinsky.[24] Although Levinsky achieves an extraordinary measure of material success in America, in some vital respects he remains an unchanged shtetl (traditional Eastern European Jewish small town) dweller.

The exceptional quality of Cahan's novel has been widely noted. Like other immigrant novels, it depicts the rise of an eager immigrant ready to exchange his wretched shtetl past for an affluent American present. But there is also in Levinsky, as Isaac Rosenfeld has said, a "constant longing for the conditions of his past," a spirit of "permanent dissatisfaction" that determines his perception of his experiences.[25] Rosenfeld equates Levinsky's metaphysical hunger for his wretched past with the Diaspora, the yearning for Messiah, and the return to Jerusalem. But in Levinsky these causes for spiritual discontent are neither acknowledged nor radicalized by the protagonist. Levinsky receives no ethical or spiritual nourishment from his past nor does his impoverished boyhood inspire him with the desire for social justice. According to Rosenfeld, Levinsky "had relatively little to overcome (speaking inwardly) to grow into the typical American of fortune" because he anticipated the "inner loneliness of the American environment in his own."[26]

The superficiality of David's commitment to his Jewish background is demonstrated in his casual doffing of all the outward signs of orthodoxy. Levinsky arrives in America in traditional regalia, complete with earlocks and beard, and almost immediately exchanges them for American-style clothing and a shave. It is fitting that the future successful garment manufacturer sees himself as a new man in his new clothes. Superficiality is also evident in his response to his best friend's atheism—shock followed immediately by the recognition that "my interest in the matter was not keen, however, and soon it died down altogether [p. 56]." But this "loss of faith" took place in the shtetl, not in "atheistic" America.

David's easy assimilation is predicted by the saintly Reb Sender, who warns him that "one becomes a Gentile in America" (p. 61). Sender is an early example of a *tsadik*. Significantly, Sender, unlike later fictional mentors and guides, does not emigrate to America. Nor does Levinsky, in contrast to post-Holocaust immigrants, ever seriously confront the question of the existence and meaning of God.

Levinsky is self-deceived, opportunistic, and a conformist, traits that help him to achieve, according to Rosenfeld, a "virtually flawless Americanization."[27] Yet Cahan's protagonist is sometimes allowed to speak for the author, as he does at a Catskill Mountain resort:

> Men and women were offering thanksgiving to the flag under which they were eating this good dinner, wearing these expensive clothes. There was the jingle of newly-acquired dollars in our applause. But there was something else in it as well. Many of those who were now paying tribute to the Stars and Stripes were listening to the tune with grave solemn mien. It was as if they were saying: "We are not persecuted under this flag. At last we have found a home." (p. 424)

The Jewish immigrant at that time did find a home in America, but David, as Cahan shows, is as isolated as a New York millionaire as he was as a pauper in his *shtetl*. David is a Diaspora Man without the collective vision that sustains others in the Diaspora. He is too selfish to preserve or transmit a meaningful heritage; his memories are personal and a way of preserving self-pity. Cahan, on the other hand, while aware of the contradictions of American life, agreed with his hero as to the potentialities for meaningful Jewish American life. In an interview in 1922 he said, "The Jews should have come to America a thousand years before they did. There is nothing to stop them from realizing the full measure of manhood here."[28] What is offered to the Jewish immigrant in Cahan's fiction is the opportunity to develop his potentialities, by no means an unalloyed gift. For in addition to the opportunity to develop one's intellect and ideals, there is offered the chance to lead a sensual, materialistic, exploitative, vulgar life—all is possible in the open society. With self-advancement comes the opportunity for self-destruction. This perception occupies later Jewish American writers as well.

Cahan and later writers believe that the immigrant has a choice. Cahan's novels and short stories show other immigrants—doctors, teachers, socialists, literary stenographers, starving poets, and other worthy inhabitants of Jewish New York—who have not succumbed to vulgarity and corruption. What frequently allows these figures of the Diaspora to avoid Levinskian despair is some aspect of the Jewish past or commitment to the collective Jewish future that enables them to transcend their individual interests.[29] Levinsky had no such talisman or insight. His particular Jewish past was insufficiently historic, his *shtetl* insufficiently nourishing, his commitment to Jewish survival too weak. In this he represents an ironic variant of the biblical story of Joseph, the model for successful Jewish immigrants. David Levinsky, however, is a Joseph manqué; he does not share his good fortune with his people. He does not send for his boyhood friend, he breaks his promise to do so. He does not even father a family to transmit his name and heritage.

For Levinsky and for other early immigrants, the voyage to America is "a second birth [p. 86]," a chance to begin anew by divesting oneself of the old. In contrast, the post-Holocaust immigrant may be said to have experienced death before his arrival in America. He comes without the outer trappings of tradition and orthodoxy, without the outer signs of difference. Instead of ridding himself of his Jewish past, he ultimately comes to treasure it, despite its horror. He attempts to retain and transmit aspects of his past just as he maintains his inward differences from those around him. Unlike Levinsky the post-Holocaust immigrant remembers his past for collective rather than for only personal reasons. But Levinsky, despite his desire to assimilate, retains "the peculiar Talmud singsong . . . which still persists in my intonation even when I talk cloaks and bank accounts and in English [p. 28]." Notwithstanding his "virtually flawless Americanization," David

Levinsky remains an identifiable "foreigner" because of his accent. He came to America as a young man in his twenties with well-established speech patterns. Questions of linguistic and cultural assimilation are treated somewhat differently in those novels of immigrant life whose protagonists grow up in America.

Second-generation novels written about children of immigrants begin to appear in the twenties and thirties. The older immigrant is no longer the central figure. Historical factors, social context, political and literary taste all contribute to the temporary disappearance of the fictional Jewish immigrant. Meanwhile, large-scale immigration to the United States had all but ceased by 1924;[30] and the American-born generation of the thirties and forties was not interested in the ethnic specificity that the immigrant novel stresses. The political dogma of the radical novel of the twenties and thirties called for class solidarity and a revolutionary Messiah for all.[31] The second generation of writers, in revolt against the foreignness of its parents, for the most part chose not to depict immigrants as major characters.

Irving Howe characterizes those second-generation novels that do center on immigrant life as following "a common pattern: a conflict between orthodox father and Americanized son in the midst of which is trapped the faithful, perplexed mother. . . . One American Jewish writer has raised this stereotype to a genuine characterization."[32] The exception is Henry Roth's *Call It Sleep*. In part what distinguishes Roth's novel from other works of the thirties is its brilliant use of transliterated Hebrew, translated Yiddish, and various levels of English. Roth uses these various parts of his protagonist's linguistic environment to convey the pattern of language disassociation and acculturation that was central to the immigrant experience of that time. Post-Holocaust immigrant fiction treats the linguistic experience quite differently. Here the immigrant-survivor is depicted as an adult with deeply imbedded language habits and an established mother tongue that he seeks to retain rather than relinquish.

The lexical background of a Jewish immigrant child, such

as the protagonist of *Call It Sleep,* is complicated by two Jewish languages, Yiddish and Hebrew, and the Germanic or
Slavic language of his parents' birthplace. The immigrant
child is in a linguistic limbo of infinite potentiality for imprisonment or liberation as he strives to learn the English of his
surrounding culture. In part the linguistic acculturation is a
reverse of the biblical myth of Babel, with the diversity of the
immigrants' languages being exchanged for the unity of
American speech. But the unity is only partial because the
American language is enriched and individualized by the immigrants' diction and cadence. For Jewish writers fragments
of Yiddish and Hebrew are part of a significant historical and
biblical past. Whether the past is preserved, rejected, or tran-
scended, it is frequently manifested in fiction in linguistic
choices. The range of choices in *Call It Sleep* is so varied and
broad that it has been correctly described "as the *noisiest*
novel ever written."[33] If David Levinsky's "rise" is economic
and social, the acculturation of Henry Roth's young David
Schearl is linguistic and psychological.

David Schearl has been victimized by language because of
his youth and immigrant speech; he has misunderstood verbal
signs and has been unable to express his feelings. But other
factors contribute to his development. At the very end of the
novel, David has been sobered by a number of initiation experiences. His need for expiation and suffering results in the
temporary but impressive mystical experience that ends the
novel. The mystical experience, like David's polyglot verbal
environment, is the product of a number of variegated traditions and influences.

David is seeking violent expiation because he has lusted
after the golden calf, here represented by Leo, a sexually precocious Polish Catholic child of the slums. To the insecure
David, the aptly named Leo is the model of courage, independ-
ence, daring, and grace. To find favor in the eyes of such a
person, David, half-innocently, acts as procurer for Leo. The
prey is the slightly sluttish stepdaughter of David's aunt. In
return Leo promises friendship, acceptance, and a broken ro-
sary which, along with Leo's roller skates, are symbols of

power. In short, Leo represents Americanization and assimilation. But David is not really ready for apostasy. Guilt, terror, and fear of punishment cause him to flee from the scene of his treason to the haven of the *kheyder* (traditional Hebrew school), "to lose himself among the rest [pp. 358–59]." There he confronts again a biblical passage that seems to allow for the possibility of the purification he has been seeking.

Roth, too, uses linguistic experience to dramatize David's situation. The raucous, sordid Hebrew school of times past is nowhere more graphically drawn than in his novel. The boys' total lack of interest and the slovenly teacher's helplessness in the face of their indifference are conveyed in scenes of high comedy. Linguistically Roth has captured the essence of the rote method of learning Hebrew by presenting many paragraphs of transliterated phonetic Hebrew. These paragraphs make little sense to David or to the reader. However, purely by chance David had previously heard an explanation, in Yiddish, of the biblical text from Jethro in which Isaiah, whose lips are unclean and who lives in an unclean land, is cleansed by an angel who touched his lips with a fiery coal (p. 227).

The paradox of something black and dirty being the instrument of purification is explored in great detail in the novel. What is central is that a significant fragment of Jewish traditional learning is combined with David's current American experiences, ultimately to form a momentarily transcendent mystical apotheosis. David's unlikely guide in his mystical experience is the irascible, sloppy, meddling Hebrew teacher, Reb Yidel Pankower, who despite his comic ineffectiveness successfully plays the role of *tsadik* to the questing David. David's journey in search of purification and expiation culminates in a flash of electricity as he forces a milk ladle into trolley tracks. The resultant electric shock plunges him into unconsciousness accompanied by a mystical vision. Implicit in David's action is a recognition of the power of American industrialization and technology. More recent immigrant novels (Edward Wallant's *The Human Season* [1960], Saul Bellow's *Mr. Sammler's Planet* [1970]) also present an encounter between immigrant and technology that usually results in an important perception for the protagonist or an important change in the action.

In David's vision, his knowledge of Isaiah is combined with memories of a previous experience during which he was coerced into throwing a homemade zinc sword into the trolley tracks. David first learns of the power of the tracks by being intimidated by older, street-wise gentile boys in an episode of conventional, not especially vicious, anti-Semitism.

In the final transcending scene David actively seeks punishment, enlightenment, and power through his experience. David's visionary experience of death and rebirth is followed by his prodigal return complete with intern, policeman, and a full retinue of tenement neighbors. He returns to an anguished mother and a shocked and repentant father. David's return is a victory that is classically Oedipal and also linguistic:

> In the kitchen, he could hear the policeman interrogating his father, and his father answering in a dazed, unsteady voice. That sense of triumph that David had felt on first being brought in, welled up within him again as he listened to him falter and knew him shaken.
>
> "Yes. Yes," he was saying. "My sawn. Mine. Yes. Auld eight. Eight en'—en' vun mawnt'. He vas bawn in—" (p. 437)

The passage contains Albert Schearl's acknowledgement of paternity, his acceptance of his son, an acceptance previously withheld by this frequently paranoid personality. It is also a linguistic victory for David. For David's rebirth, his return to consciousness after his encounter with the rails, is accompanied by increased verbal facility. When he is asked where he lives, no longer imprisoned by his family's accent he replies in an accent undistinguishable from those around him, " 'N-nint' street. . . . S-sebm fawdynine' [p. 432]." No longer "Boddeh Stritt" in imitation of his beloved mother, who only speaks Yiddish, David now speaks a coarse yet intelligible New York English. David's earlier repetition of his mother's way of mispronouncing their former address had caused him considerable anguish. Now he speaks like the other children in his lively slum. The reader is very much aware that this verbal facility is attended by considerable loss.

Although atypical in their quality, both *Call It Sleep* and *The Rise of David Levinsky* resemble other early immigrant novels to a degree that all are concerned with the depiction of assimilation into society. Yet, despite Henry Roth's Marxist associations, David Schearl's acculturation is not pictured as the corrupt fall of a David Levinsky. Roth is not critical of American life, although he portrays with painful intensity the traumas and terrors of growing up sensitive, Jewish, and Oedipal in a coarse, vulgar, but vital urban slum. Even the population is described in positive terms, friendly Irish cops, helpful passersby, ultimately admirable (if irascible and unhygienic) rabbis. It is for the most part a benign universe, sometimes brutal but comic and ready to accept a terrified small alien.

The underlying optimism of the world of *Call It Sleep* is related to the question of Roth's later career. In recent years newly awakened interest in Henry Roth's work has caused critic after critic to speculate and to ask why he ceased writing after *Call It Sleep*. Roth gives a number of answers to the question. "I was not formally religious anymore," Roth recalls when speaking of the time in which he wrote *Call It Sleep*, "but still the Hebrew uprightness of that orthodoxy was diffused in me. I could see a gleam wherever I looked." Speaking of the period after the novel, Roth comments: "I lost my creative certitude. . . . I could even imagine myself as a German Nazi, filled with ideas about Deutsche brotherhood, just as easily as an old rabbi with curling sideburns. I no longer had a point of view." [34] The choice of extremes is surely no accident, for the *deutsche Brüderschaft* destroyed the world of the rabbi with curling sideburns.

Despite Roth's detachment from American Jewish life and, indeed, from American life per se, his developing attitudes toward Jewishness are representative of a later generation of writers. Thus the stereotype of the meek victim led to the gas chambers haunted Roth, for his David was himself a sensitive victim of others who possessed superior strength. Given Roth's particular sensibilities and his virtual with-

drawal from literature and from the world, it is not surprising
that in 1963 he advised Jews "toward ceasing to be Jews." He
himself says that such hasty commentary was followed by "a
regeneration process." Roth began to feel "a profound identification with a people in the making, in the process of becoming again a people from the shadows we were." Roth's fa-
tuousness should not detract from the serious artistic dilemma
he is revealing. For what emerges from Roth's regenerative
Jewishness is his most interesting literary effort since *Call It
Sleep* when, as he tells it, "in 1965 when I was in Seville I felt
this strong urge to do something about the Inquisition. . . . I
. . . was trying to find my way back into something related to
Judaism."[35]

What Henry Roth "did" about the Inquisition was to write
a story, "The Surveyor," about a contemporary American in
Seville who lays a commemorative wreath at an unmarked, ignored site of the Inquisition.[36] It is Roth's tribute to a Jewish
heritage of martyrdom, a direct reversal of his 1963 rejection
of Jewish identity and a clear example of post-Holocaust consciousness asserting itself some twenty years after the event.
Unlike *Call It Sleep*, Roth's story is not a masterpiece. It is too
didactic and thesis-ridden. But it is of great interest to this
study of post-Holocaust consciousness that Henry Roth's most
interesting work since 1934 should be public rather than in-
tensely personal, historical rather than psychological, and fo-
cused on the particulars of the Jewish heritage. Other Jewish
American writers also felt the need somehow to recapture the
Jewish past. As a concrete manifestation of that past, the Jewish immigrant re-emerges from the *shtetl*, the concentration
camp, and elsewhere to become a major character in the fiction of the sixties and seventies.

During the 1940s and early fifties, Jewish American writers did not write about the tragedy of European Jewry. Fear
of American anti-Semitism and horror at a more virulent German strain contributed to a bland Jewish American fiction
that extolled sameness, brotherhood, and caution. Arthur
Miller's only novel, *Focus* (1946), is exemplary of the form.
Miller's hero, like Laura Hobson's hero in a 1947 best-seller

Gentleman's Agreement is not Jewish. He merely "looks Jewish" when he puts on his glasses. In 1947 Miller explained his literary *trompe l'oeil:*

> I think I gave up the Jews as literary material because I was afraid that even an innocent allusion to individual wrongdoing of an individual Jew would be inflamed by the atmosphere, ignited by the hatred I was suddenly aware of, and my love would be twisted into a weapon of persecution against the Jews.[37]

Yet many of the novels of Jewish American life of the 1940s are similar to the problem novels of anti-Semitism that Lionel Trilling faulted for stuffiness and grimness in 1929.[38]

Irving Howe, surveying the state of Jewish American literature twenty years after Trilling, dismisses the cardboard figures of the forties as "Jew as placard" characters. At the same time, Howe notes that Jewish American literature was beginning to become less tendentious and was emerging from its adolescence. Writers such as Delmore Schwartz, Isaac Rosenfeld, and Saul Bellow began "sloughing off large preconceptions and rhetorical patterns" and were turning "to the simplest facts . . . of Jewish experience as the only means of reaching its possible larger meanings."[39] The larger meanings were very large indeed, for at the same time that the brotherhood novel was being written and the adolescent novel was still in vogue, Americans were becoming aware of the Nazi death camps and of the implementation of Hitler's "final solution to the Jewish problem." The destruction of European Jewry is at the root of Daniel Bell's lucid 1946 exposition of alienation.

Bell posits alienation as the fundamental experience of our time, when brotherhood has been replaced by "otherhood." The Jew is a premature alien who has always been "other."

> The Gentile, however, is [newly] estranged from his world. His life is fragmented, his guilt large, and he suffers the tor-

ment of not even realizing the source of his estrangement. The estranged Gentile desperately seeks coherence and wants to reconcile himself to this world. The alienated Jew, self-conscious of his position, knows he is irreconcilable, and by his vocation of alienation sits in judgment on the world.[40]

Skepticism is a historically derived Jewish stance. Most modern Jews, according to Bell, grow up either casually accepting or ardently seeking the goal of assimilation to the dominant culture. Upon rejection by that culture, some return to their past and reaffirm their cultural difference from the gentile world, thereby reinforcing that world's unease with their "otherness." For the many who find themselves distanced both from the Jewish culture from which they come and from the gentile world, which they cannot or will not enter, a possible recourse is positive alienation. The Jew who consciously accepts this stance sees "as if with a double set of glasses, each blending their perspective into one, the nature of the tragedy of our time."[41]

Out of the modern consciousness of alienation comes an echo of ancient Diasporal moral responsibility:

> The assumption of alienation is a positive value, fostering a critical sense out of a role of detachment; it is, if you will, the assumption of the role of prophet, the one who through an ethical conscience indicts the baseness of the world. . . . Alienation does not mean deracination. It means the acceptance of the Jewish tradition—its compulsion to community—and the use of its ethical precepts as a prism to refract the codes and conduct of the world. As long as moral corruption exists, alienation is the only possible response. . . . A dialectic of action accelerates this course; the tragic gesture of the Bundist [Jewish Socialist] leader Szmul Zygielbojm is a relevant example. Zygielbojm had been smuggled out of the Nazi-encircled Warsaw Ghetto to plead for help for the doomed Jews. When the world refused to listen, he took his own life. For, as he wrote in his suicide note, he felt he had no right to live while his comrades lay buried in the Warsaw rubble.[42]

The grandeur and desperation of Zygielbojm's tragic gesture are well beyond the scope of Bell's exploration of alienation in America. The difference between European and American experiences clearly indicates why American writers were reluctant to write directly of the Holocaust experience. Bell himself chooses Isaac Rosenfeld's *Passage from Home* as a "parable of alienation," a novel about a "sensitive son" that on the surface appears similar to other such novels. Yet in Rosenfeld's novel can be seen an early attempt to embody significant fragments of the Jewish tradition in a *tsadik* figure capable of transmitting a meaningful heritage. *Passage from Home* represents a transitional stage in the immigrant novel for while the center of consciousness is not himself an immigrant, he is able to draw upon that heritage.[43]

Bernard, the fourteen-year-old protagonist of *Passage from Home*, feels alienated from the life around him. But he searches for a rarer world and sometimes his unlikely grandfather is a highly ambiguous source for that alternate world. The grandfather is neither the saintly Hasid of Cahan's *shtetl* nor is he the unlikely conveyor of tradition whom Henry Roth created in the superficially unsavory, but spiritually sound, Reb Yidel Pankower. Bernard's grandfather has his feet insecurely in both worlds. As Bernard expresses it:

> I was tired of it, tired of this poor overdone figure of an old man, his endless complaints and ironies, his arrogance, wit, familiarity, his pinchings and pettings, angers and cranks, his constant unalleviated schlepperei [parasitism]. . . . For he was a miserable man who happened to be profoundly satisfied with his lot. . . . Was this, then, that Jewish spirit from which I had shut myself off? (pp. 86–87)

Clearly, the grandfather's smugness, his lack of perception, his feelings of well-being, his nonalienated state make him an unsuccessful source of values for his grandson. And yet, because he is an anachronism, Bernie and the reader become aware of unexpected sources of strength in this rather unpleasant old man. Through the grandfather Bernie experiences a rare moment of association of sensibility. The grandfa-

ther, despite corruption, maintains a viable connection with a
Hasidic (mystical and pietistic) sect. Both visit Reb Feldman,
the sect's bedridden and frail *rebe*, while the traditional talmudic discussion is in progress. The archetypal chess players
in the corner add to the impression of a part of the *shtetl*
transplanted to America. Bernard waits "for some sign of their
mysticism [p. 92]." Soon the talmudic discussion becomes a
chant and the chant becomes a rhapsodic dance and the bedridden *rebe*, whose wisdom has sparked the dance, partici-
pates by snapping his fingers to the rhythm. Even the querulous grandfather, who really has little comprehension of the
intellectual play that underlies the ecstasy of the Hasidim, is
nevertheless a part of the melding of intellect and emotion.
Admittedly this momentary transcendence offers a temporary
and primarily aesthetic experience for the grandson. But
grandfather's fleeting ascent, while anachronistic in the
grandson's world, is not, therefore, irrelevant to that world.
Completeness and *communitas* exist, at least as possibilities,
and, of course, in different and as yet unknown forms:

> I could see that my grandfather was transformed into a new
> person. A look of completeness lay on his face, an expres-
> sion of gratitude as if for the ecstatic understanding to
> which Feldman had led him. Though unable to understand,
> I had shared the experience of that ecstasy, and I, too, felt
> grateful for it. (p. 101)

The experience is a talisman for what Bernard is searching for:

> I, too, would have to know the truth. . . . For, as at Feld-
> man's house, when I had seen a moment of understanding
> pass before a group of old men and had felt that this repre-
> sented what was best in their lives and in Jewish life, so I
> now felt that possession of such understanding would be the
> very best of my own life and knowing the truth, itself a kind
> of ecstasy. (p. 101)

The grandfather's experience has been incorporated into
the grandson's perception. We can only speculate as to

whether Rosenfeld would have been able to sustain a vision of *communitas* and spiritual essence in a postadolescent protagonist. Even young Bernard recognizes the difficulty of synthesis:

> The task, then, was to turn away from circumstance, to unite the here and the there, this life and the other, in a single indifference for the sake of that alone which was real in us. But the rewards of such indifference could only be mystical; and as for myself, I lacked the courage. (p. 241)

Bernard is not yet ready to relinquish the world and the world's opinion.

Rosenfeld died in 1956 at thirty-eight years of age without having created any other fictional immigrant characters. However, a 1952 essay on Cahan's *The Rise of David Levinsky* indicates a continuation of interest in the subject. Of particular interest to my study is Rosenfeld's non-Levinskian Diaspora figure: anachronistic, sometimes comic, alienated from American life, a remnant of an earlier culture and time. Frequently powerless himself, this figure is an early model of positive alienation and as such capable of transmitting some authentic substance from an older culture that has the power to counteract the Levinskian anomie. Cahan's Reb Sender stays in the *shtetl;* Roth's Reb Yidel is a small part of David Schearl's temporary transcendence. Rosenfeld's protagonist, while unable to follow in the *tsadik*'s path, is nevertheless conscious of his worth and courage. Malamud's immigrant *tsadikim* are more relevant to the needs of his younger protagonists. In Bellow and Cohen the *tsadik* figure is also the protagonist—a development that illustrates the shift in interest from the child to the parent that is characteristic of post-Holocaust immigrant fiction.

The motifs of economic rise, assimilation, and acculturation, of language loss and adjustment, which were characteristic of early immigrant literature are muted or nonexistent in post-Holocaust immigrant literature. The new immigrant novel is far more concerned with spiritual accounting than with material assets and problems of communication. Early

immigrants were immediately distinguishable in America because of the way they looked and sounded. For the most part
they attempted to eliminate differences as quickly as possible.
Post-Holocaust immigrants are not so easily distinguishable
by clothing and accent. Yet they are far more separated from
those around them by their experience of suffering and they
cannot or perhaps will not erase those differences.

Part II

Post-Holocaust Immigrant-Survivor Fiction

Three

Survivor Literature

The term *immigrant,* with its nineteenth-century connotation of movement for the sake of economic and social advancement, is imprecise as a designation for any European who came to the United States after 1933 as an exile and refugee, or later as a survivor. Those postwar remnants who survived the ghettos, mass murders, and death camps, moreover, must be distinguished from the refugees who fled from persecution before and during the war. The immigrant-survivors of this study are the fictional counterparts of those Jews who came to the United States after World War II. They represent what remains of the thousand-year-old Eastern European Jewish culture of Yiddish-speaking Jews from whom the overwhelming majority of American Jews are descended.[1]

The flowering of Jewish American literature in the 1950s at first produced few novels that confronted the Holocaust. Many have commented upon the dearth of American Holocaust novels, and some have concurred with Alfred Kazin's belief that "no one can really write an imaginative work about the Nazi terror because art implies meaning and Hitler's whole regime represented an organized annihilation of meaning."[2] Whether the power of the imagination could turn this particular darkness into art is a question raised frequently by European critics such as A. Alvarez, T. W. Adorno, and George Steiner.[3] To reduce the gas ovens and crematoria to fictional subjects would seem to many a desecration beyond belief. Yet these critics agree that survivors like Elie Wiesel, Tadeusz Borowski, Primo Levi, and others have, with superhuman effort, created art out of personally experienced horror. Survivor literature in languages other than English became an important European genre as early as in the 1940s.[4] Survivor literature consists of firsthand accounts by the victims of their wartime ordeal in the ghettos and the camps. In place of the immediate experience of the personal witness, the nonsurvivor novelist substitutes knowledge, imagination, and the strategies of memory. But it was necessary that time elapse before this knowledge could become available to and be apprehended by the imagination.

The situation for the Yiddish writer was especially poignant. Some, like the Vilna poets Chaim Grade and Abram Sutskever and the Soviet novelist David Bergelson, were themselves survivors. Others had lost their families in the Holocaust; all had lost their audience. All postwar Yiddish literature is, in a sense, then, Holocaust literature, regardless of its form and even its theme. Much of it is written directly about the Holocaust—like Elie Wiesel's *Night* (1960), which was first published in Yiddish in 1956. Survivor memoirs, novels of concentration camp life and of resistance inside and outside the camps, and commemorative poetry continue to be published for a dwindling audience in a "martyred tongue."[5] Yet it is not these works, which dwell explicitly upon the Holocaust experience and openly lament the loss of audience and language, that comprise the most important present-day Yiddish literature. It is rather the fiction of Grade, Sutskever, Jacob Glatstein, and others, who recreate the vanished world of the prewar European *shtetl* and city. American readers are familiar with similar subject matter in the translated work of Isaac Bashevis Singer. Also, recent American novels, set in part or in toto on the lower East Side in the early decades of this century, have attempted an interesting variation on the theme of recapturing the Jewish past. Among them are E. L. Doctorow's *Ragtime* (1975) and Hugh Nissenson's *My Own Ground* (1976).

Polish survivors, such as Piotr Rawicz and Tadeusz Borowski, write of the death-camp experience with immediacy and authenticity. Another remarkable achievement is Jerzy Kosinski's semiautobiographical *The Painted Bird* (1965), which explores the wartime experience of a young child. It is one of the rare works by a survivor to have been written in English. These works and important examples of survivor literature, in German and French, are subjected to extensive analysis and commentary in the first full-length study of the literature of the Holocaust, Lawrence Langer's *The Holocaust and the Literary Imagination* (1975).[6] Another critical work, Terrence Des Pres' *The Survivor* (1976), also concerns itself with European survivor literature.[7] Langer's work includes a more developed aesthetics of "the literature of atrocity" and hence is more relevant to the present study than that of Des Pres. Basic to Langer's study and to other criticism of Holocaust literature is the premise that the writers of such literature believe that they are "working with raw material unprecedented in the literature of history or the history of literature."[8] As a corollary to the uniqueness of the literature of atrocity, Langer states that

> anyone seriously concerned with the literature of atrocity must devote his primary attention to those writers who were more closely allied with the events of the Holocaust even when they were not literally survivors, since they were the ones, notwithstanding intermittent moments of despair, who were destined to recreate in their art a unique portion of contemporary reality.

Langer then proceeds to turn this experiential criterion into an aesthetic judgment, as he compares the poetry of the non-survivors Sylvia Plath and Anthony Hecht with the poetry of the survivor Paul Celan. It is possible, however, to argue the superiority of Celan's poetic gifts rather than the authenticity of his experience as the crucial factor in what Langer calls Celan's "intensity of vision."[9]

Langer's ambiguous designation of "those writers who were more closely allied with the events of the Holocaust" creates other problems, for within that category he includes the German novelist Heinrich Böll. Unlike the other writers mentioned in Langer's work, Böll does not "focus on the dilemma of the actual victim in the Holocaust, Böll turns to the problem of the civilized German—is it legitimate to call him a different kind of victim?"[10] As the inclusion of Böll indicates, the question for Langer is rhetorical. There is no question that Böll is an important author who has written movingly and honestly of German guilt and the futility of expiation (*Billiards at Half-Past Nine* [1965]). But to bracket him with Langer's other survivor-writers is very problematic. For during the time that Elie Wiesel, Primo Levi, Arnöst Lustig, Tadeusz Borowski, and other survivor-writers were in Auschwitz, Heinrich Böll served in the army of the Third Reich. Böll earns his place in Langer's discussion because of what he writes and not because he is "a different kind of victim." Langer's treatment of Böll can be contrasted with a statement by the European-born George Steiner, who became a naturalized American in 1944. If, for Langer, Heinrich Böll is a different kind of victim, for Steiner, it may be said, the American Jew is a different kind of survivor.

> The idea that Jews everywhere have been maimed by the European catastrophe, that the massacre has left all who survived (even if they were nowhere near the actual scene) off balance, as does the tearing of a limb, is one which American Jews can understand in an intellectual sense.[11]

One need not agree with Steiner to recognize the literary implications of his statement. The Holocaust cannot be declared off limits as a subject for the critical intelligence or the fictive imagination. The value and effectiveness of a work of literature are not the by-products of the writer's geographical origins or biographical credentials.

A number of themes occur in both European and American Holocaust literature. In both settings survivors must come to terms with what Langer calls "the unspeakable horrors at the heart of the Holocaust experience," while those among whom they dwell have not experienced such horror. Langer finds other recurrent tropes in the literature: "the displacement of the consciousness of life by the imminence and pervasiveness of death; the violation of the coherence of childhood; the assault on physical reality; the disintegration of the rational intelligence; and the disruption of chronological time." [12] These themes occur also in the survivor fiction of American writers. Bellow's septuaginarian Artur Sammler, Wallant's pawnbroker, I. B. Singer's Herman Broder, and Schaeffer's Anya are ever aware of the immanence of death. The American novels contain graphic references to violence perpetrated on children. Each of the immigrant-survivor protagonists manifests disorientation from his surroundings, suffers visions, dreams, and nightmares and each, from time to time, admits to madness.

There are other themes and emphases in the immigrant-survivor novel set in America that clearly differentiate it from the European Holocaust novel. For example, unlike the European writer, the American novelist does not focus primarily and directly on *l'univers concentrationnaire*. Also, the fictional survivor-immigrant necessarily must encounter the American experience, although this requirement is far less strictly enforced than it was in the earlier immigrant novels. One of the most striking contrasts, however, lies in the American writer's attention to the Jewish past.

In his discussion of Heinrich Böll, Langer emphasizes that "the failure of the retrospective imagination to find meaning in history . . . dramatizes the absurd position of man as Survivor; the act of recollection, instead of forging links with the past, only widens the . . . gulf between the dead and the living." Böll's novels do emphasize discontinuity and anomie, "the sundering of each generation from the other" and the isolation of horrible events irreconcilable with the tradition of civilization. [13]

Böll's opinions on the irrelevance of tradition, history, and heritage are for Langer evidence of the extraordinary relevance of Böll's novel to Holocaust fiction. Langer faults André Schwarz-Bart's *The Last of the Just* (1960) for attempting to endow death in the gas chamber with the transcendent martyrdom of the Jewish tradition. Langer feels that the poison-filled void alienates the protagonist "from a past and future that might justify his merging with a mythical and universalized truth." [14]

Langer appears here to be insensitive to the differences

between the German past and the Jewish past. Without doubt the Nazi genocide of Jews and gypsies, the death camps, the cattle cars, and the crematoria were events irreconcilable with "any tradition of civilization." Diasporal Jewish history, on the other hand, according to Arthur Cohen, "is an undiverting chronicle of hard work and martyrs."[15] It matters not how these Jews died; it matters only that they were murdered because they were Jews. Like the religious fanaticism of previous times the secular madness of the Nazis created Jewish martyrs.

Langer's rather casual reduction of the particulars of the Jewish past is in sharp contrast to the attitude expressed in American survivor novels. Because the novels he discusses are set in a Europe that is still a charnel house, he is unable to see what the American novelist perceives, namely that the preservation and transmission of the past are essential to the survivors' fictional world. While the time and distance that separate America and the Jewish American novelist from the Holocaust allow him to take a view of the relationship between past and present that is less despairing than Langer's view, they do not prevent him from perceiving himself as a metaphoric survivor. This personal interest has literary and moral implications for the definition of the fictional early immigrant as well as the fictional immigrant-survivor. Irving Howe points out that were it not for those early immigrants and "an accident of geography we might also be bars of soap."[16] Thus the figure of the earlier Jewish immigrant is retroactively invested with prophetic resonance by the postwar writer.

The appearance in recent fiction of immigrants from the earlier period, the reissuing of works by Abraham Cahan, Henry Roth, and Anzia Yezierska as well as other novels of early immigrant life, the success of I. B. Singer's *shtetl*-based novels and stories, his Nobel Prize—all manifest a renewed interest in Jewish particularity and the Jewish past. Their evocation of particularity and historicity and their direct portrayal of Holocaust survivors are aspects of the Jewish American writers' response to the destruction of European Jewry and are

central to their representation of post-Holocaust consciousness.

The development of this consciousness took some time.
Important imaginative literature about the Holocaust by American writers did not appear until the 1960s. Even so, writers
were preoccupied with the theme much earlier. In 1949 Isaac
Rosenfeld wrote that

> it is impossible to live, to think, to create without bearing
> witness against the terror. . . . There is no more good and
> evil—if there were the screams would have been heard.
> There is only the terror.[17]

Rosenfeld and others could, in essay form, broach a subject
that they could not as yet represent fictionally. It may be sur-
mised that the novels of the forties and early fifties—the sensitive son novels—were set in earlier, prewar times precisely to
avoid imaginative confrontation with the European Jewish experience. Numbness, horror, shock, and outrage are not conventional stances for modern novelists and poets. The group
of writers that includes Bellow, Malamud, both Henry and
Philip Roth, and others has long been wary of poetry that has
designs upon the reader. Bellow pleads in the sixties for Jewish writing that recognizes "the distinction between public
relations and art."[18] Norma Rosen in the seventies asks: "How
could the virtues of fiction—indirection, irony, ambivalence—
be used to make art out of this unspeakable occurrence?"[19]
Yet the need to imaginatively confront the unspeakable remained, for while there was a question as to whether one
could "make art" from this kind of truth, it was never doubted
that an effective way in which to recognize the truth was
through imaginative art.

Distance and displacement are used by some writers as a
means of conveying post-Holocaust consciousness. Norma
Rosen describes her novelistic stance to the Holocaust as that
of a "witness through the imagination," a "documenter of
those who have (merely) 'heard the terrible news' "![20] Practicing what she advocates, Rosen's novel, Touching Evil (1969),
focuses on the reactions of American non-Jews to the televised

proceedings of the Eichmann trial. Her elaborate distancing strategies show her reluctance to present the experience directly. Concern with the Jewish catastrophe also motivates novels that treat the American immigrant past such as Hugh Nissenson's *My Own Ground* and Jay Neugeboren's *An Orphan's Tale* (1976). Both novels center on Jewish orthodoxy and identity without apologia or sentimentality and are influenced by both postmodernism and post-Holocaust consciousness.

One of the most provocative and better known among these newer Jewish American writers is Cynthia Ozick, herself a tough-minded spokeswoman for Jewish particularity. Her credo, issued in 1970, is an attack on the universalism of many Jewish American writers. Typically, Ozick warns that

> if we blow into the narrow end of the shofar [the traditional ram's horn blown on the high holidays], we will be heard far. But if we choose to be mankind rather than Jewish and blow into the wide part, we will not be heard at all.[21]

Ozick's work projects her theory. Her successful novella, "Envy; or Yiddish in America" (1969), concerns a Yiddish poet, a survivor of the older generation of immigrants and of a once viable Yiddish literary culture.[22] A more recent work, "Bloodshed" (1976), can be compared to Philip Roth's story "Eli, the Fanatic" (1959). While Ozick's novella suffers in the comparison, juxtaposing the two works highlights the increased emphasis on Jewishness and traditionalism that is part of the post-Holocaust sensibility.

In Roth's story the parvenu Jewish inhabitants of a formerly restricted, all-gentile community are embarrassed and dismayed by the establishment of an orthodox *yeshive* in their suburban Eden of Woodenton. Eli, a young lawyer in the community, is asked to get these oddly dressed religious "fanatics" out of the homogenized suburb. That the men and boys are survivors of the Holocaust is irrelevant in the view of the embarrassed Jewish members of the community. Eli's confrontation with the head of the *yeshive* (a *tsadik* who upholds the Law while Eli discusses zoning laws) results in a reversal whereby Eli exchanges his American grey flannel uniform for the musty, traditional clothing of the Hasid. Eli's "conversion" may be temporary but it makes for a successful short story.

One of the rhetorical features of Ozick's work is that she lets her reader know that she is alluding to the work of other writers: for example, Roth's story is very much a part of the context of "Bloodshed." Ozick's protagonist is, like Eli, a liberal, secular, assimilated American Jew. It is he who journeys westward from New York City to a new small self-contained Hasidic community where his assimilation to the American way is the anomaly. Ironically the protagonist's westward journey to the mythic American wilderness is a journey back in time to a place where traditional Jewish practices survive, stubbornly unassimilated. And in a profoundly American manner, the Hasidic community, with its separation from the surrounding non-Jewish milieu, its commitment to hard work, study, and strict obedience to the Law, is an exotic variant of the Puritan heritage enunciated by John Winthrop. For the Massachusetts Bay Colony looked upon itself as a group of people chosen to be a model for others, "as a city on a hill." [23] Other religious minorities—Mormons, Shakers, Mennonites— separated themselves from the American mainstream and sought to maintain their idiosyncratic identity by moving west. But the Hasidic community contains an added dimension in that it is made up of Holocaust survivors. Bleilip, the protagonist, comes as a parasite and a voyeur and he is harshly and justly exposed and humiliated by the rebe.

While the story lacks the compassion and grace of Roth's tale, the tough-minded and rigorous Hasidism described by Ozick is infinitely more demanding than a temporarily donned Hasidic costume. But for all its resonant parallels, Ozick's work and the fiction of Nissenson and Neugeboren are not major post-Holocaust American fiction. The writers are, however, representative of a tendency to emphasize Jewish particularity and historicity that is shared by better known Jewish American writers as well.

Saul Bellow, Edward Wallant, I. B. Singer, Susan Fromberg Schaeffer, and others fictionally address the problem of how one lives in contemporary America after experiencing the horrors of the European catastrophe. The fictional survivor is of necessity an immigrant but one who differs in crucial ways from the earlier immigrants created by Abraham Cahan and Henry Roth. The immigrant-survivor is more a *luftmentsh* (one who lives on and in air) than were his predecessors. In this he is not only the product of a literary context that values myth and the absurd over the realism and socioeconomics of earlier times. Modern history as well as literary modernism is responsible for the lack of corporeality of some postwar fictional immigrants. They come as remnants of a murdered culture rather than as fragments of an atrophying one. They leave behind them no sustaining vision of a traditional *shtetl* or of urban European culture. They come out of a European past they have been forced to abandon to confront an American scene far more complex than the one encountered by earlier immigrants.

Post-Holocaust Jewish writers do not focus primarily on the problems of the immigrant's encounter with American society, nor is assimilation the central issue, although both encounter and assimilation are part of the fictional context. Most often the most crucial encounter is with the collective Jewish past. The rescue and transmission of fragments of the Jewish past require new strong emphasis on the particulars of that past no matter how disguised. Through the use of the immigrant-survivor, the novels examined in the following pages emphasize particularity, history, and tradition in rhetorically economical ways. For, regardless of how alienated the immigrant-survivor is from traditional Jewishness, his experience of the Holocaust has made it possible for him to embody, preserve, and transmit significant fragments of the Jewish past.

These works contradict Leslie Fiedler's dictum that "the writing of the American-Jewish novel is essentially, then, an act of assimilation: a demonstration that there is an American Jew . . . and that he feels at home!"[24] Fiedler's exuberant description of Jewish American interaction applies to many pre-World War II novels. More recent novels, with immigrant-survivor protagonists, are likely to stress the homelessness of the immigrant, his separation from Americans who have not experienced near-death and qualified rebirth as he has. Yet these latter-day Diasporans are more at ease in their Jewishness than was Cahan's David Levinsky. The relative openness and the pervasive anonymity of American society allow not only for the survival of these human remnants but also for the survival of the unassimilated fragments of culture, history, and religion that they embody.

The various writers discussed embody such unassimilated fragments in a variety of prose fiction forms. The anatomy, for example, with its varied subject matter and strong emphasis on ideas, is an appropriate form for the new immigrant novel. Not all the novels, however, are anatomies although all contain anatomical elements. Accordingly, the order of discussion generally moves from the more conventionally novelistic forms through the romantic mode and concludes with the most anatomical of the works. Malamud, fittingly, falls outside even such a loose schema. His works are discussed first not only because he was the earliest among important Jewish writers to seriously consider the immigrant character, but also because (with the exception of *The Fixer* [1966]) his is the most metaphoric and indirect presentation of post-Holocaust consciousness. Much more direct and novelistic are Edward Wallant's *The Human Season* and *The Pawnbroker*. These two novels feature both pre- and post-Holocaust immigrants, thereby allowing for parallels and contrasts. Juxtaposed to Wallant's naturalistic fiction is a historical novel, *Anya* by Susan Fromberg Schaeffer. Not only does Schaeffer's work present the European past in copious detail, it is elegaic in mood and includes mythical and legendary material.

The immigrant-survivor protagonists of *Mr. Sammler's Planet, Enemies,* and *In the Days of Simon Stern* are philosophers. Malamud's fixer grows intellectually during his imprisonment. These thoughtful and articulate protagonists are the post-Holocaust counterparts of the perceptive personae in the European Holocaust literature of Borowski, Rawicz, Schwarz-

Bart, and others. The protagonist of Wiesel's *Night* as a child in Auschwitz and as a survivor in retrospect ponders grave theological questions. These characters raise questions that are largely unanswerable by either character or reader. Far less aware are the bewildered child protagonist of Kosinski's *The Painted Bird* and Ladislav Fuks' elderly Jew in *Mr. Theodore Mundstock* (1968) who futilely attempt to make sense of their nightmare world. These victims' painful innocence and error coupled with the reader's prior knowledge of the historical facts result in a bitter and ironic analogue of classic "comic" distance. Since in these examples of European Holocaust literature the emphasis is often on the experience as it is happening to the victim, the reader's superior knowledge serves to increase horror and dread. In the retrospective experience of the post-Holocaust immigrant-survivor, such distance between reader and character is inappropriate. The perspective acquired by the survivor because of distance and time lends itself to intellectual and moral exploration of his experience.

Through memory and speculation the victim who was deprived of the power of action by his oppressors is frequently able to achieve self-perception by exploring his individual past and the collective Jewish past. The pain and anguish of the quest and the historic magnitude of the context endows the immigrant-survivor with a modern equivalent of tragic stature. For the most part the tragedy lies outside the individual's power and responsibility in the enormity of the catastrophe. Within this context the protagonists may perform heroic actions or they may not. Far more important in post-Holocaust literature is the action that takes place in their minds. Those who have undergone death and experienced unimaginable but historic hell are expected to emerge with uncommon insight. Not all the fictional survivors meet the challenge. Those who do undertake the painful quest for comprehension, however incomplete, mitigate the pathos of their undeserved misfortune with heroic efforts of mind.

The master novelists, Malamud, Singer, and Bellow, subsume ideas within absorbing fictional worlds. Cohen's philosophical and theological concerns are more overtly presented.

While not all immigrant-survivor novels are novels of ideas, they are all historical novels. The use of such subject matter requires attention to historical as well as imaginative truth. In this regard Aristotle's comment about the superiority of imaginative literature in depicting what may happen rather than historically relating what has happened is pertinent to the discussion of Wallant's *The Pawnbroker*, Schaeffer's *Anya*, as well as Malamud's *The Fixer*.

The works discussed vary in intellectual content and historicity and these factors, along with more conventional fictional elements, determine differences in form, emphasis, and quality. The order of discussion (with the exception of Malamud) reflects an increase in formal complexity rather than a hierarchy of quality. Bellow's Mr. Sammler is the most interesting and comprehensive of protagonists, but Cohen's novel is the last to be discussed because in form it is a complex compendium of historical, theological, and moral themes characteristic of post-Holocaust consciousness.

Four

Malamud's Secular Saints and Comic Jobs

No contemporary American writer has written about immigrants and survivors more frequently or more imaginatively than has Bernard Malamud. His fictional world is peopled with Diasporans of all kinds but, unlike Cahan's assimilated Levinsky, Malamud's characters embody significant fragments of the Jewish past. Most frequently Malamud portrays remnants of the earlier generation of immigrants, unwilling refugees from American Jewish affluence, survivors of an older Jewish community who retain unassimilated Jewish values and who do not relinquish their accents and their anachronistic occupations. Although Malamud includes some survivors of the Holocaust in his fictional Ellis Island, he has not yet directly portrayed a survivor as central figure. In *The Fixer*, however, Malamud depicts an earlier survivor of anti-Semitic persecution and this work is cited by Terrence Des Pres as an example of a survivor novel along with Albert Camus' *The Plague* (1948) and Alexandr Solzhenitsyn's *One Day in the Life of Ivan Denisovitch* (1963).

With the exception of *The Fixer*, which is historically distanced from the Nazi period, Malamud's allusive, indirect, parablelike tales of Jewish life do not confront the Holocaust experience. Nevertheless, Malamud's immigrant characters, even when they are not survivors, frequently have the insubstantiality of remnants or of dream figures. Insofar as they embody the modern sense of dream-made-real, Malamud's immigrants resemble the European survivors discussed by Lawrence Langer.[1] However, only in *The Fixer*, where the dream is a nightmare indeed, does Malamud's world contain the horrors that Langer includes in the aesthetics of atrocity. In Malamud's other fictions the grotesque elements are countered with the possibility of realizing the Diaspora dream of earthly redemption. In addition, Malamud's modern adaptation of the traditionally ironic tone of the Yiddish story teller distances and ameliorates some of the grimmer implications of his fiction.

The dreamlike insubstantiality, the redemptive vision, and the irony are frequently manifested in Malamud's modern counterparts to the East European Hasidic *rebes* and *tsadikim*. Malamud's modern *tsadikim* are considerably less saintly than their historic predecessors, but their very susceptibility to the modern world allows them to be more effective as teachers—the essential task of a *rebe*. Fictional antecedents for Malamud's *rebes* are Henry Roth's Reb Yidel Pankower and Isaac Rosenfeld's Reb Feldman. In Rosenfeld's novel the relationship of the *rebe* to the young seeker is shown as anachronistic. In the writings of Malamud, the teacher is both more ambiguous and more effective, yet the ancient Jewish paradigm is discernible. The pupil-teacher relationship may be of a younger, assimilated Jew to an older, more traditional Jew; sometimes the relationship is between Jew and gentile; usually the relationship is between a more callow seeker and one more experienced in suffering. Frequently Malamud develops the quester and the teacher as dual protagonists or *Doppelgänger* (*The Assistant*, "The Magic Barrel," "The Last Mohican" [1958]). The immigrant figure is the keeper of the Jewish past, a past that is transmitted in much the same way that the Hasidic masters passed on wisdom and lore to their pupils. Indirectly by means of parable, sometimes fragmentarily, sometimes inadvertently, unlikely modern Hasidim like Morris Bober, Pinye Salzman, Shimen Susskind, and others pass on meaningful fragments of Jewish ethics and collective Jewish history to questers and novices who are even more unlikely and unaware than their teachers.

The Malamud novice or quester is frequently in error at the beginning of his quest. Sometimes he attempts to make a new life free of his past (*Pictures of Fidelman* [1969], "Lady of the Lake" [1958]) or attempts to live a life in terms of false goals (*The Assistant,* "The Magic Barrel"). Through his encounter with an immigrant or exile, the quester once more confronts his own historic past or reforms his goals and sometimes, in classic style, achieves recognition and reversal. The contact between quester and immigrant *Doppelgänger* at times results in the quester's seeming to incorporate the older figure. The older figure may wane, even die, but some of his spirit or knowledge lives on in the now-changed quester. Three of Malamud's most widely known works are examples of this pattern—the novel *The Assistant* and the short stories "The Magic Barrel" and "The Last Mohican."

Frank Alpine, the assistant in the novel, is a climber, a man clearly destined for higher things. Unlike many of Malamud's protagonists (Fidelman, Levin, Freeman, Lesser, Bok), Frank is not Jewish, at least not at the beginning of the novel. Although an American, Frank feels alienated because he is an orphan, a Catholic, a drifter. What he learns from Morris Bober is how to be a Jew, which in Malamud's terms means how to be a human being.

It has been common to stress the ecumenicalism of Malamud's concept of Jewishness.[2] But to stress the universality and Christianity of Malamud's "conversions" and reversals is to ignore the concrete Jewish particulars in which those universals are grounded. Bober's Judaism, particularly in its unorthodoxy, in its flawed state, is thereby more relevant to the flawed seeker. Of all Malamud's immigrant *rebes,* Bober comes closest to secular sainthood. Morris is a Jobian sufferer as well as a Sabbath-breaking, ham-eating sage. In his insistence on scrupulous honesty in a dishonest world, Morris Bober is a true follower of the Torah in modern dress. Malamud evokes with loving irony, older, folkloric Jewish themes transformed by the passage of time. This occurs in the oft-quoted passage where Morris, self-conscious and under stress, explains to Frank that to be a Jew one must suffer for the Law. For Morris this does not mean Sabbath observance, or adherence to Leviticus, but rather "this means to do what is right, to be honest, to be good. This means to other people."³ Some have been offended by the simplicity of the reductivism; others have noted the resemblance to the Sermon on the Mount.⁴ But the steadfastness is Jobian and talmudic.

Malamud is reaching back to a well-known Jewish anecdote about the great Rabbi Hillel (first century B.C.E.). The rabbi was challenged by a heathen who said he would become a Jew if the wisdom of the Torah could be expressed while standing on one foot. Hillel had no difficulty in replying, "That which is hurtful to thee do not do to thy neighbors! This is the entire Torah, all the rest is commentary. Go and study it."⁵ The sources do not tell us whether the conversion took place; but in Malamud's novel the seeker, perhaps more sincere than his ancient predecessor, by action, experience, and precept does indeed become Jewish. Somewhat vulgarized by an immigrant accent (of which more later), an ancient Jewish truth is transmitted.

Bober himself survives in a depressionlike atmosphere that has been noted for its timelessness.⁶ Yet the time of the novel is more easily set than seems apparent. Malamud is careful to show that although time stands still for the unsuccessful Bobers, history relentlessly moves forward. The time is that of late thirties to early forties—after the rise of Hitler and just before America's entry into the war. Much of the novel is formed by the Holocaust in a peripheral, nonfrontal manner. The Assistant, although it refers back to the late thirties, was published in 1957 and reflects Malamud's awareness of the horror.

There is, for example, the omnipresence of anti-Semitism in the work. Frank Alpine, despite his potential for spiritual growth, acquiesces in robbing Morris, in part because Morris is a Jew. The instigator of the robbery, Ward Minogue, is full of generalized hatred for Jews. He mouths stereotypes about Jewish wealth while robbing the pauper Bober. He attempts to rape Bober's daughter because he heard "those Jew girls make nice ripe lays [p. 74]." The Bobers feel isolated among their predominantly gentile neighbors as do the other Jews in the neighborhood. Thus Otto, the German butcher, who has sold

Morris meat for years and who knows what kind of economic misery he suffers, nevertheless warns Frank, " 'Don't work for a Yid, Kiddo. They will steal your ass while you are sitting on it' [p. 60]." Morris strains to pay cash to Otto because "from a German he wanted no favors [p. 6]." Even the new grocery, which is such a devastating threat to Morris, is owned by a German. And Morris's decent Italian tenants buy their groceries at the new store to "be waited on by Heinrich Schmitz, an energetic German dressed like a doctor, in a white duck jacket [p. 12]."

The highly unlikely prospective buyer of Morris's miserable business is a "refugee." That he has escaped some as yet unknown horror is the only glimpse we are given of this man who is still refugee, not yet survivor: "He wore a small foreign-looking hat and carried a loose umbrella. His face was innocent and his eyes glistened with good will [p. 203]." Morris was "overwhelmed by pity for the poor refugee, at what he had in all probability lived through, a man who had sweated blood to save a few brutal dollars [p. 203]." But Morris and the refugee are innocent also in that neither yet knows of the totality of the European catastrophe that is dimly perceived in the background. Yet with care Malamud presents the imminence of war to the reader. At the end of the work, after Morris's death, his wife supplements her meager income "sewing epaulettes for military uniforms [p. 233]."

The presence of history is more dramatically rendered in the form of the novel. Frank Alpine is converted from a conventional Jew-hater, who admits that he "didn't have use for the Jews [p. 125]," into a definite Jew-lover, who first craves Morris's daughter carnally and then loves Morris filially. The ultimate action, almost a ritualized punishment for lust, is Frank's circumcision, which "enraged and inspired him [p. 192]." Significantly it is spring when Frank becomes a Jew. Though the Easter story of death and resurrection is surely part of Malamud's rich allusiveness, Malamud's text says "Passover," which celebrates redemption from pagan bondage and anticipates the giving of the Law. In addition, the ironist in Malamud should never be dismissed. Passover is the traditional time for anti-Semitic blood-libels and persecutions of Jews in Eastern Europe, a theme Malamud pursues pointedly in *The Fixer.* Spring renewal with its pogroms and suffering often has a bitter taste in Yiddish literature. Morris has been sacrificed and Frank has metonymously taken part in his sacrifice through the ritual of circumcision.

Far more self-serving than the saintly grocer is the ephemeral Pinye Salzman, the matchmaker of the title story in the collection *The Magic Barrel.*[7] He is even more a survivor of the earlier pre-Holocaust European culture: as a matchmaker his occupation is more anachronistic than that of the "Ma and Pa" grocery store owner. Yet because of Pinye, whether by intention or not, Leo Finkle changes his quest from an opportunistic search for a proper bride for a rabbi to a spiritual journey in search of redemption for himself and for Pinye's wayward daughter. The matchmaker appears and disappears like some orthodox-unorthodox fairy godfather; but he is a materialist nonetheless. Leo's oxymoron for him is "commercial cupid."

Pinye is literally a *luftmentsh;* his wife says his office is "in the air" and "in his socks [MB, p. 189]." Pinye's measure of a successful match is the traditional one: it should join piety and learning to money and status. Leo at first is as practical as Pinye: he seeks a bride to acquire a congregation. Of course, Leo's learning and piety are shown to be shallow and his eventual bride may be nothing but a poor prostitute. In the end Pinye remains with feet in both worlds, while Leo has perceived that he can now love everyone and that redemption can come through love and suffering. In the final tableau Leo, with flowers in outstretched arms, runs to meet his love, who stands under a street lamp, smoking. Pinye waits around the corner, chanting the prayer for the dead. Leo has already been "afflicted by the tormenting suspicion that Salzman had planned it all to happen this way [MB, p. 213]." But what of the reader's suspicions? For whom, ask critic and reader, does Pinye pray? Sidney Richman, who describes Pinye as half criminal, half messenger of God, offers a range of possibilities:

It is impossible to tell for whom Pinye chants—for himself and his guilt . . . for Finkle's past or Finkle's future, or for all these reasons. . . . that Salzman chants for everything seems only proper; for if Leo has graduated into saint and rabbi, it is only by succumbing to the terrors which the role prescribes. What better reason to chant when to win means to lose.[8]

In the Malamudian world the "evil" of an orthodox rabbi married to a reformed prostitute would only be mourned by a practical *luftmentsh* like Salzman. It is surely too cynical and literal to suggest that Pinye is mourning his matchmaking fee, yet it is not too far-fetched to feel that he may be mourning his own loss of integrity or Leo's loss of success. The reversal has taken place: Pinye, now ascetic, dignified, and orthodox, stands motionless while a flower-bedecked Leo runs, lured by visions of violins and lighted candles. No explication suffices or seems really called for—it is a bravely ambiguous ending. Pinye now shares with Leo the suffering his daughter has previously inflicted on him alone. Malamud's critics may not have recognized his unique brand of negative capability.

Malamud exhibits courage in the ease with which he treats sacrosanct subjects in his fictional use of holocaust survivors. Few of his contemporaries have been so casual or so comic, although Wallant and I. B. Singer have presented unpleasant and opportunistic Holocaust survivors. But only Malamud, with his fabulist's license, has created such a comic survivor as the artful Susskind of "The Last Mohican."

Susskind, the quintessential *shnorer* ('clever beggar'), can also be a teacher, even a Virgilian spiritual leader. He is truly a remnant of remnants, a survivor of survivors, and the last of his tribe. He has survived the death camps and is a "refugee" from Israel. His reasons for leaving Israel are an indication of his incorrigible marginality: " 'Too much heavy labor for a man of my modest health. Also I couldn't stand the suspense' [MB, p. 143]." So this remnant looks for shady deals, quick profits, and Jews to sponge on in Rome. Fidelman is the comic Dante to Susskind's Virgil.

Fidelman, at the beginning, is involved in a pretentious and alien occupation, that of academic art critic writing a study of the fourteenth-century Florentine artist Giotto, a painter of Christian subjects. In one of the most patent of Malamudian rebirths, Fidelman is literally led through his Jewish past in a search for Susskind, who has stolen the first and only chapter of the manuscript. Significantly on a Friday night, Fidelman goes from synagogue to ghetto, symbolically traversing two thousand years of Jewish history in Europe, a history that culminates for him in the old Jewish cemetery with its memorial to Auschwitz. Previously Italian Renaissance history, aesthetic and Christian, had "exalted" him (MB, p. 141); European-Jewish history oppressed him, attached him to a past he had tried to ignore, "although, he joked to himself, it added years to his life [MB, p. 159]."

The usual reversal completes the story. Fidelman, now resembling his shabby quarry, sees Susskind engaged in what appears to be an alien occupation, that of selling beads and rosaries in front of the Vatican. Malamud has done his ironic homework, for the selling of Christian religious objects has long been a traditional occupation among Rome's Jews. Even in this, the surface shnorer Susskind has more integrity than the secret shnorer Fidelman. But Fidelman is worthy of regeneration, for he has a moment of "triumphant insight" in which he recognizes that Susskind was right to burn Fidelman's Giotto chapter. Susskind has said that "the words were there but the spirit was missing [MB, p. 164]." What endows the unlikely Susskind with exemplary artistic integrity in a world of pretentious sham is his superiority in suffering, his experience of Jewish history. And what finally gives the pretender, Fidelman, his insight is his own condensed, removed recapitulation of that experience heightened by his own sense of loss. For Fidelman has been the parasite—living off his sister and, as dilettante, poaching on Roman history, Italian art, and Christian subject matter. In a dream Susskind asks Fidelman if he has read Tolstoy, and then enquires, " 'Why is art?' [MB, p. 164]." The morality is Tolstoyan. Art must illuminate the human; the human takes precedence over the aesthetic. The human is the way toward the aesthetic.

The Magic Barrel contains other stories of survivors and immigrants. Frequently Malamud presents a learning situation. In "The First Seven Years" the immigrant Feld learns from his younger helper, Sobel. Sobel's superiority in suffering, his experience as a survivor, give him the moral advantage and it is Feld who ends with material aspirations subsumed by insight. The dreary setting is alleviated not only by the book culture that surrounds Sobel but also by the biblical overtones that Malamud invokes. Sobel has labored for five years for his modern Laban; but he must "pound leather for his love" for two years more to conform to the biblical seven. One can only hope that the title does not suggest that Sobel, like Jacob, will have to labor an additional seven years for his Rachel.

Two more stories, "Take Pity" and "The Loan," directly involve immigrants and survivors and in neither story is there redemption or resurrection. Eva, the refugee widow of "Take Pity," has learned only one thing, to refuse pity, and has gained in fierce pride. This bleak tale pits Rosen's need to give against Eva's inability to take. Not all the characters in Malamud's universe are capable of transcending suffering: the sufferer is not necessarily ennobled.

In "The Loan," however, Malamud's imaginative boldness asserts itself. The immigrant baker Lieb (from the verb "to love") sells the "bread of affliction," which is the designation for the unleavened bread of the Passover service. Lieb's bread is leavened with his own tears. It is extremely popular; all come to buy where the body of the world's ills is shared as in communion. An old friend appears in the bakery to request a loan. Lieb's second wife, suspicious, possessive, self-conscious of her status as second wife, refuses to leave them alone, yet by the pervasive Malamudian pattern of reversal—epiphanylike in this story—Bessie is seen as the superior sufferer despite her apparent selfishness and lack of charity. Kobotsky, the friend, despite his Job-like afflictions (he even suffers from boils), is not as pitiable. He appears to have been Lieb's betrayer, and he is self-pitying. Yet, honorably, he is seeking money to buy a headstone for his wife's grave, and his tale makes even Bessie weep.

Kobotsky's sad tale is given perspective by the weight of Bessie's suffering. Her recital of twentieth-century Jewish woes is authorially and soberly presented:

> But Bessie, though weeping, shook her head and before they could guess what, had blurted out the story of her afflictions: how the Bolsheviki came . . . and dragged her beloved father into snowy fields without his shoes; the shots scattered the blackbirds in the trees and the snow oozed blood; . . . how she, . . . years later found sanctuary in the home of an older brother in Germany, who sacrificed his own chances to send her, before the war, to America, and himself ended, with wife and daughter, in one of Hitler's incinerators. (MB, p. 172)

The passage has dignity, yet in the placement of modifiers (before the war, himself ended) there is a foreshadowing of Bessie's own voice, which speaks out in the subsequent paragraph:

> "Working day and night, I fixed up for him his piece of business and we make now, after twelve years, a little living. But Lieb is not a healthy man, also with his eyes that he needs an operation, and this is not yet everything." (MB, p. 172)

The differences in tone and diction are obvious, but even more striking are the similarities in rhythm and structure. And, in Malamud's story, "this is not yet everything." For, during Bessie's dramatic recital, Lieb's tear-moistened loaves are burning. The unmarked grave of Kobotsky's wife is seen in the context of millions of unmarked graves: "The loaves in the trays were blackened bricks—charred corpses [MB, p. 173]." The diction is deliberate and the parallels point to no easy morality. It would be beyond the boundaries of this study to analyze all Malamud's short stories in which immigrant characters figure. It should be noted, however, that of the thirteen stories in the 1958 collection, *The Magic Barrel*, seven directly focus on immigrants and an eighth has a Holocaust survivor as heroine.

In *Idiots First* (1963),[9] Malamud continues to write about the lives of European-born Jews. In one story in the collection, "The German Refugee," he depicts an actual refugee. Malamud here writes of an educated immigrant like the secular and intellectual Jews favored in the fiction of Bellow. The narrator is a "dangling man" who teaches English to refugees. It is 1939 and the narrator says, " 'Here I was palpitating to get going, and across the ocean Adolf Hitler, in black boots and a square mustache, was tearing up and spitting out all the flowers' [IF, p. 175]." The irony, the innocence, and the brutality are American.

The story gives Malamud the opportunity to use accent in varying ways. The refugee, Oskar Gassner, despondent over his lack of progress, asks his tutor, " 'do you sink I will succezz?' " and immediately the stage German is followed by a sensitive analysis of what loss of language means for the refugee. Here were cultivated European intellectuals who felt "you had some subtle thought and it comes out like a piece of broken bottle," who expressed their loss of linguistic identity with despair: " 'What I know, indeed, what I am, becomes to me a burden. My tongue hangs useless.' " In contrast to the articulate older exile, Oskar is comic but moving: " 'If I do not this legture prepare, I will take my life' [IF, p. 181]."

But, for all the pity Oskar evokes, he is in error and must learn a bitter lesson. He is self-concerned and, like Kobotsky, self-pitying. He does not listen to news broadcasts. Instead, "in tormented English he conveyed his intense and everlasting hatred of the Nazis for destroying his career, uprooting his life after half a century, and flinging him like a piece of bleeding meat to the hawks [IF, p. 182]." Oskar is shown as insufficiently compassionate, despite his suffering. Thus, after twenty-seven years of marriage and despite her protestations of faithfulness, he left his gentile wife behind in Germany.

Oskar does not think about his wife. Indeed it is despair about his lecture that causes him to attempt suicide. Finally, with the narrator's help, he prepares his lecture on Whitman. He shows that the Whitmanesque idea of brotherhood influenced German poets but, he adds ironically, not for long. Yet a greater irony is revealed in the dénouement: the idea of brotherhood survived in Oskar's abandoned wife who converted to Judaism in outrage and despair after he left Germany. For this romantic gesture she is arrested, "she is shot in the head and topples into an open tank ditch, with the naked Jewish men, their wives and children, some Polish soldiers and a handful of Gypsies [IF, p. 191]." When Oskar learns of his wife's death, he once more attempts suicide and this time succeeds.

The Fixer (1966) is relevant to the discussion of postwar immigrant fiction because of the novel's evocation of the Holocaust in the oblique manner of some Jewish American writers. Malamud says that the story of Mendl Beilis, the history upon which the fiction is based, was paradigmatic for him: "Somewhere along the line, what had happened in Nazi Germany began to be important to me in terms of the book, and that too is part of Yakov's story." [10] To include the Jewish catastrophe, Malamud confronts it indirectly, in microcosm, in the past. For what actually happened to Mendl Beilis is far less important than what the fixer and the reader experience of the condition of Jewish life in Eastern Europe. In addition, Malamud avails himself of the reader's knowledge of the contemporary Jewish tragedy to illuminate both past and recent history. The fact that there was a Beilis case allows Malamud to ignore its historic particulars and thereby create an imaginative truth that is more effective than fictionalized history.

The Fixer is the only one of Malamud's novels that is completely set in the European past and it is both distinctly European and Jewish. [11] Yakov Bok, an unsuccessful husband and handyman, leaves the traditional shtetl for the city (Kiev), doffs his Jewish identity, and rises economically for a short time only to find himself unjustly accused of ritual murder. His imprisonment and its accompanying torture, cruelty, and humiliation are the concrete manifestations of a virulent and irrational anti-Semitism exploited by a corrupt and frightened Czarist government. Yakov comes to realize that "being born a Jew meant being vulnerable to history, including its worst errors [p. 128]." Although Yakov is in some measure responsible for his plight, he recognizes that his parents, humble *shtetl* dwellers all their lives, were not therefore safe when "the historical evil had galloped in to murder them there [p. 255]." The future of Jews in Europe is succinctly stated by the lawyer Ostrovsky: "Rich or poor, those of our brethren who can run out of here are running. Some who can't are already mourning. They sniff at the air and it stinks of pogrom [p. 247]."

The desperation of the European Jewish condition is skillfully underscored by the Dostoyevskian motifs in the novel. Kogin, the prison guard, sorrows over his son who kills "a harmless old man" for "no particular reason" and is tried and sentenced to twenty years in Siberia (pp. 219–20). In terms of "crime and punishment" Kogin's son was treated justly and properly. Such procedures are not available to the Jew Bok. That Yakov is not completely innocent is allusively shown when he, like Raskolnikov, dreams of beating a poor, bloody horse. The horse was given to Yakov by his *tsadik* father-in-law, but Yakov condemns the horse to death by trading the animal to a Charon-like vicious anti-Semite in exchange for transportation to the non-Jewish world. Yakov betrays the horse, the symbol of his Jewish identity, at the same time that his prayer sack falls into the Dnieper (p. 29).

Yakov is guilty of refusing the burden of his Jewish heritage but ultimately he endures because of his acceptance of the responsibility of Jewish identity. In this he may be seen to resemble other Malamudian heroes who learn to relinquish personal advancement in exchange for spiritual growth. Yakov's final recognition, however, has naught to do with the power of love. On the contrary, he triumphs when he fears less and hates more (p. 259). In a perception unique in the Malamud canon, Yakov endorses revolution and political activism:

As for history, Yakov thought, there are ways to reverse it. What the Tsar deserves is a bullet in the gut. Better him than us. . . . One thing I've learned, he thought, there's no such thing as an unpolitical man, especially a Jew. You can't be one without the other, that's clear enough. You can't sit still and see yourself destroyed. (p. 271)

The role of the victim and the importance of personal redemption through suffering (whether in Dostoyevsky or Malamud himself) are here rejected in favor of collective commitment and political violence. Whether Yakov's perception is historically correct or not, there is no question that his own extreme but historically valid experience of Jewish life in Europe justifies his conclusion. Malamud's highly selective use of history and his detailed portrayal of the growth of Yakov's perception result in a highly individual hero who also has collective identity and universality. But the historic particulars of the Holocaust are overwhelming in quantity and kind and therefore present a far more difficult problem in selection than Malamud's. That Malamud has not attempted a more direct rendering of the Holocaust experience despite his obvious interest is perhaps indicative of his recognition of the difficulty.

On another level entirely Malamud transmits past history and traditional values by his bold use of idiosyncratic language. It is language that creates discomfort given the seriousness of Malamud's subject matter, and it has discomfited a number of critics. Alfred Kazin feels that "Malamud's problem is to form a creative synthesis out of the Yiddish world of his childhood and his natural sophistication and heretical training as a modern writer."[12] Frank Kermode sees the problem of synthesis slightly differently and calls Malamud a writer of alien sensibility: "You have to know whether the occasional corruptness of style and invention is there because a dream is out of control or as a justifiable complexity of tone."[13] Neither Kazin nor Kermode has expanded his comments about Malamud's language. But the reader is aware of the conscious incongruity that Kermode stresses and that makes Kazin uneasy.

Malamud does not fuse his styles, he deliberately contains them. His bits and pieces of dialogue are startling, designed to pull the reader's attention to the incongruence of the language. He draws attention to comic possibilities in moments of pathos and tragedy, not with the intention of melding language, but rather with the idea of encapsulating these unassimilated, unmeltable, and unadaptable bits. These are remnants that correspond to the survivor aspects of the characters themselves. Failure to recognize unhomogenized "bone in the throat" quality of much of Malamud's language causes critical problems in analysis.

In discussing Pinye Salzman, one critic stresses the correlation between language and character, as evidenced in the following passage: " 'In what else will you be interested,' Salzman went on, 'if you not interested in this fine girl that she speaks four languages and has personally in the bank ten thousand dollars? Also her father guarantees further twelve thousand.' " It has been suggested that the passage presents in inferior language similarly inferior Jewish values (money, status) as though they were the ultimate goods in marriage.[14] Yet it is the inferior Pinye who makes possible Leo's spiritual renewal, that same Pinye who conveys somber dignity in the final scene of the story.

More crucially, a key passage from *The Assistant* is also couched in this "reductive" dialect. Morris Bober is the speaker. Frank is challenging Morris's "Jewishness": " 'Sometimes,' Morris answered flushing, 'to have to eat, you must keep open on holidays. . . . What I worry is to follow the Jewish Law.' " Frank, like any bright talmudic pupil, keeps on questioning:

> "And don't the law say you can't eat pig, but I have seen you taste ham."
> "This is not important to me if I taste pig or if I don't.
> . . . Nobody will tell me that I am not Jewish because I put in my mouth once in a while, when my tongue is dry, a piece of ham. But they will tell me, and I will believe them, if I forget the Law. This means to do what is right, to be honest, to be good. . . . For everybody should be the best,

> not only for you or me. We ain't animals. This is why we
> need the Law. . . . If you live, you suffer. . . . But I think if
> a Jew don't suffer for the Law, he will suffer for nothing."
> (pp. 184–85)

When Frank responds to Morris's question about the reason
for his interest, Frank admits that he once thought little of
Jews. Morris responds in idiomatic "Yinglish": " 'Happens
like this many times' [124–25]."

Here is another passage with parenthetical modifiers and
verb disagreements, but the values described are superior.
Typical Morris talk abounds in turns that would be comic in
another context: " 'Frank, I think from now on till it comes
summer I will raise your wages to straight fifteen dollars without any commission. I would like to pay you more, but you
know how much we do here business' [p. 129]."

There is no attempt here at phonetic realism. Malamud
does not transcribe language as Henry Roth attempted to do in
Call It Sleep. Morris Bober neither drops his final "g's" nor
turns them into "k's." He does not mispronounce "th" or "w."
But the rhythms of "Yinglish" are captured to assert that
marginal *luftmentshn* like Pinye and Susskind, and the dull
and plodding, like Morris, remain in some ways attached to
other values. Although they are speaking an adopted language, their native language colors and conditions their
speech. Aspects of language, like values from an older culture,
stubbornly persist as anomalous remnants despite changes in
time and circumstance. The language also establishes an incongruence between what is said and the way it is said. Truth,
integrity, and feelings for the past are represented by unedu-
cated, indecorous, and unintentionally (on the part of the
speaker) comic speech. Other twentieth-century writers,
among them John Steinbeck, William Faulkner, and Ralph
Ellison, have attempted to show that speakers of regional dialects are worthy of serious attention. But Malamud uses dialect and accent unrealistically to deliberately startle and un-
nerve.

In "Angel Levine" values are expressed by an unlikely
black Jewish angel (a bizarrely modern Elijah) and a comic Job

named Manischevitz. The point of view is that of the immigrant Manischevitz but the conversion pattern is the same. Manischevitz's imaginative act of faith, his belief in the black Jewish angel, redeems Levine and, at least temporarily, saves Manischevitz's wife. Manischevitz speaks to God both in his own words and through the narrator:

> Throughout his trials Manischevitz had remained somewhat stoic, almost unbelieving that all this had descended upon his head, as if it were happening, let us say, to an acquaintance or some distant relative; it was in sheer quantity of woe incomprehensible. It was ridiculous, unjust, and because he had always been a religious man, it was in a way an affront to God. . . . When his burden had grown too crushingly heavy to be borne he prayed in his chair with shut hollow eyes. "My dear God, sweetheart, did I deserve that this should happen to me?" Then recognizing the worthlessness of it, he put aside the complaint and prayed dumbly for assistance: "Give Fanny back her health, and to me myself that I shouldn't feel pain in every step. Help now or tomorrow is too late. This I don't have to tell you." And Manischevitz wept. (MB, p. 48)

And what of the reader? Does he weep? The echoes from the Book of Job and the sober but ironic narrative tone mitigate the bathetic end of the prayer. Manischevitz retains his dignity, and his intimate relationship with God is manifest. Perhaps out of context the "Yinglish" might cause one to laugh, but in Malamud's work the laugh is a lament.

Critics have been aware of the complex and paradoxical effects of Malamud's style. Kazin calls it "tense expressiveness." Hassan detects "a Hemingway cleanness in this dialogue, a kind of humility and courage, but also a softness Hemingway never strove to communicate."[15] The almost contradictory quality of the commentary suggests the uncertainty and tension that the style conveys. The style is unsynthesized and uneasy, like the lives of the characters. Perhaps the model is not Hemingway but rather the Joycean style in *Dubliners* (1916), which conveys tension and ambiguity with admirable economy. In *Dubliners* what is expressed is stasis and paralysis. Malamud's characters, Diaspora Men, are not static. Leo Finkle moves toward his ambiguous love while Pinye oddly chants; Fidelman, with newly acquired insight, runs toward a disappearing Susskind. Even Frank Alpine's tomblike grocery contains the possibility of rebirth through Helen Bober's redemptive love.

In Malamud's fictional world, with its emphasis on the unexpected, Jewish characters do not enjoy an innate moral superiority. Some, like Julius Karp and Nat Pearl in *The Assistant*, are demonstrably inferior, especially to the gentile Frank. But history, economics, circumstances, and the unsought experience of suffering are what define the Malamudian teachers and *tsadikim*, and Malamud's Jews qualify. Even among the less admirable, like Karp, Feld, and the appropriately named Harry Lesser of *The Tenants*, there is a potentiality for moral growth. The reader is induced to see embodied in the most unlikely spirit a spark of righteousness. Only the ambitious accountants and lawyers, those who follow the American Dream of worldly success, are refused Malamud's mercy and are denied possibilities for moral development.

The prime rhetorical manifestations of the potential for moral development lie in unexpected turns of inappropriate language and in unexpected, non-self-serving gestures like Susskind's theft of the manuscript, Pinye's recitation of the *Kaddish*, and, in "The Mourners," the landlord's joining his pariah tenant in lamentation. In one of the bleakest of Malamud's novels, *The Tenants*, the stereotypical figure of the Jewish slum landlord is endowed with moral consciousness. He is the one who begs for mutual pity from the embattled Negro and Jew.[16] What is stressed is not the integration of language and personality but rather the anomalous, the infinite variety of the good, the difficulty of rendering judgment on human character, the error of basing judgment on outward appearance and speech.

Malamud's use of dialect is varied. In "Angel Levine," for example, he uses Negro minstrel dialect in a passage that satirizes Jewish talmudic disputation. His disregard for verisimilitude also gives him the freedom to use immigrant dialect where those who speak are not immigrants, for example, in the speech of Frank in *The Assistant* and of the protagonist in *The Fixer*. One would assume that in this Czarist Russian setting Malamud would dispense with Yiddish-American speech patterns and sentence structures. Yet the characters speak with that same "accent" no matter what language they are speaking. The opening dialogue between the fixer and his father-in-law is similar to other conversations in which an older Jew argues for a more spiritual life with a quester who is seeking a new life.

Both are presumably speaking Yiddish, yet the older man speaks with more of an "accent." Yakov, the fixer, speaks first:

> "What little I know I learned on my own—some history and geography, a little science, arithmetic, and a book or two of Spinoza's. Not much but better than nothing."
> "Though most is *treyf* ['unclean'] I give you credit—" said Shmuel. . . .
> "Opportunity here is born dead. I'm frankly in a foul mood."
> "Opportunity you don't have to tell me about. . . ."
> "So please don't mention charity because I have no charity to give."
> "Charity you can give even when you haven't got. . . ."
> (F, pp. 11–12)

There is little to differentiate this dialogue from one between Frank and Morris except for the absence of usage errors and the presence of aphorisms and proverbs, which enrich Yiddish speech. As with Morris and Frank, Shmuel's speech contains more than Yakov's. Among Shmuel's proverbs are "cut off your beard and you no longer resemble your creator" and "He who gives us teeth will give us bread [F, p. 13]." Yakov's skepticism is established: " 'In this shtetl everything is falling apart—who bothers with leaks in his roof if he's peeking through the cracks to spy on God?' [F, p. 12]." Yakov has a talent for talmudic wit. When he is approached by a beggar who reminds him that "charity saves from death," he replies that "death is the last of my worries [F, p. 17]." But Shmuel may well win the battle of the aphorism with "for misery don't blame God. He gives the food but we cook it [F, p. 265]."

Unlike Saul Bellow's Machiavels, the aphorist in Malamud frequently has something valid to say. Thus the lawyer Ostrovsky visits Yakov in prison and supposedly in a Russian Jew's Yiddish discusses the Talmud and quotes the sages. He is a more secular *tsadik* than Shmuel. Ostrovsky speaks Yiddish-American although he is a Russian: " 'I'm sorry that your father-in-law, Shmuel Rabinovitch, who I had the pleasure to meet and talk to last summer—a gifted man—is now, I'm sorry to tell you, dead from diabetes. This your wife wrote me in a letter [F, p. 304]." Admittedly the delayed predications and hesitations illustrate the interaction of sound and sense. Ostrovsky is unwilling to break bad news. But the rhythms are Morris Bober's. Even in the fixer's grim world the use of comical locutions and mangled "Yinglish" does not detract from the seriousness or even the tragedy of the utterance.

In a one-act play based on his first published story, Malamud's artistic credo is placed in the mouth of an old Yiddish actor:

> "A writer writes tragedy so people don't forget they are human. He organizes for us the meaning of our lives so it is clear to our eyes. . . . My best roles were tragic roles . . . though I was also marvelous in comedy. 'Leid macht auch lachen.' " (IF, p. 177)

This last may be translated as "suffering also causes laughter." Distorted syntax does not imply a distorted soul. The voice of the immigrant is a fitting vehicle for Malamud's rhetorical purposes.

Like the language that conveys the sound and feeling of Yiddish-American but is not meant to be realistic, the works include much that is fantastic. The title story of the collection *Idiots First* demonstrates a virtuoso use of idiosyncratic language and fantasy. Mendel is the dying father of Isaac, a thirty-nine-year-old idiot. Mendel hopes to get Isaac off to California before Ginzburg, the absurdly named Angel of Death, "gets" Mendel. The story is anthropomorphic from the beginning as Mendel draws on "cold, embittered clothing." When Mendel speaks of his death he does so in accents that would be comic in another context: " 'Look me in my face,' said Mendel, 'and tell me if I got time till tomorrow morning?' [IF, p. 6]." " 'For what I got chicken won't cure it' [IF, p. 8]."

But the climax of the story is Mendel's debate with Ginzburg, now disguised as a ticket collector. The metaphysical discussion sounds like a vaudeville routine. Mendel wants Ginzburg to allow him to put Isaac on the train to California. He asks Ginzburg what his duties are and Ginzburg responds like a typical employer: " 'To create conditions. To make happen what happens. I ain't in the anthropomorphic business.' " Mendel's reply suggests that he does not know the meaning of "anthropomorphic": " 'Whatever business you in, where is your pity?' " Ginzburg lowers his diction although his manner has never been elegant. " 'This ain't my commodity. The law is the law.' " (Note lower case.) Despite Mendel's pleading, Ginzburg, embodying the "cosmic universal law," is obdurate. Mendel tells of his wretched life and begs:

> "Now I ask you a small favor. Be so kind, Mr. Ginzburg."
>
> The ticket collector was picking his teeth with a match stick. "You ain't the only one, my friend, some got it worse than you. That's how it goes in this country."
>
> "You dog you." Mendel lunged at Ginzburg's throat. . . .
>
> "You bastard, don't you understand what it means human?" (IF, pp. 20–21)

Mendel's question is as absurd as his attempt to murder the Angel of Death. But Mendel is also heroic because he is incapable of recognizing the inhuman even in the nonhuman. And the biblical tale of Abraham, Isaac, and a less colloquial Angel of Death adds another dimension to Mendel's struggle. The battle continues: "They struggled nose to nose, Ginzburg, though his astonished eyes bulged, began to laugh. 'You pipsqueak nothing. I'll freeze you to pieces.' His eyes lit in rage.

. . ." Now Ginzburg makes a discovery; indeed, he is in "the anthropomorphic business":

> Clinging to Ginzburg in his last agony, Mendel saw reflected in the ticket collector's eyes the depth of his terror. But he saw that Ginzburg, staring at himself in Mendel's eyes, saw mirrored in them the extent of his own awful wrath. He beheld a shimmering starry, blinding light that produced darkness.
> Ginzburg looked astonished. "Who me?"
> His grip on the squirming old man slowly loosened, and Mendel, his heart barely beating, slumped to the ground. "Go." Ginzburg muttered, "Take him to the train." (IF, pp. 20–21)

If there is terror and wrath why not pity as well? All are part of "what it means human" and even the Angel of Death is not excluded from the human. That all this superhuman effort is expended to send a thirty-nine-year-old idiot to his eighty-one-year-old uncle in California only emphasizes Malamud's stubborn insistence on salvation and survival, no matter how absurd.

Fittingly, unlike Abraham Cahan and Henry Roth, Malamud does not place his fabulous characters in a realistic urban setting. Unlike his contemporaries Bellow, Wallant, and I. B. Singer, he does not emphasize the concrete urban matrix, the subway station, the West Side cafeteria. Malamud's remnants are isolated among isolates, separated even from experiencing the city as wasteland, always unrooted, always threatening to move on.

Robert Alter, among others, complains of Malamud "that nowhere does he attempt to represent a Jewish milieu, that a Jewish community never enters into his books except as the shadow of a vestige of a specter."[17] Clearly it is not because Malamud cannot write realistic, socially and historically rooted fiction. *The Tenants, The Fixer,* and *A New Life* are all strongly rooted in history, event, and social milieu. But in the immigrant stories the particular strength of these Diaspora Men resides in their not being rooted in space, in their unassimilated, alien transcendence of milieu. Unlike the prewar immigrant, Malamud's Jews do not perceive of America as a "promised land." Alfred Kazin complains of Malamud's "abstractness" and contrasts him to the Yiddish masters who "gave the earth of Russia, the old village, a solid reality, as if it were all the world they had to cherish." But Malamud, although close to them in spirit according to Kazin, does not show "the world, but the spectral Jew in his beggarly clothes—always ready to take flight."[18] Is this not precisely what Malamud intends? The setting, like the language, attempts to capture that which is essential, that which can be distilled into something ultimately portable.

Malamud is not, as Kazin avers, abstract out of despair; rather, he attempts in language, setting, and character to preserve what is most ephemeral and yet what can best be preserved. That which an immigrant can carry with him may be nonmaterial, may suffer a sea change, may even be debased, but it is transmittable, capable of living under the most adverse conditions, and hence the only heritage worthy of transmission. It is ambiguously compounded of common suffering, common humanity, common responsibility, and common peril. And how well Kazin (still carping) sees what Malamud is trying to do with his surreal language: "He makes you think not that Jews really talk that way but how violent, fear fraught, always on edge, Jewish talk can be."[19]

Lawrence Langer's previously cited study of the "literature of atrocity" is, of course, concerned with European examples of Holocaust literature. It would be unseemly and incorrect to suggest that Malamud writes a "literature of atrocity." The essentially comic form, albeit qualified, of Malamud's work points to the distance that separates America and Americans from much European experience of the Holocaust, although Malamud, like other Jewish American writers, is in the position of a "witness-through-the-imagination," one who has "(merely) 'heard the terrible news'." And news of such magnitude has considerable effect as Malamud's prose shares with the "schizophrenic art" of the Holocaust a metaphoric language employed to "sustain the tensions that inspire it" rather than to resolve those tensions.[20] Like the "literature of atrocity," Malamud's works are characterized by "irrealism"—"a reality whose quality is unreal. The line between the comic and the tragic often becomes blurred as the authors struggle to express the inexpressible."[21]

In this context Frank Alpine's musing about Jews, "that there are more of them around than you think [p. 231]," and Manischevitz's perception that "there are Jews everywhere [MB, p. 58]" may be more somber than sanguine. Recently Malamud commented that his well-known statement, "all men are Jews," was an "understandable statement and a metaphoric way of indicating how history, sooner or later, treats all men."[22] Langer points out that in the "literature of atrocity" the non-Jewish characters "read in the fate of the Jew a dramatic pantomime of their own destiny as men."[23] Jewish history then becomes a paradigm for the relationship of the individual to history, a corollary to Daniel Bell's previously cited analysis of the Jew as a symbol of twentieth-century alienation. Yet the emphasis on the Jew as the symbol of universal humanity should not obscure the increasing importance of the particulars of Jewish life in the fiction of Malamud and other more recent writers.

In contrast to such universalism is Irving Howe's stress on the particulars of Jewish life in the important Jewish American fiction that he saw emerging in the late forties. Howe here echoes the Yiddish writer Y. L. Peretz who, in an article entitled "Escaping Jewishness," warns would-be universalists that "humanity must be the sum, the quintessence of national cultural forms and philosophies."[24] Malamud has integrated significant unassimilated linguistic, ethical, cultural, and historic Jewish elements into his fictional world as have other recent writers.

As exemplary twentieth-century Jewish characters, Malamud's personae are alienated, but not quite in the sense explored by Bell. They are not "sensitive sons" of the second generation but immigrant fathers. They are essentially homeless because they have never felt at ease in the world around them and they are not part of that world. Malamud's European-born remnants—those reminiscent of Sholem Aleichem's characters like Manischevitz, Mendel, and Morris—are fragments of a dead culture who live in the new world but cannot be said to interact with it. Yet these *luftmentshn* are capable of transmitting an important if fragmented heritage to younger protagonists. Like their immigrant mentors, these younger heroes do not enter into the mainstream of American life. Frank Alpine in his grocery, Fidelman divested of his dream of status as an art historian, Finkle, the ambitious rabbi, destined for a misalliance—none of these are "making it." From the older immigrant each has learned to give up the dream of conventional success for failure in conventional terms. Some achieve moral ascendency, not as rebels rejecting bourgeois society, but as former strivers who have sacrifice thrust upon them and who then accept it willingly.

The fluid, pluralistic American scene as depicted by Malamud, even at its bleakest, allows for such alternatives. Malamud's most consciously political book, *The Fixer*, describes a corrupt and brutal Czarist system that forces men like Bok into unaccustomed heroic roles. In his anti-Prometheanism Malamud again shows his similarity to Yiddish writers, especially Sholem Aleichem. Although both writers sometimes use subject matter that is somber indeed, neither writer chooses to confront the tragic directly.[25] Always present are the possibilities of redemption and rebirth, however slim. Even in *The Fixer*, which Malamud presents as a metaphoric Holocaust novel, the ending is ambiguous. If the reader wishes to take comfort from the historic fact that Mendl Beilis, the historic Yakov Bok, was finally released from prison, the comfort lies well outside the fictional bounds of the novel.

Malamud's fictional world contains many immigrants and fewer refugees and survivors. Malamud embodies post-Holocaust sensibility in the very insubstantiality of his immigrant remnants. In Susskind and Salzmann, in Mendel and Manischevitz, in Yakov Bok, in Morris Bober, and in others Malamud commemorates the vanished world of East European Jewry. The primary means he uses is the nontechnical rendering of idiosyncratic speech that conveys the essence of Yiddish through rhythm, abrupt juxtaposition, and nonstandard word order, rather than through phonetic transcription. This stylized language is used by the immigrant father figures to convey parts of the Jewish heritage to metaphoric sons. Both father and son share the center of Malamud's fictional stage. In other post-Holocaust immigrant literature, the center of consciousness is the parent figure. The shift of attention to the parent figure makes possible some of the important differences between pre- and post-Holocaust immigrant fiction.

While Diasporal homelessness, language loss and replacement, and the relationship of the Jewish past to the American present are common themes in all immigrant literature, the significance of these concerns is different in pre- and post-Holocaust fiction. The homelessness that was a problem for David Levinsky and, according to Leslie Fiedler, ceased to be a problem in the Jewish American novel of assimilation is accepted as part of the human condition in the later novels. The experience of language loss is less significant in the immigrant-survivor novel than it is in the earlier novels and the emphasis is on retention rather than acculturation. Since the survivor is depicted as an adult when he emigrates to America, he is likely to retain former language patterns. Unlike earlier fictional immigrants, immigrant-survivors are not intent upon fulfilling the dream of American economic success. Age and their experience of suffering make them unlikely candidates for economic and social rise. The interaction of the survivor with the American present, while important, is less so than the survivor's interaction with the Jewish past, both ancient and traditional, historic and recent.

Most of all recent immigrant novels seek to commemorate the Holocaust. Accordingly the individual character's past is seen as representing or encompassing some part of the collective experience of the Jewish people. The protagonists are therefore placed in a fictional milieu of Jewish refugees that may include German Jews who escaped in the thirties, recent emigrés from Israel, former inmates of Soviet slave labor camps, and Nazi death-camp survivors. Through the sensibilities of their protagonists, to varying degrees these novels attempt the difficult task of rendering imaginatively the horrors of twentieth-century Jewish history.

The questions raised by the inclusion of the recent Jewish past in novels with an American context are treacherous and delicate. How does one who has lived through the unlivable integrate that tortured past into his consciousness? How does the survivor live with his past in manic, metropolitan New York (where immigrant-survivor novels are set)? What, if anything, from that past can be transmitted—given the hedonism of modern life? In these recent novels the question of the survival of the Jewish experience becomes crucial. It has already been shown that the transmission of aspects of Jewish heritage, no matter how secularized, is an important theme in the work of Bernard Malamud. Malamud has also suggested a hierarchy of suffering in some of his works (*The Assistant, The Fixer*, "The Last Mohican"). In works with immigrant-survivor protagonists the transmission of a heritage and the experience of suffering become even more important themes. The figure of Job, the archetypal sufferer, is frequently evoked along with the purposeful wanderer Elijah. Yet despite biblical evocations and traditional allusions and references, the protagonists of four of the novels under discussion are products of a secular Polish academic system rather than the *kheyder* (traditional *shtetl* Hebrew school) and *yeshive* (Talmudic academy), which formed part of the background of earlier immigrants.

Fittingly, all four fictional survivors, despite their different novelistic contexts, came out of the rich and varied urban Jewish life of pre-World War II Poland, whose Jews accounted for 10 percent of the population. By chance, but not without reason, three protagonists are presented as academically trained philosophers with degrees from Polish universities. The fourth survivor, a woman, is presented as a former medical student. It is understandable, of course, that the American-born novelists Edward Wallant, Susan Fromberg Schaeffer, and Saul Bellow avoid the depiction of a traditionally educated *shtetl*-reared central character. But Isaac Bashevis Singer, of orthodox background and *shtetl*-reared, also chooses a modernist skeptic as representative survivor. These fictional immigrants differ from their prewar immigrant forebears in that they come to this country as secularly educated, assimilated European Jews. As youths, all three men typically rejected the traditional orthodoxy of their parents' generation. Anya, Schaeffer's heroine, came from a partially assimilated home where an accommodation between old and new had been accomplished. As middle-aged and elderly people and Holocaust survivors, they are in the process of attempting new syntheses that take into account the extremity of their experience as twentieth-century Jews.

Five

Wallant's
Reborn Immigrant
and Redeemed Survivor

Only two of Edward Wallant's four novels were published during his brief lifetime. His first published novel has for its central character an immigrant plumber; his second, *The Pawnbroker*, is essentially the story of a Holocaust survivor. Despite critical differences in background among the protagonists and despite differences in setting, all four novels are strikingly similar in action since all four begin with isolated protagonists who ultimately learn to love and are thus reborn. Wallant is a naturalistic, Dreiserian novelist who employs an omniscient narrator in all his works. It is not surprising then that his first novel, *The Human Season* (1960), is a throwback to the immigrant novels that appeared decades before. Indeed this work is far less "modern" than Cahan's prototypical 1917 novel.

In *The Human Season*, Wallant's straightforward technique is effective because the subject matter is so reminiscent of earlier fiction about Jewish immigrants.[1] Joe Berman, the immigrant protagonist, must review his past life to overcome his grief at the brutally sudden death of his beloved wife. The work is simply structured, with one sequence of events in the fictional present going forward in time, while another dated sequence moves backward in time. The earliest memories are involuntary dreams while the last memory is deliberately evoked by Joe, thereby indicating that he has regained control of his life. Through these complementary journeys backward and forward, Joe relives the tragedies and triumphs of his life and begins to perceive that tragedy, like death, is part of life, that to struggle to birth is to become susceptible to death.

Joe curses and rails against God with Jobian bitterness but in colloquial, homely Yiddish to make his curses "more personal and sincere [p. 17]." The reader does not see Joe as a kind of Job although Wallant may have intended the parallel. For Joe is a successful example of what Isaac Rosenfeld calls flawless Americanization. He is at ease out of Zion, a successful plumber with his own home, kind friends, loving children, and the memory of a good marriage. In this modest story Wallant succeeds in conveying the importance of Joe's immigrant past to his movement toward self-perception. Through reliving the deaths of his wife and only son in his dreams, through the re-creation of his *shtetl* past, Joe is able to free himself of his corroding, isolating bitterness and rejoin family and community.

What brings Joe Berman back to life is an amalgam of vaguely Wordsworthian intimations of immortality and the evocation of his father, a dignified *shtetl* patriarch. Joe's father, dying in full consciousness, within the confines of a traditional Jewish Sabbath in the Russian Pale, accepts death, firm in the knowledge that death is part of life. He knows that he will live with God and in the memory of his children. What saves the amalgam of the romantic and the Judaic from inappropriate glibness is the correspondence between the two for, for traditional Jews, immortality is the belief that the dead and their deeds live on in the memory of the living. The evocation of the memory of the powerful father is depicted as having a lifelong effect on Joe's conduct. Out of Joe's childhood comes a sense of continuity, of something transmitted from one generation to another.

The evocation of the elder Berman transforms Joe's vision of God by replacing the anthropomorphic vision of "God with a beard just out to get you [p. 191]" with a more evanescent, metaphoric insight

> . . . phrased in the hidden eloquence of his brain. Answers come in little glimmers to your soul, most clearly in child-

hood, in the sounds of certain voices and faces and things, when you feel the miracle and the wonder; and he knew then that the Torahs and prayer shawls and churches and saints were just the art men tried to create to express the other deeper feelings. (p. 192)

Joe's powerful father lived as he died, with dignity and firmness. One of Joe's memories is of his father in the role of an avenging Jehovah-like figure, turning on his anti-Semitic Russian tormentor and killing him. The elder Berman strides away, saying, " 'Lord forgive me, I was sorely pressed. Thus be it' [p. 156]." The small boy experiences "strange magic" when "he felt the presence of God in unique vestments and the world was filled with a peculiar singing mystery [p. 157]."

It is possible to cavil at the probability of such an event as it is possible to squirm at the imprecision of Wallant's language. Clearly Wallant wants to include in the Jewish heritage what are admittedly atypical elements of individual violence and muscle. Here Wallant's ambivalent attitude toward the Jewish past manifests itself, for just prior to the violence Jews are described as "those feeble, cheek-turning people of such marvelous resiliency, such amazing memory." The unlikely describer is another Russian peasant whose respect for Berman's father "was sincere and based on fear [p. 154]." Wallant's celebration of the right of might is repeated in Joe Berman's later experience in America. Joe's encounter is with a less virulent Irish American anti-Semitism. Joe fights with honor, loses a finger, but gains the approbation of his peers: "Berman felt pain, strong and living in his head and where his finger had been, and he was swollen with the joy of it, burned with recognition, as though it were the overpowering evidence, irrefutable, of some towering presence [p. 92]." The American experience of anti-Semitism is more ritualistic than vicious: the Irishman sends a get-well card. Berman's son in turn carries on a "fighting tradition," but he dies in Europe in World War II, a more serious enemy requiring a greater sacrifice.

Wallant's demonstrated tendencies toward simplistic reductionism are far less troubling in this novel of a simple plumber than they are in his far more somber novel about a Holocaust survivor. Joe Berman is rather heavy-handedly "shocked" into rebirth with the aid of the television set that he has substituted for human interaction: "He gave a loud cry as the electricity shot through him. He felt himself thrown, as though by a gigantic hand, down to the floor [p. 171]." The shock acts as a restorative; Joe "begged with no memory of pride, to come out of that living death he had made for himself [p. 171]." He comes to recognize that his particular grief is not unique, that he can and should join with his mourning daughter for mutual comfort and communion. The striking parallel between Berman's restoration by electric shock and David Schearl's being "shocked" into rebirth is more likely to be an accident rather than the influence of Henry Roth on Wallant. Contrasted with Roth's careful development of David's associations with the live rail, Wallant's use of electric shock appears clumsy and gratuitous. Perhaps, like Roth, Wallant is using American technology to exemplify the possibilities for rebirth that are available in American society. The rebirth of Wallant's next protagonist is considerably less mechanistic although it may be considered equally mechanical.

The Human Season succeeds in presenting Joe Berman's simple story with directness and economy. *The Pawnbroker* (1962) is quite different in intention and execution.[2] It is one of the earliest American novels to portray an immigrant-survivor as central figure and is a less than successful treatment of a most challenging subject. Significantly Sol Nazerman is the only protagonist among those discussed who is specifically a death-camp survivor although Schaeffer's heroine, Anya, spends time in a camp. Sol's body, unlike Anya's, is the distorted product of experiments in death-camp surgery. Sol's experience of suffering is one of the most extreme among the survivor-protagonists and yet he is the only one who appears to have been reborn. With what may be deliberate irony, rebirth occurs in a traditionally Christian manner. The incident is strikingly parallel to Frank Alpine's attempted robbery of

Morris Bober in *The Assistant*. In Malamud's novel the gentile becomes the "saviour" of the Jew. The post-Holocaust setting of Wallant's novel requires a more extreme sacrifice on the part of the gentile.

Sol's rebirth occurs through the sacrifice of his delicately handsome black-Latino assistant, appropriately named Jesus Ortiz. Jesus conspires with others to rob Sol's pawnshop with the caveat that Sol not be injured. When plans go awry and Sol's life is in danger, Jesus dies for Sol. The irony of the non-Jew, Jesus, dying for the Jew is compounded by the recognition that Sol, who already considers himself a corpse, was courting death at the hands of the robbers. Perhaps Jesus' martyrdom, which is redemptive for both himself and Sol, is meant to contrast with the meaningless and gruesome martyrdom of Sol's family in Europe. For Sol is seeking death as a relief from his unspeakable dreams in which he relives in unbearable detail the brutal and hideous destruction of his family. Jesus' sacrifice acts like the electric shock does on Berman. The rocklike pawnbroker becomes vulnerable as a result of Jesus' death:

> The sound of weeping . . . filling the Pawnbroker's ears, flooding him, . . . dragging him back to that sea of tears he had thought to escape . . . his body becoming worn down under the flood of it, washed down to the one polished stone of grief. All his anesthetic numbness left him. . . . What was this great agonizing sensitivity and what was it for? Good God, what was all this? *Love*? Could this be *love*? (p. 200)

Wallant's relatively positive ending makes it possible for Sol, like Berman, to mourn as an individual and as part of humanity. It is a dénouement that sharply distinguishes Wallant's work from other survivor novels that end on a more ambiguous note.

Similarly in his depiction of Sol's homelessness, Wallant is more positive than other novelists. The pawnbroker, like other immigrant-survivor protagonists, is a displaced person with an excess of places to sleep but no "home." Nazerman inhabits a room in a house he has purchased for his odious sister and her parasitic family. This suburban American Eden was purchased with Sol's tainted money to assure him of the privacy and isolation that he craves. It is a fragile plastic cover for Sol's terrible past, a superficially clean, well-lighted place where the members of Sol's family feed on each other and on him and where Sol's horrible nightmares do not allow him to sleep. Nazerman supports another home that is kept secret and distinctly separate from his official home. In a decaying Bronx apartment house, Sol maintains Tessie Rubin and her aged father, Mendel. Tessie (Sol's mistress) and her father were in the concentration camp with Sol and their smelly apartment represents Sol's European camp past. Not surprisingly Sol sleeps better in this fetid, slummy atmosphere than in homogenized Westchester. The hideous nightmares that torture Sol in Westchester do not afflict him at Tessie's where the camp past is always in evidence and where memorial candles are always lit for the many dead.

Sol's Harlem pawnshop is yet another "home" enclosing within itself the detritus of Western civilization. Behind his wire cage Sol can be withdrawn from the world and can traffic with the world on his own terms. It is another false haven, for Sol's privacy and economic security are purchased by his passive cooperation with the Mafia empire of corruption and exploitation. Sol attempts to insulate himself from awareness of evil just as he attempts to ignore the brutality and poverty of his Harlem environment. At the end of the novel Sol has been converted to love and his fragmented "homes" seem to converge. When he asks his pitiful nephew, Morton, to become his assistant in the pawnshop, Sol is moving toward bringing his public and private lives together. The integrative movement is supported by Sol's joining Tessie in mourning for her father and belatedly for his own murdered family. There is even the possibility of a future home with the American social worker Marilyn Birchfield, whose very name is symbolic of Edenic America. Sol is as yet "too dirty" for the virginal Marilyn (p. 201).

Other survivor novels end more uncertainly for their protagonists. The patterned "rebirth through love" ending of

Wallant's novel and the hint of a possible future for Sol and Marilyn cause *The Pawnbroker* to superficially resemble earlier immigrant works of assimilation, like Mary Antin's *The Promised Land*. Given the detailed depiction of Sol's grisly past, which the novel emphasizes, such archaisms are out of place as Sol is out of place in suburban America. Another technique that is out of place is Wallant's use of the dream as history. Wallant focuses as with a camera eye directly on the death-camp past. But as George Steiner, Lawrence Langer, and Terrence Des Pres have pointed out, the fictional representation of *l'univers concentrationnaire* is an unprecedented aesthetic and moral challenge and Wallant's realism and naturalism do not provide the most effective means of meeting that challenge.

European writers of Holocaust literature are often themselves survivors and often depict their pasts as directly experienced. The American writer who chooses a related subject is more likely to employ the American setting and the retrospective point of view characteristic of immigrant literature. The technical problem of the fictional presentation of memory is of a major importance in works with survivor protagonists. Unlike Malamud who obliquely and indirectly uses the European past as background and context, Wallant, Singer, Schaeffer, and Bellow attempt to integrate unprecedented past experience into the ongoing present of their central characters. Just as the fictional characters seek rapprochement with an intolerable past experience, their creators attempt to present that experience honestly and aesthetically.

The confrontation of past and present takes place within the survivor himself in the novels under discussion. It will be recalled that in Malamud's more indirect presentation the experience of tragic history is vicarious in much of his fiction and analogic in *The Fixer*. Thus his protagonist Fidelman's "experience" of Jewish history is that of a rapidly moving observer. Fidelman's loss of his second-rate manuscript is only comically analogous to Susskind's unknown losses. When Malamud portrays direct suffering, as in *The Fixer*, the experience is historically and geographically distanced from Ameri-

can and Nazi contexts. Malamud distances the Holocaust experience also by not focusing on it in time but in the
consciousness of his readers. Morris Bober of *The Assistant*
only imagines the horrors the early "refugee" suffered. The
survivor Susskind does not speak of his experiences; the
reader and Fidelman imagine them. The hideous death of the
wife in "The German Refugee" is relayed through a letter
written to the refugee, which is read by the American narrator
after the refugee's suicide. Malamud is creating and maintaining distance between audience and experience. For Wallant,
Schaeffer, I. B. Singer, and Bellow, the choice of an immigrant-survivor as center of consciousness involves a more
direct presentation of the Jewish past. The Jewish European
past has been an important element in the literature of the immigrant, but pre-Holocaust writers did not have to include (or
exclude) brutally sensational raw material nor did they face
the problem of writing of and for the survivor without having
the credentials of the survivor.

An earlier immigrant writer, Abraham Caha⬛ only employs a first-person narrator who, in the course of his confession, condemns himself more than he intends. David Levinsky's *shtetl* past and his wealthy present are only different in
material particulars; his ambitious opportunism remains
unchanged. In Henry Roth's novel, the protagonist's past is
defined by his ten-year-old consciousness. His is a received
past, transmitted by his aunt and his Hebrew teacher and,
above all, conveyed and preserved by his mother in the sanc-
tified *shtetl* atmosphere of her flat. Malamud's secular *rebes,*
teachers, and comic sages embody the past unconsciously in
vestiges and convey it to wavering questers in nervous idiosyncratic speech. But the survivor-protagonist contains within
himself the bloody past that obsesses him. He is in turn surrounded by other survivors who are obsessed to varying degrees and who embody various aspects of the recent Jewish
past. Some continually ruminate upon the past; some attempt
to suppress memory; all manifest emotional wounds.

Wallant's pawnbroker rigidly attempts to keep his past re-
pressed and unremembered. Like some real-life survivors, Sol

Nazerman hates his survival. But his brutal past experience must obtrude upon his supposedly numb present. As the "anniversary" of the annihilation of his family approaches, Sol's horrendous dreams recreate in vivid and unbearable detail his death-camp experiences. Wallant presents these searing memories in chronological order, moving from the bestiality of the cattle cars to the grisly pile of corpses ready for the burning. This is the world of nightmare made real.

Wallant overdoes the realism, for Sol's dreams are more cinematographic than "nightmarish." Sol's unbearable death-camp experiences are presented as expository flashbacks that are neither symbolic nor metaphoric. The dreams are naturalistic presentations of unnatural Holocaust experiences, recounted by an omniscient consciousness that presents them like a sequence of film. They are italicized to emphasize their detachment from Sol's life and from the thrust of the novel. There is no commentary or reflection on the dreams. Such "objective" reportage gives an impression of completeness, verisimilitude, and order that is not only undreamlike but is also very unlike the survivor dreams in the "literature of atrocity." Lawrence Langer quotes from a representative survivor-writer whose dreams embody "the prevalence of the unreal over the real. Everyone dreamed past and future dreams . . . of improbable paradises, of equally mythical and improbable enemies; cosmic enemies, perverse and subtle, who pervade everything like the air."[3]

Sol's dreams are neither surreal nor "irreal" but realistic, quasi-documentary in impact. As such they are more successful on film than as fiction. In the novel more than just the presentation of these horrors is needed—they need to have happened to someone. Sol does not confront his experiences nor does he reflect upon them. The element of *dianoia* is missing from the novel, a disturbing lack in a central character who is an erstwhile philosopher reliving his horrible past with spatial and temporal distance. Wallant does relate the dreams thematically to Sol's present life with rather heavy-handed crudity. The first dream of horror, for example, is a revolting episode that shows the Nazerman family in the closed cattle car. Sol stands helpless and compressed while his small son slips from his arms and appears about to suffocate in a sea of excrement. This unforgettable dream is preceded by a scene in the present that shows Sol at dinner with his unpleasant sister and her parasitical family. Morton, the weakest, most despised member of the family, is depicted as being verbally "shat upon" by his mother, father, and sister (pp. 27–32).

Other dreams of the past are more elaborately related to Sol's present life and eventually penetrate his rocklike insulation. The insulation is the sought-for economic result of Sol's business association with the gangster Murillio. Sol, no longer committed to those ethical principles that were so brutally betrayed by his experience of contemporary history, is willing to close his eyes to the unsavory "businesses" that are the sources of his economic security. Neither drugs, nor thievery, nor gambling is sufficiently criminal to affect Sol's conscience. But he is anxious to determine the extent of Murillio's association with the local brothel. Sol's confrontation with Murillio and the dream that follows constitute the turning point of the novel. The confrontation ends in an ugly scene:

> Sol felt the cold touch of metal against his cheek. When he swung his head to see what it was, something unbelievably hard crashed against his teeth; opening his mouth at the pain, he felt the cold metal thrust between his teeth and he tasted the bitterness of steel.
>
> "Now don't move, Uncle," Murillio said, his eyes on the man behind Sol. "Stand absolutely still and lick on that gun barrel for a while." (p. 123)

The section of the novel that follows this scene explores forms of "love" that include the bestial and the banal. Sol returns home, shaken, to the phony family love of his parasitical sister and brother-in-law and retires in disgust to read *Anna Karenina*. His reading of this great love story is interrupted by the sounds of suburban, domesticated sex emanating from his sister's bedroom. Sol chooses the terrors of sleep to avoid overhearing, but the results of the choice are unbearable. The memory of his helplessness at Murillio's causes Sol to relive the nadir of his experiences in the death camp. There he was made to watch through a peephole, helpless and degraded, as his pretty wife, an inmate of the camp brothel, was forced to perform fellatio. In Sol's agonized memory his wife's realization that her helpless husband had been a witness to her degradation makes the event even more lacerating. The Pawnbroker's dreams are among the most loathsome scenes in the literature of atrocity and the unintended effect is numbing.

Wallant further relates the bestial sexual exploitation of the concentration camp to the unused and wasted sexuality of the healthy and virginal American social worker Marilyn Birchfield. In brutal counterpoint to her wasted body is the overused body of the pretty black whore Mabel Wheatly. In a grotesque parody, Mabel offers herself to the uninterested Sol to earn money for her true love, Jesus Ortiz. The distasteful climax to these sexual scenes comes with Sol's visit to his survivor-dependents, Tessie and her dying father. While the father is slowly dying in the bedroom, Sol is momentarily moved to grim laughter by the naïve Tessie. "She shushed him, reminding him of the old man. Later on, she lit a memorial candle for one or another of her dead. Then she began to cry and Sol had to make love to her after all [p. 143]."

Wallant here presents a roster of perversions of the act of "love," from the aesthetic adultery of Anna Karenina to the bestial degradation of the death camp. Sol's powerlessness in the face of his wife's humiliation is cruelly and crudely paralleled in his own humiliation by Murillio. But Sol can begin his return to life by demonstrating that he is not afraid of death, by defying Murillio, and by losing his economic protection if not his life. He must also relive his experience of hell to live again; he must be brought back to life by being brought back to love.

Once he has decided that his insulation from life is not worth the price of cooperating with the deadly Murillio, Sol is allowed a nonharrowing dream of his past. This is a bucolic if stereotyped picnic scene in which Sol acts as father to his family while Sol's own father reads a holy book under a tree. This nostalgic backward glance is a static tableau and does not represent any integration of past and present. Only after Jesus' sacrifice and Sol's rebirth, through love, is Sol able to make a communal gesture and join Tessie in mourning for her father. At the same time Sol is able to mourn and commemorate the death of his own family in atonement for his previous efforts to forget.

Although Sol has recaptured his past, the novel in general transmits an apologetic and ambivalent attitude toward the Jewish past. Sol's occupation provides Wallant with the opportunity to present a self-conscious defense of Jewish mercantilism. Until his rebirth Sol has only been a commercial "uncle," the argot term for pawnbroker. After Jesus Ortiz's death Sol perceives that he has failed to function as a father to his own family and to Ortiz. Now he takes on the role of father-saviour to his nephew Morton, the legatee of Sol's Jewish mercantile heritage. If the secularist Sol Nazerman has been a combination of Nazarene and "Naziman" in his relationship with people, as pawnbroker he has been Jehovah-like in his sternness and rectitude untinged with mercy. Wallant goes to great lengths to rationalize the Jewish occupation of pawnbrokering by showing it can be honorable, even if it is not honored.

Specifically Wallant has used Sol as mouthpiece to enunciate an apologia for Jewish business success. Precipitated by Jesus' provocative question, " 'How come you Jews come to business so natural?' " Sol responds with a historically sound if tendentious rationale for Jewish success (p. 43). In a novel that presents the most extreme examples of modern persecution of Jews, such a sociological defense seems gratuitous. Yet it points to Wallant's unease with Jewish materials, ancient and modern. Survivor guilt, so often expressed by fictional characters themselves, is here supported by the author. The apologia, however gratuitous, does allow Wallant to demonstrate that his protagonist is or has been a thoughtful, educated man. Sol's speech is also one of the few occasions when he is allowed to comment on his background or display any evidence of training or education. If he does not display any of the philosophical training with which his creator credits him, at least he sounds well informed.

Sol becomes, on Wallant's value scale, more of a human being when he is no longer interested in survival. Tessie's martyred husband who sought death after his son was killed by the Nazis, Sol's suffering wife, and even the ambiguously sacrificed Jesus are endowed with a nobility unavailable to the living. Sol's passive behavior in the concentration camp is implicitly condemned along with his present rocklike attitude. At the same time that Wallant is depicting scenes of unprecedented horror, he appears to be equating Nazi barbarity with Sol's lack of mercy toward his victimized Harlem customers. Other uneasy parallels are left ambiguous and unexplored. Are we meant to see Mabel Wheatley and Sol's dead wife as equally debased and exploited? Are Morton and Jesus meant to correspond to Sol's butchered daughter with the hook in her heart? For in Sol's dream there appear on her mutilated body not only the faces of Morton and Jesus but also the faces of many of Sol's customers, of Tessie and her father, and others (p. 144). If Wallant is using scenes of lacerating horror to point to the continuing presence of evil in the world, he is overstating his case. If he is drawing parallels, the extremity of the Nazi scenes undermines the similarities. At the same time there is no reflection by author or character that could aid the reader in determining the authorial position.

The incompleteness of Wallant's approach in *The Pawnbroker* also can be seen in the world of other survivors and immigrants which he creates for his hero. Like I. B. Singer's Herman Broder, Sol Nazerman has a mistress with an aged parent, both death camp survivors. Tessie Rubin is depicted as slovenly, unappealing, greedy, and self-pitying. Her aged and orthodox father is a querulous, suspicious, whining old man. Wallant also includes in his roster of survivors an extreme example of the grotesquely comic survivor who appears in more complex and interesting forms as Singer's Yashe Kotik, Malamud's clever Susskind, and Bellow's ludicrous but talented Walter Bruch. In the revolting Goberman, however, Wallant descends to the level of anti-Semitic caricature.

Goberman is a vicious embodiment of the quintessential parasitical figure; he is consumed with guilt for having survived. To assuage his conscience he preys on other survivors and attempts to involve them in his own guilt. Sol "recognizes" him and accuses him of having informed on members of his own family. What follows is a gruesomely comic scene wherein Goberman responds to the accusation:

> "Not my own family, never my own family. . . . No one can say to my face that I . . . *never* in a million years would I have done a thing like that to my *immediate* family." His mouth sagged like a too-wet formulation of clay, "I NEVER . . . SOLD . . . MY . . . OWN . . . FAMILY . . . NEVERNEVER- NEVERNEVER!" (p. 94)

The literary echoes of a mouth borrowed from Faulkner's Flem Snopes and reiteration borrowed from *King Lear* are, to say the least, inappropriate, if they are indeed intentional.

Sol finds the repellent Goberman amusing and sees him as "a professional sufferer, a practicing refugee." At the same time Goberman "recognizes" Sol: " 'Are you any better than I am? Don't tell me you didn't leave your dead there and run as fast as a rabbit, saying good riddance to all this, to all the smelly dead.' " Significantly, at this moment Sol's special glasses acquired in a pile of corpses are off and he is laughing at Goberman, frightening Tessie and her father. The reader is meant to see the justice of Goberman's attack, yet the only alternative to leaving the dead behind is joining the 6 million who perished. Sol, who is now wearing his glasses, continues to bait Goberman

> . . . and his [Sol's] face turned to inhuman stone. "*Make me laugh some more*," the Pawnbroker snarled. Goberman wailed "I'll go, I'll go. You are worse than all the Nazis, you are worse than my nightmares." "You are *dreck*, Goberman: you should be washed away. Now go SHVEINHUNDT!" Gober-

man leaped into the air as though the word had electrocuted him. He gave one whimper, bumped softly into the wall with a cry of pain, and then ran clumsily but very swiftly out the door. The racket of his heels on the tiles of the hallway was like a machine gun. (pp. 95–96)

The scene is a distasteful parody of the concentration-camp experience. The victim Goberman is a parasite and toady who embodies the humiliation of the concentration-camp experience. Another victim, Sol, is here representative of the sadistic Nazi and, by implication, guilty of complicity in the Nazi experience. This implication of complicity and inner filth is clearly expressed by Sol after his conversion by love at the end of the novel. There in his semi-delirium he sees the immaculate face of Marilyn Birchfield and responds, " 'No, no, I am too dirty; you must go away from me' [p. 201]." This attitude is shared by the author: the dead, like Sol's wife and Tessie's husband, are mourned and respected; living Jews are tainted.

The Jews who are not survivors are also presented as parasitical, from the Jewish cop on the take to Sol's revolting sister. She is representative of the older generation of Jewish immigrants, ready to give up all Jewish identity in obeisance to the pretty, the plastic, and the "American." She is depicted with authorial venom in all her vulgarity. Wallant does show compassion for the weak Morton, for the beautiful martyr Jesus Ortiz, for Mabel, the whore with the heart of gold, for the good black intern, for the citizens of Harlem, and even for the deadly Murillio. Because he wishes to convey something about the nature of evil and the nature of man, Wallant suspends his compassion when he depicts Jewish victims of the Holocaust. This undefined "something" about evil remains undeveloped in Wallant's novel despite the stark historical particulars that he freely presents in brutal detail. Instead the novel seeks to transmit clichés of love and brotherhood.

The traditionalism of Wallant's novelistic methods is manifested also in his symbolic use of the Hudson River, an important focus in the immigrant experience in *Call It Sleep* and elsewhere. Wallant's Hudson is an example of pathetic fallacy. At the beginning of the work the rocklike Sol Nazerman "ironically" notes "the river's deceptive beauty. Despite its oil-green opacity and the indecipherable things floating on its filthy surface, somehow its insistent direction made it impressive [p. 6]." The river's "life" contrasts with Nazerman's stasis and lack of direction. Midway in the novel, under Marilyn Birchfield's wholesome American influence, Nazerman sees the Hudson north of New York and perceives it as "wide and generous, bordered by green hills and full of great sweeping turns. The steady hum and vibration of the boat filled him with a restless feeling, and he dared deep breaths of the persistent breeze [p. 153]." After his rebirth Nazerman is able through his redemptive tears to clearly "see" the river in Harlem.

> He wiped his eyes clear again and he stood watching the river as it slid obscurely under the bridges toward the sea, bright and glittery in the boat lights on its surface, so vast in its total, never anything here and now, as it hurried slowly toward the obscurity of the salty ocean; so great, so touching in its fleeting presence. The wetness dried on his cheeks and a great calm came over him. (p. 205)

Sol Nazerman's tears, an emblem of his human nature, rejoin him to nature. Nazerman is consoled by the American landscape in a manner similar to that of earlier immigrants. After the inhuman and unnatural horrors that the novel presents so graphically, this pantheism appears inadequate.

The trope of language disassociation is an important component of exile literature in general and of Jewish immigrant literature in particular. Malamud specifically treats the desolation of the cultured refugee who has been torn from his verbal context in "The German Refugee," but he does not use refugees and survivors as centers of consciousness. His immigrant remnants speak in idiosyncratic rhythms and use non-English word order to draw the reader's attention to their Jewish origins and to show complex interaction between the tragic and the comic. The more openly somber subject matter of the

novels by Wallant, Singer, Schaeffer, Bellow, and Cohen calls
for a more muted treatment of language. Wallant's treatment
illustrates some of the difficulties.

Sol Nazerman speaks the careful English of the educated
foreigner who has known the language for some time. He appears to have no accent and he makes no errors. His only
speech idiosyncrasy appears to be his precise English, which
includes no contractions and where all final "g's" are
sounded. Wallant does endow his other characters with accents—black and Puerto Rican urban speech, bad Yiddish-
English. Wallant is afraid to detract from Nazerman's dignity
and culture by making any reference to immigrant language
problems. But Wallant has a sensitive ear for the painful inar-
ticulateness of the black, Buck White:

> "I almos went there . . . once. . . . It was like I was in there
> the army but not befo', not, when I was getting out like, ony
> this guy don remember which because he wasn't in like me
> the army, ony he said if." . . . He felt himself drowning in a
> sea of words, but he continued to thrash around, making a
> great show of swimming. (p. 66)

Wallant has not lavished such care and such compassion on
his Yiddish-speaking characters.

Sol, like other Polish Jewish survivors in the novel, is intended to be a native speaker of Yiddish. He groans in Yiddish
in the unbearable scene when he dreams of the mutilated
body of his baby daughter. The pain of this scene is dimin-
ished by a trivial error: Sol cries, " 'Naomi, Naomi kinder, my
baby' [p. 44]." The assumption here is that Wallant intends
Sol to say "Naomi child"; instead, Sol says "Naomi children,"
where use of the plural makes no syntactical sense. Similarly,
Mendel, Tessie's pitiable father, is insightfully depicted as
responding to the Puerto-Rican Spanish of his neighbors as if
it were the German of the Nazis. But he also is made to say the
impossible for a native speaker of Yiddish. Like Sol, Mendel
makes the same error in number with the same word, *kinder*.
These are Mendel's dying words: " 'A long . . . time ago vhen
I vas . . . a klayna kinder . . . ve had volves in duh snow' [p.

169]." On an earlier occasion, Mendel also spoke the impossible: " 'Vat is the pounding,' asks Mendel. 'Ich shtab svai huntret yourn! I haf died too many times already' [p. 69]." Aside from the phonetic mangling of both accented English and Yiddish, Mendel is unintentionally made to mouth nonsense. Mendel supposedly glosses his Yiddish as "I haf died too many times already." What Mendel actually said in mangled Yiddish is "I die two hundred years," a nonsensical string of words. A refugee-survivor and native speaker of Yiddish who is capable of asking about "pounding" in a newly borrowed tongue is surely capable of constructing a correct sentence in his mother tongue—or would be if his creator paid attention to what he was placing in his character's mouth.

The parasite Goberman, no matter how despicable, would not on first meeting address a stranger with the familiar *du*, nor would he say "Du bist ein Yid?" Both the familiar *du* and the article *ein* are not used in this way by a native speaker. Nor is it likely that a man with Goberman's limited English vocabulary would refer to Sol as "an interloper [p. 93]." Wallant, unlike Malamud and Bellow, is careless in his diction. Given such carelessness it was wise of Wallant to refrain from depicting any of the customary linguistic problems of the immigrant in his central character. More seriously, Wallant's carelessness with language indicates his ambivalence toward his central character and toward the Holocaust experience.

Wallant's novel was one of the earliest American works to treat this complex theme; the necessary time, distance, and data were lacking. Later novels—those of Bellow, I. B. Singer, Cohen, and Schaeffer—reflect their authors' awareness of the growing body of knowledge about the Holocaust, knowledge that was not yet available in the late 1950s.

But if Wallant cannot be faulted for not making use of information that was unavailable, he can be criticized for withholding compassion from his survivor characters while sentimentally depicting Sol's exploited Harlem customers. Wallant depicts even the most barbarous and murderous of the would-be robbers as dignified and clean in contrast to the slovenly Tessie. Robinson, the ex-convict, has a disease, diabetes, and a talent, the ability to play the harmonica. Robinson is so dedicated a musician that he would kill Sol to get the harmonica back (pp. 148–49). No such sympathetic internal views are presented of the survivors. Tessie's expression "was wicked and vindictive" says the authorial voice, and Mendel uses "a sly and vicious tone [pp. 91–92]." Wallant manifests little compassion in *The Pawnbroker* for the people whose suffering he has so sensationally exploited.

It would be unfair to Wallant, however, not to take note of a palpable increase in sophistication in his treatment of the survivor that appears, regrettably, in the posthumously published novel *The Tenants of Moonbloom*.[4] Norman Moonbloom's bizarre tenants are the means of his rebirth. Among them is a family of survivors who embody family values, tradition, and accept their responsibilities. Even the numb Norman becomes aware of "the strangely discreet torments of these pale foreign people [p. 142]" but he is understandably annoyed when Sarah Lubin loses her habitual calm over the results of a minor kitchen fire:

> "What's so terrible about your leaving the wall like that for a while?"
> Sarah's look embarrassed him, made him feel he was being measured, and he worried perversely that he might be found wanting. In the other rooms he could hear the soft, mouselike sounds of the family being quiet. The old lumpy putty on the window glistened and made the room seem like a cave. *"I cannot stand the signs of the fire,"* she said slowly, placing each word in him like a dart. Her eyes were like mirrors, and he saw a tiny Norman Moonbloom in each of them. He smelled the burned odor, but it seemed to him to come from her. . . . She looked wild, and he was afraid. (pp. 143–44)

Wallant does not attempt to present the horrors of the death camps here. Instead Moonbloom is granted a perception of the crematoria that allows him, however briefly, vicariously, and metaphorically, to share in the horror of the survivor experience. Such identification is impossible in the far more graphic world of *The Pawnbroker*, but not because an excess of horror results in distancing and detachment. Rather because no one—not even Sol—responds or reflects on the horror; the terrible past is only told but not experienced within the fictional world of the novel.

It was Wallant's practice to draw upon his experiences for his predominantly realistic novels. His father was a plumber; his uncle owned a pawnshop in which Wallant worked. Wallant allows his plumbers and pawnshop owners to think about the significance of their roles analogically and historically. His portrayal of the plumber Berman and the experiential depiction of Sol's pawnshop have a verisimilitude and depth that are lacking in the survivors. Yet Sol's European experiences are also based on the firsthand accounts of a relative of Wallant's. The experience of atrocity remains raw material, as if Wallant was both reluctant to tamper with real-life events and also ambivalent about his own attitudes toward the subject. Uncertainty and ambivalence are indicated by Wallant's unwillingness to turn the particulars of an individual history into the universals of imaginative literature: he fails to transform what has happened into what may happen. Hampered by realistic novel form and lack of intellectual exploration, *The Pawnbroker* evades the aesthetic and metaphysical challenge that the use of such tragic historic material demands.

Six

Schaeffer's Romantic Survivor

Susan Fromberg Schaeffer is neither the offspring of immigrants, like Malamud, Wallant, Bellow, and Cohen, nor is she an immigrant like I. B. Singer. She was born in 1941 and, unlike the older novelists, she grew up without knowledge of the Holocaust. Her interest in the subject arose from encounters with actual survivors.[1] Schaeffer's youth, her distance from European Jewish life and from the immigrant experience together with her background as a poet and scholar, result in a work of post-Holocaust fiction that differs markedly in form and subject matter from the other works discussed here. *Anya* is unique among American immigrant-survivor novels in that the major action takes place in Eastern Europe before, during, and after the war.[2] In addition, *Anya* is the only new immigrant novel discussed here that is told in the first person by the survivor.

The use of the first person provides authenticity and intensity while allowing for authorial distance. Anya's voice is the only one in this lengthy novel and the reader is always aware that it is the voice of a woman who has witnessed the brutal destruction of her world and who has survived hell. She has not survived intact—she has received a number of brutal blows on the head and suffers severe headaches as a result. Anya possesses enormous strength and resources but her ordeal has affected her telling, and her inconsistencies and incoherence demonstrate how harrowing experiences leave their mark on the mind. Anya's strengths and frailties are thus revealed without authorial intervention.

In contrast to other immigrant-survivors, Anya is not a thinker. As she says, "I have been lucky in everything but my mind [p. 419]." She received some medical school training and her strengths are mainly physical and emotional. Her primary commitment is to survival—her own, her child's, and her family's. Her imagery is frequently biological. After the war she visits the camp where she was a prisoner and perceives that "I would be forever attached to this camp by an invisible umbilical cord, infinitely elastic and infinitely strong, one that could never be cut [p. 362]." Her attachment to her European past is just as strong and eternal. Surveying the now pastoral scene, she envies

> the earth which is swallowing all those things. . . . What it took in, it broke down and used; what I took in stayed as it was; I broke down. What I took in built great walls, like the Great Wall of China in paths of my mind; I was losing so much every day. (p. 362)

Anya does not "take in" her experiences; they are not assimilated, broken down, and reformed. Her concern is with the fateful interaction of her loved ones with catastrophic events. She extracts no wisdom and draws no conclusions.

Long after the war she asks herself, "So what are my experiences? [p. 472]" and "So what have I learned from the war? [p. 473]" And again, "So what have I learned? I have learned not to believe in suffering [p. 474]." But on the next page, "Suffering is the best teacher; I have learned that [p. 475]." Anya senses that no explanation suffices: "Events were so ridiculous no explanation could be ridiculous enough [p. 472]." It is a perception expressed more elaborately and explored more profoundly by Bellow's and I. B. Singer's wiser protagonists. Anya's lack of intellectual sophistication does not, however, invalidate her insight.

Anya is victim and witness but, above all, recorder of the past. The novel is a historic romance of the Holocaust and, like I. B. Singer's work, is concerned with the fictional preservation of the destroyed European Jewish past. That Schaeffer attempts to present prewar Jewish life in Poland without

Singer's credentials is, like her use of the first person, indicative of her courage and, at the same time, symptomatic of her distance from her subject matter.

The novel's divisions reflect its historicity and its preoccupation with the past. The short opening and closing sections, prosaically entitled "Prologue" and "Epilogue," are set in America in the present. They consist of Anya's dreams of her dead family, of her incomplete and unsuccessful attempts to understand her horrendous experiences. Anya's language in these two minor sections reflects her present-day inconsistencies and uncertainties. In sharp contrast are the major sections of the novel, which are a precise, doggedly chronological, and detailed account of Anya's life from golden girlhood to marriage and motherhood, through her harrowing experience of the Holocaust, to her eventual arrival in America. The first section, significantly entitled "In History," is a concrete, loving evocation of the lives of upper middle-class, worldly European Jews who were at ease with both their worldliness and their traditions. Schaeffer uses the form of the family novel, rich with details of home life, food, clothing, and country vacations. The rhetorical purposes are directly stated by the narrator from the very beginning:

> My name is Anya Savikin, and I am going to take you into the apartment of my parents . . . in Vilno, Poland. I want to be sure that you can see this apartment. . . . I want you to go through this apartment so you have a memory of it: my memory. (p. 9)

Anya wants the details she depicts to "grow into a film" wherein the reader is an extra. "You will have the feel of the polished wood table on your fingertips; you will have the smells of the kitchen in your nostrils. This is my ambition. Perhaps it is too much to ask [p. 9]."

Anya wants to convey concrete authentic experience and at the same time transmit *her* memory of her life. She is, at once, an accurate recorder and the heroine of a fairy tale "in which the ordinary laws of nature are slightly suspended."[3] The novel is a historic romance of the Holocaust populated by wondrous beings of almost mythic stature. Anya's father is a saintly and skeptical intellectual, the kindest and most cultured of fathers. Her extraordinary mother is the apotheosis of survival—practical, prophetic, remarkably wise, and dedicated to raising healthy, accomplished children. Anya's brothers and sisters are admirable, the servants are colorful and loyal. The parents and servants are gifted storytellers who enjoy sharing superstitions, tales, fables, and parables. The fairy tale world contains grotesque and frightening products of the imagination but the grim reality of history invades the Savikins' kingdom. A kindly psychiatrist is thrown into a boiling cauldron of soup by his mad patients; anti-Semitic Polish students use iron nails to destroy the faces of Jewish girl students. The grotesque death of the psychiatrist is probable in the fictional context; the incident of the nails is based on historic fact.

Schaeffer creates "a reality whose quality is unreal," the "irreality" that Langer posits as characteristic of the literature of the Holocaust. The memories of survivors are the "source of *information* for the novel" (italics Schaeffer's).[4] The realities of the survivor experience are embedded in the romance form and combine with the heroic and the marvelous. The synthesis of history and romance reveal Schaeffer's reverence toward her subject matter. It is not only in Anya's flawed imagination that loved ones appear larger than life, survival miraculous, and the universe mysterious. In her creator's literary imagination the martyred dead are heroic, the events of the Holocaust are awesome, and the task of making characters and events into a fictional whole prodigious. Malamud, I. B. Singer, Bellow, and Cohen present their protagonists through their thoughts, as preoccupied with the moral and the intellectual, and thus their works dramatize the range of human behavior and the extraordinary power of the human mind. *Anya* is presented cinematographically, as numerous references make clear, and the intellectual dimension is expressed through literary allusion and the poetic imagination.

Schaeffer's highly individual use of biblical and other literary motifs is exemplified in the section fittingly entitled

"Biblical Times." The section begins with the fable of the grasshopper and the ant, but in this context the moral has less to do with the grasshopper's fecklessness than with the human inability to see imminent evil. The doomed innocence of the victims is sounded early in the novel when, in the early thirties, Anya reads *Mein Kampf* and declares, "It's really a fairy tale [p. 78]." In 1939, with the Nazis outside of Vilna, Anya's wise mother quotes the refugees who "say the Germans aren't so bad. . . . *Mein Kampf* is only a fairy tale, that's what the last one said, just like you did [p. 148]." The painful innocence is replaced by even more painful wisdom as the section movingly depicts the mass shootings, selections, and other brutalities that result in the annihilation of Anya's family. Anya's mother then recognizes that they were "living through biblical times [when] . . . the living will come to envy the dead [p. 149]."

However, the searing events, part of the history of the occupation of Vilna, are modified in this work by the manner of death. Anya's cultured father, an omnivorous reader, is shot by the Nazis on his way to get a book to ease his confinement. Anya's gentle and angelic sister chooses to die with the man she loves. Anya's husband gives up the chance to escape in order to stay with her and their child. Her mother hides and allows herself to be selected for death in order that Anya may live. Within the fictional world the victims are granted meaningful deaths.

The historic particulars of Schaeffer's chronicle of the slaughter of the innocents in the Vilna ghetto are verified in historical accounts. Lucy Dawidowicz makes reference to the elaborate hiding places set up in the ghetto.[5] In *Anya* people are hidden into made-up beds, in walls, behind credenzas. Anya's mother hides from the Gestapo by crawling into an oven like the witch in *Hansel and Gretel*. Treasure is buried in yards, under city streets, in jars of preserves. Anya's precocious baby is told animal tales and grisly fairy stories "about a man who murders his wives, and a boy who was eaten by wolves [p. 187]" as well as more conventional nursery tales. The imaginary cruelties collected by the Brothers Grimm comport with the day-to-day barbarism of the Nazis. In *Anya* people read *The Three Musketeers* and *The Scarlet Pimpernel*—romantic, escapist literature full of daring and courage where right always triumphs and virtue is rewarded. Says Emanuel Ringelblum, the historian and archivist who perished in the Warsaw Ghetto, "in a word, being unable to take revenge on the enemy in reality, we are seeking it in fantasy, in literature."[6] By the end of this portion of *Anya*, the novel has become a tragic romance "where the theme of inevitable death works against the marvelous and often forces it into the background."[7]

The biblical motifs in *Anya* are not the Jobian probings favored in other novels of post-Holocaust consciousness. Instead the disguise and guile practiced by the patriarchs on their enemies are repeated throughout the book. Like Joseph and Jacob, characters assume disguises and change their identity. To prevent the slaying of her first-born, Anya disguises the child as a gentile and arranges for her to be rescued like baby Moses. Yet another pervasive biblical motif is in the family talisman. It is a silver filigreed bowl that depicts the story of Noah's ark. Fittingly, the bowl, which represents survival in the face of the destruction of the world, is the one family heirloom that survives the destruction of Anya's family. But more somberly and ironically the legend of Noah marks a significant break in the relationship between God and man. After the Flood God vows never to destroy the world because of man "since the devisings of man's heart are evil from the start [Gen. vii. 22]." The destruction of Anya's world is an act of man, not God.

In place of the world they destroyed the Nazis created *l'univers concentrationnaire*. The account of the boxcar journey, the casual cruelty of the soldiers, the degradation and humiliation of existence in the camp with the constant danger from starvation, disease, magotty food, jealous prisoners as well as the routine threat of murder or selection to the death camp—these form a grim litany of systematized but not banal evil. No matter how often it has been chronicled in fact or fiction, the gratuitous violence and institutional sadism create disbelief in the reader as well as in the disoriented victim who is undergoing the ordeal.

Like other Jewish American writers, Schaeffer does not presume to portray a Nazi death camp in the manner of the eyewitnesses Wiesel and Borowski. But she does include a displaced and metaphoric equivalent of the crematoria in the burning of the barracks next to Anya's. Anya fears that she too would be burned to death: "This is the most terrible way to die; dear God, . . . let me die any other way. . . . And the flames came to a stop at our barracks [p. 234]." In the documented but unbelievable world of the camps such "miraculous" survivals did occur. There are graphic descriptions of rotten food, filth, and primitive camp hospital procedures but Schaeffer excludes the excremental experience so much a part of the "literature of atrocity." And, although the novel contains much about love, courtship, marriage, childbirth, motherhood, and family life, there is no sexuality in *Anya*. This reticence is consistent with the nineteenth-century decorum inherent in the family novel and in the romance. The exclusion of the excremental and the sexual is another indication of the formal coherence that underlies the chaos of the events depicted and the disorientation of the narrator.

The section that includes the camp experience, appropriately titled "The Lion's Jaws," includes a bizarre "fairy godmother" in the person of a German soldier who is really a disguised Jew. In this context such a figure is not unlikely. Survival is a miracle and miraculous escapes occur in fact and fiction. Erdmann (earth man, a natural man in contrast to the unnatural men around him) provides Anya with a disguise and "a magic thing," a cross that will serve as her charm and help her to pose as a gentile (p. 251).

The work contains other heroic actions, hair-breadth escapes, and remarkable coincidences—the literary conventions common to the romance. Anya is exceptionally beautiful, as is her daughter. The daughter is protected by an extraordinarily brave Lithuanian judge who is murdered because he sheltered Jews. The novel depicts people who sacrifice much, and who are more courageous than seems humanly possible, against a background of the Nazi horror whose perpetrators are inhumanly brutal and sadistic. Among the many documents testifying to the bestiality of the Nazis, there are also accounts of the nobility and courage of the victims (Primo Levi, Emmanuel Ringelblum, Szmul Zygielbojm, and Janusz Korczak among others). Schaeffer's romantic fiction celebrates the heroic extremes.

Anya's own courage and determination come from her vividly portrayed background and are most obviously manifested in her fierce devotion to her child and to her family. Anya and her daughter survive the Holocaust and Anya attempts to rebuild her life in postwar Poland. What convinces her to leave Europe occurs on a highly improbable plane trip to Warsaw which, according to Schaeffer, was necessary in terms of the novel's structure. Anya goes to Warsaw in search of remnants of her husband's family. By means of the plane ride and a fruitless and agonizing journey through the city, Anya gains perspective on the complete devastation and ruin of Europe. "It was as if the city had fallen into some solution of time that was dissolving it [p. 373]." The Germans killed people and buildings and trees and even furniture because "they didn't know the difference between what was living and what was dead [p. 370]." Anya now recognizes but does not articulate that her beloved past is dead and vanished. It can only live in her memory. But Anya must leave Europe carrying only the Noah's ark symbolic of the new life she was to create after the deluge. Her detailed and corporeal re-creation of the past would not occur until considerable time had elapsed.

Barely 40 pages of the novel's 489 are set in America, and they are understandably anticlimactic as Anya unsuccessfully attempts to evaluate her extraordinary life. But when she discovers that she has to fight for Jewish survival (albeit on a drastically different level) in the new world, she temporarily regains her previous vigor. The irony is that Anya's daughter, Ninka, who was saved from annihilation by superhuman effort and whose life involved the sacrifice of so many other lives, falls in love with a non-Jew. Anya then resorts to masquerading as a gentile again to prevent Ninka from making a mockery of all the sacrifice. Anya and Ninka's survival of the Holocaust was accomplished by infinitely more perilous and resourceful subterfuges and disguises. Here Schaeffer echoes I. B. Singer, who believes that survival in a demonic world is based on guile, flight, and stealth. Anya prevails again and Ninka marries a Jew.

The European setting, the first-person narration, and the romance form set *Anya* apart from other immigrant-survivor novels, but it shares important similarities with the genre as well. Schaeffer's work presents the theme of survivor homelessness, which appears in the other novels. Anya's home is in her memories of her Vilna girlhood and her brief glowing experience as a newlywed in Warsaw. These places are described in vivid detail to evoke the beloved vanished past. Of Anya's American homes, only one is recounted in any detail. And it too is imbued with the sense of the past that combines the European with a fleeting, incomplete aspect of the Jewish American immigrant past.

In the manner of the older immigrant novelists, Schaeffer includes a metaphor of rebirth in Anya's postwar voyage to America. Anya's extreme seasickness is an earthy symbol of her attempt to purge herself of her unspeakable memories. Her first sight of the New York skyline "wiped everything out of my mind; they were so many gray erasers." A sudden pleasant memory from her girlhood flashes across her mind, then "I walked into the street . . . my mind empty as a slate [p. 455]." Like Singer's Yadwiga, the more sophisticated Anya succeeds in creating a pale analogue of the warmth and color of her Vilna home in a modest apartment in New York. Like the other survivors Nazerman and Sammler, Anya at first would like to forget all the wartime horrors and not even remember the prelapsarian Vilna days. But her attempt, like that of the others, is doomed and Anya's only "home" must ultimately be with the totality of her experience.

Yet she does go to a psychiatrist-hypnotist in an attempt to remove the memory of what took place before her arrival in America. The doctor, another survivor, refuses because " 'the

Jews get fewer . . . and what will you have left? At least now you have your memories' [p. 485]." The memoir is proof that Anya is committed to opening "the rooms to the house in the past which were kept locked so long" for "the rooms I live in now seem to have filled with the artificial snow of sealed globes and thickened; moving into them is like moving into an ice cube [p. 469]." Therefore she attempts to integrate her present with her wartime past by living in a building where "there are more people from the camps." What is re-created is not the prewar warmth but "the neighborhoods that haunted us after the war in Europe. We are reliving it again [p. 475]." Like Wallant's Tessie Rubin and Singer's Masha, Anya is at home in her tragic past and she exists among others like herself.

Like Bellow's elderly Sammler, Schaeffer's middle-aged Anya is contemplating her final "home," which appears to her in joyous dreams where her parents welcome her. They are *tsadikim*, who inquire as to her health, offer advice and guidance, and, of course, tell stories. Anya

> can picture the new house as clearly as the camps or the ghetto, or the apartment we live in now. . . . And more and more I have this feeling . . . that I will dream about the house and . . . they will not vanish; they will be there. (p. 489)

Anya's home is with her dead family. What disturbs her idyllic vision is the vision of her own burial without her parents near. Like I. B. Singer's Masha, Anya wants to uphold the tradition of family burial:

> I want to be buried near my mother. . . . But I don't even know where her grave is. You don't know how terrible that is, not even to have her grave. If I had it, I could pretend she was there; she *would* be there. (p. 6)

Anya's dreams, visions, and her entire fictional world are triumphs of the imagination over grim reality, but they afford her neither perception nor solace.

The novel is a different kind of triumph for Schaeffer. The romantic and fairy tale elements indicate that, despite the horror of the events recounted, much of *Anya* is a fiction that depicts life as it ought to have been. Schaeffer endows her protagonist with her own poetic gifts, but she does not inject authorial rhetoric to modify Anya's perception of truth. Instead Schaeffer employs the literary devices and allusions of the romance to create a respectful distance between the products of the literary imagination and the realities of the Holocaust. The effect is the opposite of the reductivism of the banality of evil. Instead, twentieth-century evil is uglier and more inexplicable in a fictional context where courageous, high-minded, admirable characters who live vivid, idealized lives are wantonly destroyed. The narrative method and the romance form are as effective as distancing devices as are Malamud's indirection and the use of American settings by I. B. Singer, Bellow, and Cohen.

The survivor narrator is a remarkable but broken woman whose testimony reveals the mental, emotional, and physical scars of her devastating experience. Schaeffer has created a gifted and promising persona, whose gifts were destroyed and whose promise was aborted by historic evil. The successful medical student could not even work in a hospital after the war; the woman who was quick at languages never could learn English even after many years in America. The resourceful and clever worker becomes a part-time antique dealer because she is only truly alive in the vanished past. In that past, as daughter, sister, wife, and friend, Anya displayed a limitless love that was an energizing force. Such love confined to Ninka grows obsessive and constricting for mother and daughter. This prematurely old woman who longs for death does not achieve tragic perception, but the novel conveys a sense of tragic loss to the reader. With all its vividness and authenticity, the overall effect of *Anya* is elegiac. The novel begins with references to the memorial candles with which Jews traditionally commemorate their dead and ends in a lament for the prematurely destroyed people and their vanished world.

Seven

Singer's Diasporan Survivor

In contrast to Edward Wallant and Susan Fromberg Schaeffer stands Isaac Bashevis Singer, whose background, education, experience, and philosophical bent equip him to be relatively at ease with the difficult subject of the Holocaust. Singer is the only postwar "American" novelist who is himself an immigrant. Not technically a survivor (he left Poland in 1935) but a refugee, he is the scion of a family that represented two opposing strains within traditional Judaism, Hasidism and rabbinic Judaism. He is also a product of urban, secular, antitraditional Jewish life. His embodiment of these paradoxes and antinomies is evident in the tortured and complex fictional characters whom Singer creates. Herman Broder, the protagonist of *Enemies,* is typically Singerian in that he is craven, lecherous, inconsistent; at times he retreats toward orthodoxy, only to be pulled again to his customary hedonism.[1]

Singer's fiction resembles Wallant's only in its particulars. Like Nazerman's family, Broder's wife and children were all (apparently) murdered by the Nazis. Herman, like Sol, has a mistress who lives with an elderly parent; all are death-camp survivors. Herman also has a new wife, Yadwiga, who formerly was a servant in his mother's home. She is a gentile and a Pole, who risked her life to shelter Herman in a hayloft during the Nazi occupation. She is another "good gentile," like Malamud's Alpine and Wallant's Ortiz, but her motives are more direct for she truly loves Broder. The most "Christlike" of the characters in *Enemies* is Herman's first wife,

Tamar, who unexpectedly reappears—having escaped the Nazis after all. The frequency of such instances in the lives of actual survivors removes the comic aspects from the absurd situation of a man with three "wives" and at least as many "homes."

Herman, again like Sol, has attempted to create a kind of "Eden" in Yadwiga's prelapsarian Brighton Beach apartment, complete with parakeets flying free and bucolic odors. It is the pre-Holocaust vision of the European village and is as fragile as Sol's precarious "privacy." In contrast, Masha, Herman's tortured and passionate mistress, lives in a decaying Bronx apartment house much like Tessie Rubin's. Herman's nights with his mistress are quite different from Sol's passionless encounters with his matronly mistress. Masha mixes moments of sexual abandon with equally passionate reenactments and retellings of her life in the camps. Masha's apartment, more overtly than the Rubins', embodies the recent collective Jewish past. Herman's particular and personal past is represented in yet another place, when Tamar comes to America and creates still another "home," this time in Manhattan.

Herman's "homes" are static incarnations of his past and present life as well as of collective Jewish history. Prewar innocence is enshrined in Brooklyn, while the febrile, smelly Bronx neighborhood is a pale analogue of wartime suffering. In the bedroom that is the setting for their illicit love, Masha re-creates more than recent history. She goes through a ritual sequence of love-making, smoking, talking, and eating that "reminded Herman of the ancients who would relate the miracle of the exodus from Egypt until the morning star rose [p. 46]." Implicit in Herman's recollection of the Exodus is the injunction of the Passover Haggadah: "In every generation let each man look on himself as if he came forth out of Egypt."[2] Exodus and Redemption are meant to be relived and taken as personal experience.

Tamar Broder's Manhattan apartment is the scene of more ideological discussion and considerably less love-making than is Masha's bedroom. Tamar's presence is associated with Herman's adult past and his failures as husband and father. Yet, because Tamar conveys the strengths of the survivor, her apartment is still another refuge, another surrogate hayloft, for the peripatetic Herman. He, who begins the novel with two "homes" and acquires a third, continues to wander. In addition to spending nights in the beds of assorted wives and mistresses, Herman, in the year's time portrayed in the novel, makes two trips to the Catskills.

In the countryside the theme of homelessness is somewhat modified by the characters' positive response to the American landscape, a response evident in earlier immigrant fiction and in the works of Wallant. Schaeffer's heroine, of course, cannot respond to the American landscape. Her love of nature is expressed in her longing for the now mythic Polish countryside of her youth. In Singer's case the response is colored by appropriate irony. Gazing at the bucolic scene at Lake George, Masha says playfully, " 'Where are the Nazis? What kind of a world is this without Nazis? A backward country, this America' [p. 104]." Herman too relaxes to some degree for "surrounded by the light-blue sky, the yellow-green water, he . . . felt less guilty. The birds had announced the new day as if it were the morning after creation." But the smell of food causes Herman to imagine "that he heard the screech of a chicken or a duck. Somewhere on this lovely summer morning, fowl were being slaughtered; Treblinka was everywhere [p. 105]." Singer, a vegetarian, is not employing bathos. On Herman's second trip to the Catskills, this time to visit the more spiritual Tamar, the American landscape has become even more familiar. On his way to Tamar's cottage he

> tried to memorize each tree, shrub, and stone along the way, as if America were destined for the same destruction as Poland. . . . A nocturnal melancholy descended from the heavens. The stars gleamed like memorial candles in some cosmic synagogue. (p. 124)

Even the Edenic American landscape is susceptible to evil.

Nevertheless, Herman is in the main soothed and consoled by the American countryside though his vacation with Masha is like that of displaced persons who cannot remain in one place. Tamar, who has suffered most, is the most stable. She stays in one place. At the end of the novel, when Herman has abandoned all his "homes" and his "wives," Tamar is capable of establishing a new home for Yadwiga and her baby daughter. Tamar is also capable of Jobian steadfastness and thus can create and maintain a traditional Jewish environment for Yadwiga and her child. Tamar's stability makes her a most unusual modern Singerian character. She speculates at the end of the novel that the wandering Herman "had either killed himself or was hiding in an American version of his Polish hayloft [p. 254]."

Herman, like many of Singer's protagonists, is a heavy-hearted *picaro*, as lost in New York as others are in Tel Aviv, Wisconsin, Buenos Aires, or the other cities that Singer uses as settings. In 1973 Singer wrote that

> my stories deal only with Yiddish-speaking immigrants from Poland so as to ensure that I know well not only their present way of life but their *roots*—their culture, history, ways of thinking and expressing themselves. . . . Some of these people have helped to build Warsaw and New York and are now helping to build Tel Aviv. They lived in the midst of almost all the social movements of our time. Their illusions were the illusions of mankind. The vandals who murdered millions of these people have destroyed a treasure of individuality that no literature dare try to bring back.[3]

Singer's juxtaposition of the slaughtered community of Warsaw with the living communities of New York and Tel Aviv is no accident. His fiction reveals an unchanging world in which evil is constant and history is cyclical. This is a world of *goles*, a fallen universe deserted by God and presided over by malicious powers. The Singer character is in exile whether in Israel or in the Diaspora. Neither man nor God is at home in this fallen world where all are condemned to repeat the same errors. Herman's superficially ridiculous fantasies of the Nazis invading New York are buttressed by Singer's cyclical view of history, his knowledge of ancient and modern Jewish history, and his perception of the relativity of time.

For the Singerian exile a home exists with the saintly sufferers like Tamar and with others who re-create fragments of the past. These in their turn have no homeland except in their memories of a destroyed world. Neither in the "promised land" of Israel nor in the "golden land" America is there a permanent home. For homelessness is the human condition and permanent homes are not needed. Diasporans do not yearn for a spatial homeland. They may, however, yearn for an irretrievable time before the Holocaust, which appears in retrospect innocent, even idyllic. The Jew, according to George Steiner, "has his anchorage not in place but in his highly developed sense of history as personal context. Six thousand years of self-awareness are his homeland."[4] The fictional Holocaust survivor and his creator are faced with the problem of developing a personal context that includes the most devastating event in the collective Jewish past.

To some degree all of Singer's characters share in the same collective past. The craven but not unsympathetic Herman Broder spent three years hiding in a Polish hayloft. In safe America he dreams of the Nazi bayonets he managed to escape and awakes with a dream stigmata, a black and blue mark on the forehead. Shifrah Puah, the mother of Herman's mistress, has a real Nazi bayonet mark on her cheek. Herman is as "marked" by his experience as is Shifrah Puah.

Certain experiences recur in many works dealing with the Holocaust whether fiction, memoir, film, or history. Among the most arresting are the excremental experiences, which are recounted in the novels under discussion. Wallant and Singer present an interesting contrast in the use of this devastating material. It will be recalled that Sol's nauseating dream emphasizes his impotence and helplessness as his son appears about to drown in excrement. In *Enemies*, Shifrah Puah's memory of a similar incident is as involuntary as Sol's: "That very moment as she stood at the stove, she had seen in her mind's eye a young Jewish girl stripped naked and balancing on a log over a pit of excrement [p. 50]." This is one of "a hundred such incidents" that the old woman recalls to Herman. Singer's novel conveys a sense of the day-to-day horrors of the Nazi war against the Jews without the sensational detail that Wallant stresses. Yet Singer's novel is more moving because each survivor reflects his or her reaction to the particular experience of horror. Shifrah Puah's excremental memory is more horrible for her because the young woman, "this daughter of rabbis and esteemed Jews, slipped and fell into the offal [p. 50]." If the memory had been Masha's or Tamar's the reaction would have reflected their particular values. Singer's people have experienced degradation as individuals; they are not passive viewers watching something happen to someone else. Throughout the novel is the humbling and sobering recognition on the part of the author, characters, and reader that much more was left unsaid than said. Singer's characters live in and with their horrendous memories.

Withal Singer does not ennoble his gallery of survivors and immigrants, just as their experience of suffering has not necessarily ennobled them. Singer's commitment is to the recapturing of the experience of suffering despite explicit recognition "that the whole truth would never be learned from those who had survived the concentration camps or the wandering through Russia—not because they lied but because it was impossible to tell it all! [p. 70]" Singer has reverence for the experience of suffering—if not for the sufferers—and is himself engaged in telling the survivor story in its infinite variety. He thus preserves valuable fragments in fictional form.

Even Herman Broder, despite his hypocrisy, cowardice, and hedonism, is a valuable fragment. Herman is obsessed with his own survival, but is perceptive and ironic about himself as he looks for surrogate haylofts in Brooklyn, Manhattan, the Bronx, and the Catskills. His mind dwells on

> fantasies of vengeance in which he discovered methods for destroying whole armies, for ruining industries. He managed to bring to trial all those who had been involved in the annihilation of the Jews. He was ashamed of these reveries which filled his mind at the slightest provocation, but they persisted with childish stubbornness. (p. 123)

Herman's recurrent obsession that a Nazi invasion of New York is imminent is less childish, in Singer's eyes, since it is buttressed by Singer's cyclical view of history and his understanding of modern philosophy:

> If time is just a form of perception, or a category of reason, the past is as present as today: Cain continues to murder Abel, Nebuchadnezzar is still slaughtering the sons of Zedekiah and putting out Zedekiah's eyes. The pogrom in Kesheniev never ceases. Jews are forever being burned in Auschwitz. Those without courage to make an end to their existence have only one other way out: to deaden their consciousness, choke their memory, extinguish the last vestige of hope. (p. 33)

Herman's pessimism is in part a rationale for his own hedonistic behavior and in part sincere belief based on knowledge of the historical past and observation of human behavior. Thousands of years of Jewish history and its cycles of persecution and catastrophe are an integral part of the fictional world of *Enemies.*

It is a world that is presided over by demonic powers, capricious if not malicious. According to Herman,

> survival itself was based on guile. From microbe to man, life prevailed generation to generation by sneaking past the jealous powers of destruction. . . . Animals had accepted the precariousness of existence and the necessity for flight and stealth; only man sought certainty and instead succeeded in accomplishing his own downfall. (pp. 225–26)

Herman, in this frame of mind, has no use for Jewish law. He "had not sealed a convenant with God and had no use for Him. He didn't want to have his seed multiply like sands by the sea. His whole life was a game of stealth [p. 226]." Despite Herman's pessimism and personal alienation, he displays reverence for those who keep the past and disdain for those who seek to forget.

Herman's disdain is conveyed at a Catskill resort when he comments on the German refugees:

> "In what way are they my brothers and sisters?" Herman asked himself. "What does their Jewishness consist of? What of my Jewishness?" They all had the same wish: to assimilate as quickly as possible and get rid of their accents. Herman belonged neither to them nor to the American, Polish, or Russian Jews. Like the ant on the table that morning, he had torn himself away from the community. (p. 107)

Like Cahan's David Levinsky, Herman feels cut off from his community. But David is self-deceived and his past is used to trap him in solipsism and self-pity. Herman, far more aware than Levinsky, is nevertheless unable to make the meaningful and positive connections between present and past that make community possible. Herman's skepticism, his hedonism, and his selfishness paralyze him spiritually and morally.

Singer's fictional world contains characters who do maintain past values and thereby retain a sense of community. The community may no longer exist as an entity and the past values may appear to have little relevance to contemporary life, but within the confines of the novel these preservers embody and re-create what was worthy in the Jewish European past and ceaselessly commemorate the recent Jewish catastrophe. The most traditional among these is the *tsadik* Reb Abraham Nissen and his wife who remain unchanged in their spiritual strength and in their commitment to orthodoxy. Shifrah Puah, Masha's mother, another saintly survivor, seeks to indict herself:

> She had rebelled against her parents, she had treated her husband badly, she had paid too little attention to Masha when she was growing up, when it would have been possible to instill the fear of God in her. And the greatest sin she had committed was to have remained alive when so many innocent men and women had been martyred. (p. 45)

Shifrah Puah, despite her own piety, tolerates the complexities of Herman's marital and sexual relationships. So does the *tsadik*, Reb Nissen. He understands modern skepticism:

> Why should these young people be expected to have faith when he himself was plagued by doubts? How could those who had lived through the destruction believe in the Almighty and in His mercy? Deep in his heart, Reb Abraham Nissen had no sympathy for those Orthodox Jews who tried to pretend that the holocaust in Europe had never taken place. (p. 224)

But his faith remains whole. He and his wife journey to Israel because he does not want to be buried among the shaved Jews of New York and because he wants to "save himself the arduous journey through the underground caverns which the dead must traverse before reaching the Holy Land, there to be resurrected when the Messiah came [p. 224]."

Singer admires these pious remnants and is one of the few contemporary writers who can portray them from within, without sanctimoniousness or sentimentality. Yet Reb Nissen and the others, while admirable, are remote from the modern skeptics who are their descendants. Herman's three wives also maintain commitment to past values, offering a more germane contrast to Herman's modern paralysis. All three—Yadwiga, Tamar, and Masha—despite their various failings, are capable of deriving sustenance from the Jewish past. Not surprisingly it is Tamar, the supreme sufferer, who is capable of a productive synthesis of past and present.

The loving Yadwiga not only re-creates the Polish village in Brooklyn; she remains a simple, loyal, bovine peasant untouched by her surroundings. Even her conversion to Judaism is mindless, emotional, and ritualistic, and therefore equivalent to the watered-down Judaism of the Americanized Jewish immigrant whom Singer satirizes. She will be a faithful Jew as she was a faithful servant and a faithful wife. Yadwiga's fidelity is rewarded in Singer's fictional world with a child. The beautiful, intelligent Masha is punished both by Herman and by Singer. She is an angel of death, a Jungian succubus who can only produce a hysterical pregnancy. Masha has committed the sin of being "unfaithful" for she has slept with her husband, Leon Tortshiner. This was the price Tortshiner demanded before he would grant her the divorce that Masha wanted so that she could be married by a rabbi to the already twice-married Herman. Of the three women, Tamar is the noblest. Not only has she been faithful to the philandering Herman, she is consistently unselfish. Perhaps one of the most ironic instances of her unselfishness is her typing of Herman's dissertation. Even before the war Tamar saw the dissertation as "anti-humanist, anti-feminist, and depressing in outlook [p. 63]." Singer's writings have been similarly judged.

Singer, however, is an ironist, and while Singer and Broder may indeed share male-supremacist double standards, Singer recognizes the hypocrisy and incongruity of these standards. Tamar, who represents whatever moral center the novel contains, remarks that "men love virgins. If men had their way, every woman would lie down a prostitute and get up a virgin [p. 174]." Herman, the extra- and intra-marital adventurer, is uncomfortable with modern, educated, and potentially liberated women: "What kind of women are these? How is it that they are so well-informed? . . . I don't belong here. I should have remained a Talmudist [pp. 197–98]." Herman's distaste is hypocritical, but Singer is ironically defending the inconsistencies.

Singer's knowledge of Jewish law and his ease with traditional materials add a dimension to his treatment of Herman's difficulties. Although adultery is condemned in biblical and other sources, "the extra marital intercourse of a married man is not per se a crime in biblical or later Jewish law." Adultery is defined "as voluntary sexual intercourse between a married woman . . . and a man other than her husband."[5] Such legalistic discrimination, while not articulated in Singer's works, may influence the severe fictional punishments meted out to sexually adventuresome females and not equally visited upon straying males. Herman's desire for his three wives is de-

plored in the novel because of possible legal complications
and the danger of deportation. Herman does not worry over
the moral question, nor does he express guilt. Other men,
such as Rabbi Lampert and the immigrant Pesheles, are rather
admiring.

Even Herman's three "marriages" are rendered more ambiguous by time-worn Jewish marital and sexual mores. "The
law is different in the case of a married man who purports to
take a second wife while still married. According to Jewish
law this second marriage (and any others) is valid."[6] Singer's
imtimate knowledge of these traditions enriches even his most
trivial subjects with the constant interplay of past and present.
All materials are potentially germane regardless of the passage
of time.

Singer ignores the passage of time and changes in place
and custom to emphasize the continuous presence of the past
in his works. Masha's "adultery" is punished in traditional
terms. Masha has always wanted to bear Herman's child. For
Holocaust survivors there has been deep-rooted conflict between the desire to replenish the destroyed people and the
revulsion against populating an evil world. The biblical com-
mandment to "go forth and multiply" is countered by Tamar's
observation that Jewish children exist "so that the Gentiles
will have someone to burn [p. 95]." Tamar has experienced
the ultimate in suffering for she has witnessed the murder of
her children. Masha, deformed by concentration-camp life, as
she claims, or perhaps because of her passionate, histrionic
nature, is incapable of conceiving a child. Only the simple
Yadwiga is allowed to bear Herman's child.

Singer is too accomplished a story teller and Masha is too
fascinating a character for her to constitute only an object lesson. Masha, like Tamar, is a sufferer, an incarnation of the
death camp. Masha, like other defiant, God-cursing unbelievers in Singer's fiction, practices Jewish rituals while expressing her contempt and defiance. She too is committed to
the preservation of the significant past. The typically hedonistic Masha has repeatedly urged Herman to run away with her
to the warmth of Florida, Gehenna being her proper milieu. In

the end she is incapable of freeing herself from her responsibilities. Although Masha appears to want to run away from her symbiotic relationship with her mother, Shifrah Puah's death reveals the traditional Masha beneath the iconoclast. She cannot leave her mother's corpse for fear of being damned in the life to come. Like Reb Nissen, Masha does not want to lie among strangers. She wants to be buried next to her mother. Masha's final words to Herman are traditional and admirably inconsistent. Although she has long urged Herman to desert Yadwiga, she now begs him not to leave her and his unborn child.

If Masha is sirenlike, Herman's first wife, Tamar, is saintlike. But her nobility and unselfishness are not only the result of her experience of suffering. Herman admits that she is "essentially a spiritual person [p. 63]." Rather sarcastically Herman describes the prewar Tamar as "the incarnation of the masses, always following some leader, hypnotized by slogans, never having an opinion of her own [p. 64]." But Tamar was also a devoted mother, and through all her years of wandering, a faithful wife as well as successively a communist, Zionist, and neoreligious Jew. Tamar, unlike Masha and Herman, is not a hedonist. As Reb Nissen embodies the religious tradition of the *tsadik*, Tamar represents what is worthy in the secular, collective Jewish heritage. Her spirituality and idealism allow her to live with her searingly tragic past and to be a preserver and transmitter of that past. She has wished for death but does not take her own life as Masha does. Nor are her reasons for self-preservation hedonistic and cowardly as Herman's are. She relates present discomfort to earlier deprivation:

> "Thank God, my time of suffering isn't over. I'm still in the midst of it. This more or less is the way we had to struggle in Jambul. You won't believe me, Herman, but I find some comfort in it. I don't want to forget what we went through. When it's warm in the room, I imagine that I've betrayed all the Jews in Europe. My uncle [Reb Nissen] feels that Jews

should observe an eternal shiva [mourning period]. The entire people should squat on low stools and read from the Book of Job." (pp. 217–18)

In contrast to those refugees, whom Herman disdains, who wish to forget and assimilate as quickly as possible, Tamar bears witness to her past by partly re-experiencing that past in present experiences of want. Her reliving of her past is itself analogous to the retelling of the story of the Exodus at Passover, in which the participants attempt to experience what their ancestors experienced. It will be recalled that the less than saintly Masha also "retells" her past in this *seder*-like manner. The references to the Book of Job increase our awareness of the magnitude of Tamar's undescribed wartime ordeal. In contrast, Wallant's detailed flashbacks are facilely integrated into Sol's present life, and their unexamined implication of similarity between past and present is reductive and shallow. Tamar's hard-won strength, which enables her to help others survive, is best symbolized by the German bullet that after so many years in her body, has become Jewish. "It reminds me that I once had a home, parents, children [p. 175]." Sol Nazerman's distorted body is also a German product, the result of a Nazi experiment in surgery. The memory is exploited for its grisliness. Sol's body bears visible stigmata, but Sol's mind and emotions never confront his experiences except as screaming victim. Sol's death-camp experiences appear almost gratuitous, while for Singer's survivors they are forever a part of present life in memory, in dream, in silence, and in questioning consciousness.

Tamar cannot be said to be ennobled because of her suffering; her experiences only strengthened her potential for the spiritual and the communal. The unbeliever Tamar creates for Yadwiga and her child an anomalous Eden behind an anachronistic Jewish bookstore that precariously preserves a Jewish character. Perceptive survivors like Herman, Masha, and Tamar recognize the difficulty of maintaining their particular Jewishness in the free atmosphere of America. The sense of Diasporal alienation, so pervasive in Cahan's works, returns in Singer's novels, perhaps because both Cahan and Singer were themselves immigrants. Tamar expresses her anomie in striking comparative terms:

> "It really is strange. In Russia, things were pretty bad but at least people were together; whether we were in the camp or in the forest, we were always a group of prisoners. In Stockholm we stayed together too. Here, for the first time, I'm alone. I look out of the window and I feel I don't belong here." (p. 93)

Tamar is referring to her Russian slave-labor camp experiences rather than to her time in the Nazi death camp. Nevertheless she is mourning her participation in a collective identity, even that identity that is possessed by a group of prisoners. She is mourning the destruction of the European Jewish community with all its social ferment. Her sense of the past is quite different from Anya's elegaic reconstructions in Schaeffer's more romantic treatment. But Tamar, who has always been committed to group goals, whose strength lies in her socialization, is, like Anya, out of place in the seemingly chaotic individualism of modern America. Tamar, unlike Anya, will forge a new group identity for herself in America. The self-absorbed, solitary Herman also feels a sense of anomie in America, although he was as isolated in Europe as he is here. Herman is negative about American Jewish life, which is satirized in the characterization of the American rabbi Lampert. Singer draws a venomous portrait of a modern rabbi who, having made an industry of himself, complete with nursing homes, real-estate holdings, Proustian "allrightnik" cocktail parties, and ghost-written sermons and books, is symbolic of Jewish American spiritual corruption and decay. Herman, although not a crass materialist like the rabbi, is presented as an opportunist who prostitutes his learning to supply the rabbi with the necessary scholarly writings and materials. Fittingly it is at the rabbi's party that Herman's triple life catches up with him.

Appropriately the party is the setting for the appearance

of Yasha Kotik, an example of a recurrent figure in European Holocaust literature. Lawrence Langer builds a hypothesis on the work of Jakov Lind, Günter Grass, and others that recognizes that there is "humor" present even in *l'univers concentrationnaire,*

> a humor dwelling on the verge of horror and never far from hysteria—the "humor," one might say, of awakening one fine morning to find yourself transformed into an enormous insect (or, in a grimmer and more literal version, to find yourself a candidate for the gas chamber for the "logical" reason that your barrack is overcrowded).[7]

Yasha Kotik, Singer's survivor-clown, might have appreciated the comic aspect of Langer's example. Yasha, though related to Wallant's Goberman (but more like Bellow's engaging Walter Bruch), is gallant and humorous, tragic and comic, and, like Tamar, a contrast to Herman Broder.

Kotik is by profession a Yiddish actor-comedian. "Everything about him moved with acrobatic agility. His face was in constant motion, grimacing and mimicking simultaneously. He raised one eye in mock surprise while the other one drooped as if crying [p. 200]." Singer, in the Yiddish version, described Kotik's comedy as *galgen humor* ('gallows humor'). Yasha describes his attempts to perform in Europe during the war:

> "When they didn't let me perform in Warsaw, I went to Vilna, Lodz, Ishikok. I performed in the ghetto too. Even a hungry audience is better than a deaf one. . . . During the war none of us was human. The Nazis made soap out of us, kosher soap. And to the Bolsheviks we were manure for the revolution. What can you expect of manure?" (pp. 201–202)

These examples of Kotik's wit may seem crude and tasteless, but what is to be expected of a performer whose audience was destroyed in a gas chamber? Kotik is the comic equivalent of Singer, who also has to perform his antics before "audiences who have forgotten their Yiddish. How can you be a comedian before an audience that doesn't hear you and couldn't understand if they did? [p. 202]"

Kotik is paradoxical. Like Singer he wants his audience to understand the dehumanizing experience of the survivor. But Kotik himself is depicted as having used his wit, his human essence, to keep himself alive. Herman recalls that "it was said he told jokes while digging his own grave and the Nazis had been so amused by him that they let him go. Similarly, his buffoonery also stood him in good stead with the Bolsheviks [p. 200]." Here it is well to turn to the original Yiddish version, which states that Kotik *hot arayngezogt di bolshevikn.* This is decidedly more active and less formal than the rather passive and stiff "buffoonery" that vaguely "stood him in good stead." What the Yiddish says is that Kotik "told off" the Bolsheviks, a braver and more direct construction.[8] Despite Kotik's vulgarity he is to be admired; he is not a coward and, unlike Herman, under the most difficult of circumstances he is trying to rebuild his life among the remnants of Yiddish-speaking Jews.

Considerably less gallant than Kotik is Masha's first husband, Leon Tortshiner, an opportunistic and malicious braggart, parasite, and troublemaker. Tortshiner, like the "allrightnik" philanthropist Pesheles, is a comic figure, unworthy but not revolting. Pesheles is of the older immigrant generation, a generous man who expects to be amply thanked and praised for his generosity. Tortshiner is a charlatan and one of Singer's ways of desentimentalizing the survivor. Tortshiner is a liar, but his lively and scandalous view of survivors has a ring of truth:

> "In a hundred years the ghettos will be idealized and the impression created that they were inhabited only by saints [*tsadikim*]. There could be no greater lie. First of all, how many saints are there in any generation? Second of all, most of the really pious Jews perished. . . . My theory is that the human species is getting worse, not better. I believe, so to speak, in an evolution in reverse. The last man on earth will be both a criminal and a madman." (p. 150)

If Kotik represents a gallantry and bravery that Herman cannot aspire to, Tortshiner embodies, in heightened degree, Herman's pessimism and his need to rationalize his own weaknesses by thinking ill of others.

Just as Masha is exposed by Tortshiner, Herman's instrument of truth is the unworthy Pesheles. In the course of being purged of his falsehoods, Herman achieves a mock transcendence. He vomits, thus purging himself, and achieves a "feeling of indifference to himself" that his learning associates with the Hasidic "disintegration of the limbs," the mystics' "description of a state of selflessness [p. 208]." Masha deserts Herman when she learns of the return of Tamar and, without his siren, Herman enters upon a period of talmudic study. This interlude is climaxed by a traditional *seder* celebrated by Herman and two of his three wives. In Singer's world, however, human nature does not change and Masha and Herman resume their relationship. The death of Masha's mother, public knowledge of Herman's illegal and multiple marriages, and their love for each other move Herman and Masha to plan mutual suicide. Typically Herman backs out when Masha, in a predeath confession, admits that she slept with Tortshiner. Herman abandons Masha to her death, leaves Yadwiga and their unborn child to Tamar, and takes off for parts unknown.

Like Singer, Herman is the unsynthesized product of both orthodox and modern Polish Jewish life. Pervasive in the Singerian canon is the cynical disbelief in secular progress and the recurrent theme that "if a Jew departed in so much as one step from the Shulcan Aruch [orthodox code of law] he found himself spiritually in the sphere of everything base—Fascism, Bolshevism, murder, adultery, drunkenness [p. 156]." Undercutting the righteous extremism of this position is the ironic and sobering awareness that few of Singer's protagonists are able to keep to the Law for very long. Herman is anything but righteous but, like Singer's other Eastern European Jews, he is on intimate terms with the God whom he reviles, curses, and condemns, and in whom he supposedly no longer believes.

Herman no longer believes in a God of mercy and his approach is talmudic: "If a God of mercy did exist in the heavenly hierarchy, then he was only a helpless godlet. A kind of heavenly Jew among the heavenly Nazis [pp. 115–16]." Sometimes Herman's speculations are cabalistic rather than talmudic. For when Masha asserts that God wants Jews slaughtered, Herman, the product of the *yeshive* and university, joins cabala and Spinoza: "It could be that suffering is an attribute of God. If one agrees that everything is God, then we are God too." Masha is too earthy for such sophistry: "If the Jew is God and the Nazi is God, then there is nothing to talk about. Mama baked a kuchen. I'll bring you a piece [pp. 39–40]." This is not bathos. The characters are continuously asking metaphysical questions in the homeliest of contexts. Holy writ, the Torah, and the Talmud are concerned with the minutiae of life and the interaction of earthly and spiritual is uninterrupted even among these bitter remnants. Pertinent also is the old tradition of *krign zikh mit got* (quarreling with God), a tradition that begins, long before Hasidism, with Job and the patriarchs. It is a tradition that is frequently revived in post-Holocaust Yiddish literature, another rescued fragment of the traditional Jewish past. Paradoxically, skeptics and unbelievers like Herman, Masha, and Tamar, understandably bitter because of the horror of their experience, are concerned, even obsessed, with questions about the existence of God and the moral nature of the universe. The economic and social emphasis of the earlier immigrant novel is thus superceded by theological and metaphysical questions, often expressed in simple terms and in commonplace circumstances, as in the fiction of Malamud and Singer.

In another sense Singer's novel *is* reminiscent of earlier immigrant novels. Singer is reluctant to use native-born Americans in his fiction. *Enemies* is his first novel to have an American setting and it was written after he had lived more than thirty years in America. In Singer's own words, "I would never dare to write, almost never, about a person born here because I know that I don't know him enough."[9] Herman manifests the bewilderment of the newly arrived immigrant as described in *The Rise of David Levinsky* and *Call It Sleep*.

Like Cahan, Singer recognizes the value of American freedom because "Jews were allowed to live freely here [p. 20]," but both authors temper their gratitude with the knowledge of the eventual Americanization of Jewish life. Like the parvenu Levinsky, even the unconventional Herman "felt the common ambition of the refugee: to show that he had achieved a degree of success in America [pp. 61–62]." However, it is important to note that the major characters in Singer's novel are not likely to wish to join the mainstream of American life. Cahan's immigrant novel of 1917 and Singer's of 1972 offer valuable contrasts in the fictional portrayals of Diasporans.

Both Cahan and Singer are themselves Jewish immigrants who, despite their long sojourn in America, remain essentially European writers. Both achieved success in the larger world of letters, but both chose to remain committed to the Yiddish-speaking milieu. Their novels, separated by fifty-five years of eventful world and Jewish history, reflect such changes. Cahan records the rapid rise of an "allrightnik" immigrant eager to exchange partly understood Jewish values and culture for the dream of American success. That David Levinsky still feels out of place despite his millions is in part the result of his own lack of self-perception. In addition, Cahan, while cognizant of the opportunities American society provides for its citizens, is also aware that Jewish immigrants, no matter how eager, are not eagerly accepted by that society. In Singer's fiction the question of acceptance by American society is not even raised. His immigrants, refugees, and survivors function in a predominantly Jewish world that rarely, if ever, interacts with the surrounding majority culture. Although both Cahan and Singer show that America offers alternatives to assimilation, it is only in Singer's post-Holocaust fiction that most of the characters *choose* to live apart from the majority culture. Further, in Singer's fiction those who fiercely cling to the Jewish past are authorially admired and allowed, like Tamar, to achieve qualified transcendence.

The very act of writing in Yiddish is for Singer yet another way of preserving the significant past. The original Yiddish version of *Enemies* began to appear in the *Forverts* in October 1966. Singer, who has lived in the United States since

1935, supervises the English translations of his works and makes many changes:

> One would be surprised to see what divergences, what differences there are between the translation and the Yiddish original. . . . In Yiddish you can use a lot of overstatement but you cannot use it in English. English is a language of understatement.[10]

A random comparison of the Yiddish and English versions indicates that the Yiddish is usually longer, not because of overstatement or hyperbole but because of the more leisurely, digressive pace of Yiddish writing.[11] Yiddish writing grows out of a tradition of story telling and embellishment with ancient roots in parable, exemplum, and Midrashic commentary. The cliché that language is culture is particularly evident in Yiddish literature where allusions and references to biblical, talmudic, and midrashic sources are incorporated into the text as are Yiddish proverbs and curses. The form is aggadic.

For his non-Yiddish-reading audience Singer tightens the prose and eliminates some of the proverbs and references. It has been noted that Yasha Kotik's idiomatic, earthy speech has been altered in the English version. Singer prefers to leave idiomatic speech untranslated when literal translation would be, in his view, barbarous or ludicrous. Singer's "gentilizing" appears in Kotik's comment on America. In the English version Kotik is amazed to see Masha at an American cocktail party after not having seen her since they were in the displaced persons' camp in Europe. He exclaims, " 'That's America for you, crazy Columbus, ha! [p. 200]." In the Yiddish version Kotik's opinion of America is rendered with a typical mock curse that literally translates as "that's America—a demon in Columbus's belly button, ha!" Singer seeks to eliminate specific ethnicity but some loss of idiomatic flavor is the result. Similarly Yasha describes the Rumanian-Jewish-American cabaret where he worked as a place where "Jewish ex-truck drivers go with their shiksehs [p. 202]." In the Yiddish original Yasha adds that the old men want to hear "A brivele der mamen"—a sentimental Yiddish song—while their young gentile girlfriends want to hear "When Irish Eyes Are Smiling."[12]

Interestingly Singer does not translate *shikseh, yeshive, landslayt,* and other Yiddish words for his American readers. He usually leaves such words in transcription without italics or gloss. He does not condescend to his readers by annotating references to talmudic and midrashic texts. He casually mentions obscure holidays and customs with the insouciance of an author writing for an audience of Jews well versed in law, lore, and custom. Sometimes Singer does translate, but inconsistently. For example, he makes reference to the "Shulhan Aruk" and at another time he translates it as "the prepared table [p. 24]," a reference that makes no sense to the reader who is unaware that the Shulhan Aruk (prepared table) is the Jewish Code of Laws first set forth by Joseph Karo (1488–1575). This is the underlying Singerian fiction that fortifies the elegiac and particularist aspects of his work. There is no need for gloss, for the intricacies of Jewish background are problems for the fictional characters; the reader is swept up in the story. He is assumed to know as much as he has to in order to experience the fictional world.

Throughout the novel Singer has allowed for the inclusion of talmudic commentary, philosophical digression, and bits and pieces of traditional lore. The following is but one example:

> He sat over his Gemara, staring at the letters. . . . These writings were home. On these pages dwelt his parents, his grandparents, all his ancestors. These words could never be adequately translated, they could only be interpreted. . . . Could this be explained to an outsider? The Jew took words from the marketplace, from the workshop, from the bedroom, and sanctified them. . . . The sinners in the Gemara stole and cheated solely so that Jews would have a lesson to learn—so that Rashi could make a commentary, so that Tosafoth could write the great supercommentaries on Rashi; so that the learned teachers such as Reb Samuel Idish, Reb Meir of Lublin, and Reb Shlomo Luria could seek even clearer answers and ferret out new subtleties and new insights. (p. 158)

Singer's reader is left, like the outsider in the preceding paragraph, without explanations for the many references. Singer feels free to expand the novel form to allow for the aggadic and anatomical elements that are so integral a part of Yiddish literature. He freely moves also from the sacred to the profane, from Rashi to Masha: "Reading Rashi's annotations to the Talmud, he still couldn't keep her peppery words from intruding—her teasing remarks, her contempt for those who desired her, running after her like hounds after a bitch [p. 158]." Only a flexible fictional form could contain such diverse elements.

The Yiddish version includes linguistic complexities that are eliminated in the English translation. The charlatan American rabbi Lampert is referred to as "rabay," a set of phonemes for which there is no equivalent Yiddish word. Singer's contempt for this fraudulent type is conveyed by the orthography. The rabbi's speech is peppered with English and "Yinglish" words as is the speech of older immigrants, whose Yiddish has been corrupted. Much more is made, in the Yiddish version, of Herman's own linguistic discomfort. Singer elaborates on Herman's fluency in Yiddish, Polish, and Hebrew, and on how Herman's less adequate English contributes to his sense of anomie. Herman has been in America for only three years, a fictional choice that is fitting for the immigrant Singer. Immigrant-survivor protagonists in the works of American-born novelists are depicted as having spent many more years in America.

Herman's distaste for the well-informed American women at the party is exacerbated in the Yiddish original by his fear that one of the women might attempt to have a conversation with him in English. In the English version Herman is "apprehensive that they might try to draw him into their conversation [p. 197]." The Yiddish version is more macaronic, with Yiddish dialects interspersed with Polish in the speech of many of the characters. As a result the Yiddish version is somewhat more comic despite the somber subject. It is also more intimate and at the same time more stratified, for Singer uses levels of diction, accent, and dialect to differentiate among his various strata of Yiddish-speaking immigrants. In this regard also, Singer's novel in its Yiddish version is like earlier immigrant novels.

Herman Broder, however, is unlike those earlier fictional immigrants such as David Levinsky who achieve "virtually flawless Americanization." More than Levinsky, Herman consciously isolates himself from Jewish and American values and community. In his very isolation Herman represents a somber variation of an American archetype, a middle-aged Huck Finn who leaves his city, his women, and his responsibilities, not in search of an Edenic territory but in search of a place to hide or die. Herman's escape, like his life, is negative. Singer characteristically leaves Herman's fate in doubt just as he detaches himself authorially from his persona. At the end of *Enemies* the narrator, previously limited for the most part to describing Herman's consciousness, distances himself by removing Herman from the scene.

The ending of *Enemies*, like the ending of *Satan in Goray* (1935), Singer's first novel, and the ending of *Shosha* (1978), Singer's recent novel, indicates movement from the individual to the social. Singer's hedonistic, individualistic heroes (*The Magician of Lublin* [1960] is another example) are ultimately judged by some kind of community or outside authority. This community epilogue (and in *Enemies* it is called an epilogue) shows that everyone, including the lecherous and fraudulent rabbi and the comic Kotik, has behaved with more responsibility than the absent Herman. The essence of their responsibility is a commitment to memorializing the past and a sense of community. Rabbi Lampert urges that Herman's daughter be named for Masha. Tortshiner, Lampert, and Kotik see to it that Masha and her mother are properly buried. The traditional joint headstone is provided by Lampert. There is also a semblance of continuity as Lampert becomes a frequent visitor to the home that Tamar has made for Yadwiga and little Masha. Only Herman remains cut off from his present and from his past and therefore is, in Singer's world, deprived of a future.

Eight

Bellow's Worldly "Tsadik"

Mr. Sammler's Planet (1970) is the most intellectually rich and challenging of the survivor novels by an American author, largely because Saul Bellow has endowed his protagonist with a mind of extraordinary range and quality.[1] Artur Sammler, approximately as old as the twentieth century, embodies the century's intellectual history enriched by traditional thought—Western and Eastern, Christian and Jewish. Sammler's early universalism, liberalism, and belief in progress were largely destroyed by the bestiality and amorality of his particular experience as a Jew. Sammler is thus a European intellectual who has experienced the Holocaust as a Polish Jew and who survives, some thirty years afterwards, as an American. Sammler's mental world may be seen as a metaphoric Diaspora wherein he attempts to see possible relationships between universal and particular, past and present, God and man, in order to find tentative answers to the question, "How does one prepare for death?"—Sammler's way of posing Bellow's usual question, "How does one live?"

Although the primary action of the novel takes place in Sammler's mind, other dramas also take place in Sammler's universe. A significant part of the novel is centered on the death of Sammler's nephew and benefactor, Dr. Elya Gruner. The novel's three days' duration also focuses on two rather bizarre "criminals." One is Sammler's daughter Shula, who has stolen a manuscript by a Dr. Lal on the subject of colonizing the moon. The other, a slightly more conventional criminal, is an elegant black pickpocket whom the curious

Sammler observes more than once as the pickpocket practices his craft on Manhattan buses. These are only "events." Even Elya's death, which affects Sammler deeply, is another opportunity for Sammler to reflect on the meaning of life, death, and morality. Bellow characterizes this novel as "my thoroughly non-apologetic venture into ideas."[2] It is in the realm of ideas, many of them incomplete and partly expressed, that Sammler is most at home.

Sammler's literal homes, like those of other survivors, are more overtly problematic than his metaphysical ones. Unlike the other survivor-protagonists, Sammler, more than seventy years old, appears to have no need to keep a mistress hidden away in an apartment. But he has a number of temporary homes, nevertheless. At the beginning of the novel Sammler occupies a room in the West Side apartment of his niece by marriage, Margotte Arkin. At one time he lived with his daughter, Shula, but her loony chaos and clutter proved too much for his shattered nerves.

Sammler also spends one of the two nights of the novel's duration in the Gruners' Westchester house. This professionally decorated suburban mansion with its sunken living room and Roman bathroom is a mausoleum, as sterile as the plastic-pretty house of Sol Nazerman's sister. No one lives in the Gruner house; Elya feels more at home in the King David Hotel in Jerusalem, but he maintains the house as a pretentious memorial to his pretentious, dead wife. Little value is attached to the memory of Mrs. Gruner; her children will undoubtedly sell the house after Elya's death. In a more sincere act of remembrance, the widow Margotte Arkin makes a shrine of her husband's study. She invites Sammler to share her husband's books and papers, thereby combining continuity with reverence. The act of memorializing the dead is, of course, of central importance in the immigrant-survivor novel.

As the title indicates, Sammler is a citizen of the whole planet, and as such he claims no particular "homeland." However, the problems of nationality and homeland are an important part of Sammler's world. Bellow is one of the few serious Jewish American novelists to explore fictionally the subject of

Israel and he does so on many levels. Sammler's deranged daughter Shula and her "smiling maniac" husband Eisen are immigrants from Israel. Sammler regrets their leaving Israel: " 'If only,' thought Sammler, 'Shula and Eisen had been a little less crazy. Just a little less. They would have gone on playing casino in Haifa, those two cuckoos, in their white-washed Mediterranean cage' [p. 294]." Sammler feels that one of the uses of Israel is "to gather in these cripples [p. 155]." Coupled with this ambivalent idea of Israel as out-patient clinic is Sammler's particular brand of "Zionism," which manifests itself during the 1967 Six-Day War. Sammler had to leave the clowning "civilian" atmosphere of New York to re-experience the harsh realities of his own wartime ordeal.

"No Zionist, Mr. Sammler, and for many years little inter-ested in Jewish affairs." Yet, half-blind and over seventy, Sammler

> could not sit in New York reading the world press. If only because for the second time in twenty-five years the same people were threatened by extermination. . . . He must reach the scene. He would be there, to send reports, to do something, perhaps to die in the massacre. Through such a thing he could not sit in New York. That! Quivering, riotous, lurid New York. . . . And Sammler himself went to an ex-treme, became perhaps too desperate, carried away, begin-ning to think of sleeping pills, poison. It was really the tan-gled nervous system, the "nerve spaghetti." These were his old Polish nerves raging. (pp. 142–43)

Nerves that cause him to say of World War II that "had the war lasted a few months more, he would have died like the rest. Not a Jew would have avoided death [p. 273]."

Among the rotting corpses and scavenger dogs of Al Arish the nauseated Sammler re-establishes his primary con-tact with the dead since "they were the one subject the soul was sure to take seriously [p. 252]." Seeing the off-duty Israeli soldiers playing soccer and studying for exams, conscious of the evidence of Israeli use of napalm, Sammler recognizes that "this war was, as human affairs went, a most minor affair."

Yet the "desperate faces" of the captured snipers appear "as if it were *not* a most minor affair [p. 252]." Sammler continues to do what is characteristic of him: he distinguishes. He distinguishes between what is peripheral and what is central, between the "civilian" and desperate matters of life and death. In Israel matters of life and death are all too clear in the Mediterranean light. In truth Sammler the philosopher prefers the more shadowy cities of the North where an elderly sage can observe with disinterest. But Sammler's credo is that it is necessary to live with all combinations of facts and survival in Israel is one of the central facts that Sammler lives with. Still Israel is not a homeland for Sammler but a historic event of the utmost importance since matters of collective life and death are involved.

Does Sammler indeed have a homeland? If so, it is not in his Eastern European childhood and youth, for, when asked by Lal if he is Polish, Sammler replies that he *was* Polish (p. 209). If one lives in New York, says Sammler, one is an American, although one cannot discern any effort on Sammler's part to become Americanized. Sammler remains what he is in all the various places he has lived. His nostalgia (like Anya's) is for a time and a place that no longer exist and that Sammler discovers are no longer relevant to the present. In Sammler's case it is for twenty halcyon years in London when he worked on a magazine appropriately named *Cosmopolis*. From the liberal universalism of the 1920s and thirties, Sammler can derive no contemporary values, for he rejects his earlier belief in the possibilities of a world state, dismissing it as "a kindhearted, ingenuous, stupid scheme [p. 41]."

No longer Polish, although born in Poland, no longer an Anglophile Polish Jew in London, although he remembers those years with affection, Sammler feels no need to visit Europe, for his Europe no longer exists. Although he is not a Zionist, he is drawn to visit Israel to pursue tentative answers to the precarious questions of Jewish life and death, questions that transcend those of home and homeland.

It is somehow fitting that Sammler's own "home" is comically threatened at the end of the novel. For despite the somberness that permeates the end, with the death of Elya Gruner, there is implied a traditional comic ending as well, in the probable marriage of Margotte and Lal. Such an event would dispossess Sammler of his West Side haven. More threatening are the intimations of Sammler's ultimate "homelessness," his death, prefigured in Lal's moon journey and Elya's death. Sammler's "homelessness," in its variations from comic to somber, and his intelligence, age, and experience serve to broaden his perspective and allow him sufficient distance to see his epoch, his history, and his planet whole.

Contributing to Sammler's authority and reliability is that quality that Wayne Booth calls his "relentlessly ironic vision." Sammler's vision and distance support his attempts to relate the present to the past and his heroic efforts to view even the Holocaust past with personal disinterest. This daring attempt may be the most significant factor in Booth's characterization of Sammler as "a character who is unambiguously (though of course haltingly) wise, wise and—what is perhaps even harder—good."[3] Sammler's acknowledged wisdom and perhaps his more ambiguous goodness were painfully acquired from unambiguously evil past experience. That wisdom and even an ambiguous goodness can be attributed to Sammler, given his particular experience, indicates how very different he is from other modern protagonists, including those in Bellow's other novels.

Among Bellow's heroes only Sammler is called "Mister," an appellation inappropriate to Augie March, Henderson, Herzog, and the others. The appellation of respect not only indicates how the inhabitants of his fictional world regard Sammler, but also reveals Bellow's attitude toward his own creation, a mixture of respect and irony not unlike Sammler's own attitude toward himself. Bellow makes an effort to distance himself from the workings of Sammler's encyclopedic mind and from his devastating past experience. Both his mind and experience are clearly differentiated from Bellow's own by the use of third-person point-of-view. However, intimacy and intensity are maintained by focusing on what Sammler is thinking. The narrative stance is a variation of Henry James'

narrative method in *The Ambassadors* with the demurrer that
Sammler, unlike Strether, not only experienced life but also
"underwent murder [p. 92]."

Sammler is not only different from other modern protagonists, he is different from the other inhabitants of his fictional
world. Sammler's distinctiveness is graphically represented.
Physically, for example, he is taller than other people, slim-
mer, with a disproportionately small head. The head is
frequently topped by an Augustus John hat, a mannered and
voluntary evocation of Sammler's Bloomsbury past. At
seventy-two Sammler is ruddy, erect, rapid; he carries a furled
umbrella with which he points his direction to oncoming
Manhattan traffic. His grey eyebrows are "canine" and his
smoked glasses protect his one good eye and cover the eye
blinded by the Nazis, a grim, involuntary, and constant re-
minder of his Holocaust past.

Sol Nazerman's distorted body is also visible evidence of
the atrocities performed upon him and also symbolizes his
distorted view of life. Sammler's blind left eye similarly con-
trols his perspective on life. Instead of limiting Sammler's
vision, this inward-turning eye contributes to the complexity
and completeness of his view. In Bellow's hands the clichéd
metaphors of sight and insight transcend the conventional.
The difference between Bellow's and Wallant's treatment of
the spectacles that shield their protagonists' eyes is instructive
and basic to a discussion of post-Holocaust consciousness as
manifested in fiction.

Both Sammler and Nazerman wear tinted spectacles,
which are associated with their European experiences. Nazerman finds his glasses in a pile of corpses and they embody his
embittered view of the world. On one of the rare occasions
when he removes his glasses, he is "seen" by the revolting
Goberman as another guilty, self-serving survivor who has left
his dead behind him. The dying Jesus Ortiz sees the pawnbroker's "great formless face that seemed to have meaning
only because of the round spectacles [p. 199]." Later, after
Nazerman's rebirth, the spectacles appear to have been
cleansed with redemptive tears, which may imply clear vi-

sion. Wallant does not develop the motif any further, in contrast to the baroque variations in Bellow's novel.

Sammler's smoked glasses are also the result of his experience of the Jewish catastrophe. A Nazi rifle butt knocked out Sammler's eye just before he and his wife were forced to dig the communal grave in which his wife lies buried. Thus Sammler, the admirer, friend, and erstwhile follower of H. G. Wells, becomes literally a one-eyed man, who might, ironically, be a king among the denizens of his country. But Sammler, in the wisdom of his experience, specifically describes Wells' "The Country of the Blind" as "not a good story [p. 211]." Sammler's experience, however, has endowed him with special insights as it has created even more special problems. For Sammler's glasses are smoked not only to protect his one good eye (and his sensitive "nerve spaghetti") from the outside world but also to protect the world from his disfigurement. Similarly, Sammler's traditional formality and courtesy are a way of distancing others from the horrors of his past, the somberness of his thoughts, and the remaining violent and arrogant fragments of the prewar Sammler.

Sammler, in his pre-1939 Polish past, was impatient and imperious. Even today he could be explosive, "under provocation more violent than other people [p. 27]." Sammler's potential for violence is exposed when he takes his glasses off at the very end of the book. He is insisting to Elya Gruner's obtuse doctor that he be allowed to see Elya's body. "Sammler removed his glasses. His eyes, one a sightless bubble, under the hair of overhanging brows, were level with Dr. Cosbie's [p. 312]." This is the only occasion in the novel when the reader views Sammler's mutilated eye from the outside. Sammler, with icy determination, threatens to make a scene in the hospital corridor unless he is allowed to do as he wishes. The doctor and the reader are impressed. Sammler avoids speaking of his wartime experiences; he usually keeps the demanding aspects of his personality under control. Only in matters of life and death does he assert those violent fragments usually kept hidden under the mien of the "ripe old refugee [p. 68]."

Bellow playfully refers to Sammler's "different looking eyes"—not only do the eyes appear different, each looks in a different direction. One looks primarily inward and to the past; the other looks outward and to the present, while Sammler attempts to find working hypotheses that can, at least temporarily, reconcile these variables. Sammler's is hardly a balanced view, for

> Mr. Sammler did feel somewhat separated from the rest of his species, if not in some fashion severed—not so much by age as by preoccupations too different and remote, disproportionate on the side of the spiritual, Platonic, Augustinian, thirteenth century. (p. 43)

In Sammler's feeling of dis-ease, in his disinterest in sexuality, in his specific reference to "mackerel crowded seas [(p. 176]" there is a Yeatsian recognition that one may say of the world of the 1970s, "that is no country for old men." This particular old man, because of his past experiences, is able to distinguish the essential from what he terms "the civilian." He is also able to see parallels and patterns emerging from the past and the present that are beyond the grasp of his companions. As the human embodiment of many cultures and as a septuaginarian, Sammler appreciates "God's entertainment from the formation of patterns which needed time for their proper development [p. 72]." One example that also demonstrates Sammler's customary irony occurs when his sexually active cousin, Angela Gruner, relates her rococo adventures. While listening for his supper, Sammler, "considering two sets of problems (at least) with two different-looking eyes," remembers Angela's orthodox Jewish grandparents and wonders about the "fitness of Jews for this erotic Roman voodoo primitivism. He questioned whether release from long Jewish mental discipline, hereditary training in lawful control, was obtainable upon individual application [pp. 72–73]." This is typical of Sammler's internal style: those who address him have no idea that he is evaluating, relating, judging, and attempting to see modern life from within historical and traditional perspectives.

Although Sammler abjures explanation he does awake "daily at five or six a.m. and tried to get a handle on the situation. . . . He could leave the handle to Shula in his will [p. 74]." This self-mockery and the use of slang are characteristic of Sammler's internal musings as is his ironically presented desire to leave some heritage of wisdom to his half-demented offspring. He does not speak aloud in this manner. As for the handle, part of it is simple and comfortless, "death was the sole visible future [p. 75]," a view eloquently expressed also by the sage of Ecclesiastes. Such seeming bleakness is tempered by Sammler's intermittent feeling that man's soul "contains a splash of God's own spirit [p. 189]." These "God adumbrations" are the temporal antitheses of Wordsworth's for they come out of Sammler's experiences in middle-life and old age. Sammler grew to adulthood as a liberal unbeliever, survived multiple deaths and rebirths and, at the very end of his life, admits that "very often, almost daily, I have strong impressions of eternity [p. 237]." Sammler's intimations of immortality are the results of his past experience with death. The extremity of Sammler's suffering and his present tentativeness lend credibility to his attempts to express the ineffable.

The use of such mythopoeic terms as "death" and "rebirth" belies the impact of Sammler's experiences on himself and on the reader. Beginning with the comic, symbolic confluence of Sammler's being literally a one-eyed man and an aficionado of Wells, Bellow tears away literary cliché, allegory, and a number of conceits. Sammler's one-eyed state and his broadened vision are the result of the historical reality of his being a Polish Jew who was in Poland in 1939. His descent to the kingdom of the dead is not the metaphoric journey of the epic hero but the grisly historic actuality of burial in a mass grave. He does not retell the tale with the art and artifice of a narrator. Instead he experiences involuntary but constant mental confrontation of self and soul.

Sammler confronts certain insufferable things

> which were not subject to control. They had to be endured. They had become a power within him which did not care

> whether he could bear them or not. Visions or nightmares
> for others, but for him daylight events in full consciousness.
> (p. 137)

Sammler's burial in the mass grave, his digging himself out
from the corpses, his time in the mausoleum in a Polish cemetery and, perhaps most crucial, his killing of a German soldier
in the Zamosht forest are events of historical magnitude, and
almost all of them are repeated in the experiences of other real
and fictional survivors. The murder is most crucial for
Sammler not only because of the moral problems that it raises
but also because it is Sammler's individual experience.

Sammler reflects on himself as murderer and at the Dostoyevskian pleasure derived from the act, and continues his
vital distinguishing by conceding that he was less than
human when he committed it. Bellow does not allow easy
moral choices. Sammler killed an unarmed German soldier for
his shoes, his bread, his socks. Nearly thirty years later
Sammler reflects that

> the thing no doubt would have happened differently to an-
> other man, a man who had been eating, drinking, smoking,
> and whose blood was brimming with fat, nicotine, alcohol,
> sexual secretions. None of these in Sammler's blood. He was
> then not entirely human. (p. 139)

Sammler at the time of the killing had been living with the
Polish partisans as a partisan until they reverted to the old-
fashioned Polish desire for a "Jewless Poland [p. 140]." Then
Sammler, starving, naked, frozen, "the dead eye like a ball of
ice in his head," derives rich warmth from the killing of the
German straggler (p. 138). Sammler, already judged as admirable by the reader, painfully attempts to evaluate his own behavior. In contrast to Wallant, who renders authorial judg-
ments on his fictional survivors, Bellow allows Sammler to
face the paradox that, under certain circumstances, a good
man can also be a murderer. Like Malamud, Bellow is exploring what it means to be human. Sammler, the courageous
humanist, and the novel itself assert that what distinguishes

the human is the recognition that life is sacred and the taking of life a sin. Sammler recognizes his own circumstantial lack of humanity.

Another part of Sammler's credo is that one must live with all combinations of fact (p. 226), and to live with the fact of murder, Sammler, characteristically, distinguishes between various ways of death and murder. Sammler's status among the denizens of his planet is the result of his

> coming back from the dead, probably. . . . by preoccupation with the subject, the dying, the mystery of dying, the state of death. Also by having been inside death. By having been given the shovel and told to dig . . . beside his digging wife . . . he tried to help her. By his digging, not speaking, he tried to convey something to her and fortify her. When they were as naked as children from the womb, and the hole supposedly deep enough, the guns began to blast. (p. 273)

This unbearable experience (told out of chronological order as befits a memory present at all times in Sammler's consciousness) is not recounted until well after the murder incident has been contemplated. The painful memory of Sammler's attempt to reach out to another human being in extremis is not directly offered as extenuation for Sammler's later action. Instead Sammler's human gesture is contrasted with the cold, nonhuman, collective power of the guns blasting at bodies "naked as children from the womb." The juxtaposition sharply conveys Sammler's manner of distinguishing even between murderers. Sammler's murder for need and perhaps unspoken revenge is an action that will always haunt him and make him aware of the limitations of his individual humanity. The institutionalized, impersonal, systematic massacre of the innocents is mechanically distanced from the holders of the blasting guns.

Another striking contrast is offered earlier in the novel when Sammler first recalls the murder and the mass grave. In a bitterly ironic parenthesis Sammler muses that "over a similar new grave Eichmann had testified that he had walked, and the fresh blood welling up at his shoes had sickened him. For a day or two, he had to lie in bed [p. 137]." Sammler offers no comment on Eichmann's testimony, but it is clear that Eichmann wanted to demonstrate his humanity by testifying to his revulsion. His "humanity" revealingly consists of attempting to protect his feelings just as he protected his consciousness from guilt or responsibility for the millions who were murdered. Eichmann was thus able to protect himself from recognition of the gruesome consequences of his exercise of power.

The implicit comparison of the fictional Sammler with the historic Eichmann is balanced by the juxtaposition of Eichmann with another historic figure, Mordechai Chaim Rumkowski, "king" of the Lodz ghetto. Rumkowski, the flamboyant, unpredictable, egotistical, vulgar "dictator" of the ghetto is the parodic counterpart to the powerful, efficient, consistent, methodical implementer of the Nazi war against the Jews, Eichmann. Rumkowski, although dangerous, held mock power, but, despite his distasteful theatricality, he appears less self-deceived than Eichmann.

An earlier version of *Mr. Sammler's Planet* appeared in the *Atlantic* magazine.[4] Bellow considerably enlarged the Rumkowski material for the final version of the novel. In the magazine Rumkowski's story, although lengthy, is confined only to the important moment when Sammler, the listener and thinker, is induced to say aloud what he has been thinking. In the novel Bellow builds more suspensefully on the Rumkowski material and more directly compares him with Eichmann.

Early in the novel good-natured Margotte wishes Sammler to discuss Hannah Arendt's theory of "the banality of evil," a concept developed in Arendt's *Eichmann in Jerusalem*.[5] Margotte makes the reader aware that Sammler and her dead husband had had "such conversations about that crazy old fellow—King Rumkowski. The man from Lodz [p. 18]." Sammler is not ready to discuss Rumkowski, but he does take time to attack Arendt's thesis by enunciating that "life is sacred" and that the Germans had "an idea of genius" in making "the century's great crime" look dull. "What better way to take the curse out of murder than by making it look ordinary, boring or trite [p. 18]." Much later in the novel Eichmann and Rumkowski are again associated, this time with Elya Gruner's son Wallace acting as *ficelle*. Wallace informs the reader that Sammler was asked to testify at the Eichmann trial but refused. Wallace adds, " 'You wrote that article about that crazy character from Lodz—King Rumkowski' [p. 188]." Sammler's reply is a simple "yes" but an extremely significant admission. The erstwhile journalist is discovered to have written only two pieces in the almost thirty years since the war. One is the series of articles for a Polish periodical that Sammler contracted to write as a means of getting to the Israeli front during the 1967 war. That Sammler's only work since the war is concerned with Israel and Rumkowski rather than H. G. Wells or metaphysics suggests how important the specifically Jewish past and future have become to the Anglophile, universalist Sammler. And through Sammler the universalist novelist Bellow demonstrates his own post-Holocaust consciousness.

Sammler neither elaborates on the Rumkowski material nor does he succeed in explaining it. Rather he tells the story and attempts, with difficulty, to comment upon it. The exposition occurs when Sammler is prevailed upon to speak his mind aloud in the communion of a shared meal with Shula, his niece, Margotte, and his new friend, Lal. The Rumkowski vignette is equivalent to one of those short views that Sammler prefers to summary or explanation.

Rumkowski is described by Sammler as a "failed business man. . . . corrupt, director of an orphanage, a fundraiser, a bad actor, a distasteful fun-figure in the Jewish community [p. 231]." As such he is a serious and all too historical equivalent of those fictional, blackly humorous figures created by Wallant and Singer. Rumkowski is crucially different; he does not survive. In his historic actuality he is a more grimly ambiguous figure than his fictional counterparts. He was one of the "horrible clowns," in this case chosen by the Nazis to be in charge of the Lodz ghetto. He became

> a parody of the thing—a mad Jewish King presiding over the death of half a million people. Perhaps his secret thought was to save a remnant. Perhaps his mad acting was meant to amuse or divert the Germans. . . . And besides, the door had been shut against these Jews; they belonged to the category written off. This theatricality of King Rumkowski evidently pleased the Germans. It further degraded the Jews to have a mock king. The Nazis liked that. (pp. 231–32)

At this point Lal protests that he has failed to make the connection, and the reader sympathizes. Here again occurs an evocative difference between the magazine and the final version of the novel. In the novel Bellow has Sammler recite a commentary on the Book of Job before continuing with his disquisition on Rumkowski. It is a daring association, but Sammler clarifies his comparison by directly posing the question: "What is the true stature of a human being? [p. 232]" Sammler comments that modern man, like Job, is subject to "too great a demand upon human consciousness and human capacities [p. 232]." But Job, the noble, stoic sufferer and endurer, is tried by God for some purpose. Modern sufferers are tried by circumstances, history, chance, by the horrible, the sordid, the trivial, and to no apparent purpose. The Jobian reference involves areas other than the central one of moral stature. For Sammler is made to say when speaking of Job, " 'I am not speaking only of moral demand, but also of the demand upon the imagination to produce a human figure of adequate stature [p. 232]." Bellow is offering insight into the challenges faced by him as creator of this particular protagonist and his particular fictional world.

The challenge of the material is manifested in the implicit but clearly intended comparison of Rumkowski and Eichmann and of Sammler and Job. Much commentary on the Book of Job points to the difficulty of relating Job's faith and endurance to his anguish and disproportionate suffering. Sammler's life is Jobian in the extremity of his suffering and he too, painfully and tentatively, moves toward faith. Sammler's faith in God is inextricably bound to his central question about the true stature of a human being.

Sammler, after posing the question, does not directly answer it. Instead he goes on:

> "This, Dr. Lal, was what I meant by speaking of the killers' delight in abasement in parody—in Rumkowski, King of rags and shit, Rumkowski, ruler of corpses . . . though the man was perhaps crazy from the start; perhaps shock made him saner; in any case, at the end, he voluntarily stepped into the train for Auschwitz." (pp. 232–33)

Sammler's discourse on Rumkowski and related subjects does not constitute a readily apprehensible explanation or theory for as Sammler says, "all is not flatly knowable [p. 236]." But implicit in the juxtaposition of Eichmann and Rumkowski is the contrast in their hideous "moments of honor." The powerful Eichmann offers an example of his "humanity" by demonstrating distasteful sentimentality, fastidiousness, and self-protection in his "sensitivity" to the horror for which he was responsible. The powerless and revolting Rumkowski exhibits courage in his ghastly role, and his final action imbues his death with uncharacteristic dignity. Mr. Sammler makes complex distinctions between these historical Holocaust figures in a context enriched by the biblical archetype of Job. Sammler's remarkable perspective reveals the considerable dimensions of his own humanity.

So accurate is Bellow's account of Mordechai Chaim Rumkowski that it is cited along with primary sources and historic documents by Lucy Dawidowicz in *The War Against the Jews: 1933–1945*.[6] There were a limited number of sources from which Bellow might have learned about Rumkowski. One of the most important is an article by the historian Solomon Bloom that appeared in 1949 in which the following statement occurs:

> For our age abhors the unexplained event. Better a dozen theories than one obstreperous fact. We are in the way of killing true knowledge by premature understanding. Far from being comprehended the Jewish catastrophe and all the other Nazi horrors bid fair to tease us out of thought. . . .

> These are matters of which it is important to know every-
> thing before concluding anything, not to speak of judging.[7]

The words are Bloom's but they might as well belong to
Sammler—Sammler, who finds theories and explanations per-
nicious, who believes that "one must live with all combinations of the facts [p. 226]." The novel opens with Sammler's
abjuration of "the roots of this, the causes of the other, the
source of events, the history, the structure, the reasons why [p.
3]." Much of *Mr. Sammler's Planet* is midrashic commentary
on the plethora of useless explanations that resists ob-
streperous facts and ignores meaningful distinctions. Sammler's insight corresponds to the insights expressed by Singer's
and Schaeffer's post-Holocaust survivors.

Mr. Sammler's serious discussion with Lal is interrupted
in a manner that exemplifies the incursion of the modern,
gaudy present on Sammler's attempts to "get a handle" on the
situation. Wallace Gruner—an undisciplined mishmash of
American technology, learning, and nonsense—has been pur-
suing the American dream by searching for money that he
believes his physician father has hidden in the house. Elya
Gruner earned the money, it seems, by performing abortions
for the Mafia. Wallace, with typical American ingenuity, attempts to find the money in the plumbing pipes, thereby
flooding the entire house. Later on in the novel Wallace, still
in quest of easy money, buzzes another house, again causing
considerable damage.

These encounters with American technology, as in Wallant's *The Human Season* and in Henry Roth's *Call It Sleep*,
may serve in Bellow to point out the playful, excessive, wan-
ton waste of American affluence and industrialization. But the
underlying contrast is with the inhuman technology of death
that the Nazis developed. Sammler's emphasis on the making
of distinctions supports such an implied contrast as does the
fact that benign American technology is exemplified in the
telephone, which makes possible Sammler's last contact with
Elya. Sammler's profound wish to be with Elya is thwarted by
the bizarre circumstances of urban contemporary life just as

his discourse with Lal is interrupted by the bizarre antics of the contemporary Wallace.

Sammler's last effort to reach the hospital to visit the dying Elya is interrupted by the sight of the ubiquitous black pickpocket wrestling with Sammler's enterprising friend Feffer. Sammler's mad son-in-law Eisen watches, smiling as the powerful black chokes Feffer in an effort to get his camera. A crowd of onlookers also watches but no one will respond to Sammler's plea to stop the violence: "No one would do anything, and suddenly Sammler felt extremely foreign—voice, accent, syntax, manner, face, mind, everything foreign [p. 287]." In extreme alienation and helplessness Sammler turns to the "amiable maniac" Eisen, who combines Russian brutality with an Israeli dedication to survival. Sammler's powerlessness causes him to turn "to an Eisen! [literally to an iron man] a man himself very far out on another track, orbiting a very different foreign center [p. 289]." At no time does Sammler believe that the black will kill Feffer, but he does wish to end the violence. Sammler's call for Eisen's help results in overkill, for Eisen hits with his bag of metal weights and he hits to kill.

After Eisen's second brutal blow fells the black, Sammler feels that "this is the worst thing yet." Frail, half-blind and old, Sammler *acts* to stop Eisen:

> Sammler seized his arm and twisted him away. . . . Eisen, still handsome, curly, still with the smile . . . seemed amused at Sammler's ludicrous inconsistency. He said, "You can't hit a man like this just once. When you hit him you must really hit him. Otherwise he'll kill you. You know. We both fought in the war. You were a partisan. You had a gun. So don't you know? . . . If in—in. No? If out—out. Yes? No? So answer." It was the reasoning that sank Sammler's heart completely. (pp. 292–93)

Eisen's reasoning causes Sammler to despair because it wrongly equates this encounter with violence in New York with the life-and-death Israeli struggle for survival and with his wartime partisan experience. Sammler's experience of

America, despite the frenzy of life on Manhattan's upper West Side, is quite different from his experiences in Israel and Europe. Eisen, a newcomer to America, whose wartime experiences were almost as unspeakable as Sammler's, is incapable of making distinctions. Sammler characteristically distinguishes: Feffer would not have been murdered, the taking of another person's life cannot be a matter of generalizing or reductivism. Reducing the humanity of the victim to "a man like this" makes it easier for the murderer to murder. The taking of another life is not a matter of fact or logic, neither is it an occasion for humor or theorizing.

At this moment in the confrontation of the amoral Feffer, the law-defying pickpocket, and the insane Eisen, Sammler, the most integrated of survivors, feels most alien from his planet and its creatures. Sammler's powerlessness in such a situation makes him acutely aware not only that he is "extremely foreign" but that he is "a past person . . . someone— poor in spirit. Someone between content and emptiness, between full and void, meaning and not meaning, between this world and no world [p. 290]." The substance of the passage reflects Ecclesiastes as well as Sammler's beloved mystic, Meister Eckhart. Sammler is no longer as capable of confronting violence as he was in the past. The physical gesture of stopping Eisen has made him extremely aware of his fragility. Sammler's helplessness is a benign analogue to the powerlessness he experienced when commanded to dig the mass grave. Yet Sammler fully recognizes the differences between violence in America in the seventies and Europe in the forties, between the natural weakness of old age and the numbed helplessness of the victims of mass murder.

Sammler's encounter with street violence in America is one of the most unusual of the confrontations that fictional immigrants have experienced. Cahan's David Levinsky in the earliest of the novels discussed tells of the anti-Semitic brutality in Europe that led to his mother's death. But Levinsky himself encounters no violence in America despite the labor struggles that Cahan's novel depicts. In *Call It Sleep* David Schearl is tormented by gentile boys largely because he is Jew-

ish, but the experience is treated as a rite of passage, a necessary step in David's assimilation to America. Wallant's
plumber, Joe Berman, battles with an anti-Semite as part of his
Americanization and here too the outcome is positive. Less
archetypal and felicitous but more conventional are the experiences of Morris Bober and Sol Nazerman, who are severely
beaten by would-be holdup men. Very unconventionally and
mythologically, and in bitter contrast to the European experience, the shopkeepers Bober and Nazerman survive because of
the conscious sacrifice of their Christian would-be assailants,
Jesus and Frank. In I. B. Singer's fiction, the potentiality for violence in America is recognized, but such violence is itself
never manifested, in marked contrast to incidents of German
and Russian brutality and anti-Semitism, which are described
in explicit detail.

In Bellow's far more complex scenes of violence the similarities and differences between Europe and America, between
native Americans and immigrant-survivors are subtly and
sharply delineated. Although Sammler has earlier responded
to the chaos and corruption of New York City by likening it to
Naples or Salonika, the differences between Europe and
America are far more significant than the similarities.

In New York Sammler is violently assaulted, but the assault is biological and sexual. The black pickpocket threatens
Sammler with his penis, a formidable object but a metaphor
for power and not power itself. Sammler is similarly attacked
when, under the aegis of the enterprising Feffer, he offers
commentary on "the British Scene in the Thirties" to a university audience. Sammler perceives his audience uncharitably
and organically as "a large, spreading, shaggy, composite
human bloom. . . . malodorous, peculiarly rancid, sul-
phurous [p. 40]." He is received in kind by at least one
member of the audience who loudly describes him as "this ef-
fete old shit" and asks, " 'What has he got to tell you? His
balls are dry. He's dead. He can't come' [p. 42]." The speaker
is crude and cruel, but Sammler recognizes the rough justice
of the comment. In the spirit of Yeats' "Sailing to Byzantium,"
Sammler has indeed wished himself to be a soul released

from nature [p. 51]. Far more violently than the speaker in Yeats' poem, Sammler is an object of the sexual scorn of the young and the primitive.

Sammler is no longer potent since he "lacked the physical force" to make the black release Feffer or to make Feffer release the camera, which has recorded the black's crime. For Feffer, the camera represents potential economic gain; for the black, the camera represents the possibility of prison and the end of profitable crime. Neither responds to Sammler's pleas. The onlookers are voyeurs of urban and television violence. Sammler, who wishes to halt the violence, is forced to call upon the mad, newly arrived Eisen, who is more violent than the Americans and responds with the extremity bred of Nazi and Soviet experiences. Ironically Eisen has obeyed Sammler only because the latter is a "past person," with a particular violent past that commands Eisen's respect. When Sammler attempts to restrain him, Eisen reminds him of the partisan past that they shared. This legacy of violence and extremity is not the heritage that Sammler wishes to transmit. Moreover, Sammler's despairing reaction to the violent scene is not consistent with the austere, qualified, almost bitter affirmation that has been his customary stance toward questions on the value and meaning of life and death. It is qualified affirmation rather than violence or despair that Sammler, as a "monument of unaging intellect" and civility, wishes to share.

That Sammler is reluctantly but resignedly concerned with the passing on of some legacy has been clear from the beginning of the novel. The opportunistic but clever Feffer is aware that Sammler has been trying to condense what he knows, his life experience, "into a Testament [p. 114]." But Feffer, while insightful and charming, is too self-serving to be the recipient of the Testament when it finally is presented. Sammler has been "eliminating the superfluous, identifying the necessary [p. 278]." Preoccupation with Rumkowski, with Elya's death, with contracts and matters of duty, with a viable spiritual legacy for Shula, all indicate the intent of Sammler's ruminations. Thus the matter of the pickpocket, manifestly an interruption, becomes an occasion for Sammler to physically assert the human and prevent a death. Shula's distracting theft of Lal's manuscript becomes the occasion for Sammler's transmission of a verbal legacy however incomplete and fragmentary.

A central tenet of the legacy is transmitted in Sammler's conversation with Lal. Lal, the pragmatic biologist, rejects the idea that "there is an implicit morality in the will-to-live" and rejects any consistent idea of duty "to one's breed." He asserts that "duty is pain [p. 220]." Sammler characteristically agrees that there is no simplistic will-to-live but counters with a nonempirical demurrer:

> "When you know what pain is, you agree that not to have been born is better. But being born one respects the power of creation, one obeys the will of God—with whatever reservations truth imposes. . . . The pain of duty makes the creature upright, and this uprightness is no negligible thing."
> (p. 220)

Sammler's complexly qualified affirmation comes from the Talmud:

> Our Rabbis taught: For two and a half years were Beth Shammai and Beth Hillel in dispute, the former asserting that it were better for man not to have been created, and the latter maintaining that it is better for man to have been created than not to have been created. They finally took a vote and decided that it were better for man not to have been created, but now that he has been created, let him investigate his past deeds, or, as others say, let him examine his future actions.[8]

The passage, while it belies conventional ideas of Jewish optimism, is a fortuitous combination of bitterness and obedience that corresponds to Sammler's characterization of Elya and probably applies to Sammler himself. The implicit irony of the passage and its explicit, somber emphasis on morality would appeal strongly to Sammler and his creator. It is another bit of wisdom to be passed on.

In Lal, Margotte, and Shula-Slawa (but not in Feffer), Sammler has an audience fit to receive his important insights. All three listeners are "refugees" and survivors who have suffered considerable loss. Both Lal and Sammler have had "personal acquaintance with the phenomenon of extermination [p. 210]." Lal may be a dandy, an intellectual *arriviste* immigrant, but he is nevertheless capable of transcending his anguish at the disappearance of his precious manuscript. He warms to Sammler and appreciates him and appears also to appreciate Margotte. Despite her Weimar shmaltz and "German wrongheadedness [p. 17]," Margotte "was prompt to help when difficulties were real. . . . Not persisting mechanically in her ways when the signal was given [p. 132]." In this Margotte is different from the sexually adventuresome Angela Gruner, who persists solipsistically in her ways despite her father's grave illness. Margotte is rewarded in Bellow's fictional world by the possibility of marriage with Lal, while the beautiful heiress, Angela, has, at the end of the novel, lost her latest lover.

Even Shula, despite her looniness, is a proper recipient for Sammler's testament. Not only is she Sammler's daughter, but she too had been written off for dead. Her wartime years were spent in a contagious hospital and in a Polish convent. Sammler describes his daughter thus:

> She might creep down on her knees and pray like a Christian; she might pull that on her father; she might crawl into dark confession boxes; she might run to Father Robles and invoke Christian protection against his Jewish anger; but in her nutty devotion to culture she couldn't have been more Jewish. (p. 198)

Sammler by the end of the novel describes Shula as the best of daughters (p. 311) and with equanimity contemplates living with her. In all he treats her as a worthy heir. In an *opéra bouffe* coda Shula becomes Elya Gruner's heir as she discovers the hidden money for which Wallace has been searching so determinedly. Shula's wartime suffering and her father's influence mitigate the eccentricity of her behavior and endow her with the moral stature that makes her a more fitting heir for Gruner than his own children.

Bellow presents the assembled Lal, Margotte, Shula, and Sammler, this strange assortment of post-Holocaust immigrants, in a particularly appropriate setting. In Elya Gruner's Westchester home the four new immigrants are enjoying the hospitality of a representative of the older generation of immigrants. Elya is a latter-day David Levinsky, who has achieved material and even moral success in America. While fictional immigrant-survivors such as Nazerman and Broder usually satirize the assimilated "allrightniks" of the earlier generation of immigrants, Sammler fully recognizes that through the generosity and family feeling of men like Elya, refugees and survivors were able to find refuge (however chaotic) in America. Admittedly it is only circumstance that caused Elya to choose surgery rather than the less prestigious garment industry as the means to success. Elya cares little for his profession and is severely disappointed in his children. Elya is most interested in the European Jewish past and in the Israeli Jewish future. He loves talking about the former with Sammler and enjoys making quixotic trips to Israel to inspect the latter. Elya goes to Israel like an American benefactor exploring the property he has helped to develop with the riches he has accumulated in the American Diaspora.

Unlike David Levinsky, Elya is not self-deceived. He recognizes his own limitations and the limitations of his particular Jewish American life. Near death he tells Sammler, " 'I ask myself what I spent so many years of my life on. I must have believed what America was telling me. I paid for the best, I never suspected that I wasn't getting it' [p. 177]." Elya perceives the emptiness of success but he also accepts responsibility. He is a Joseph figure, who has provided for his people. His American-born heirs are worthy neither of his efforts nor of his moral and material legacy. He is bitterly disappointed in his daughter, who has "fucked out eyes" and in his son, the "high-IQ moron [pp. 177–78]." But Elya is dutiful and responsible even in preparing for death. Sammler senses the imminence of tears in Elya's expression "but dignity would not permit them. Perhaps it was self-severity, not dignity [pp. 178–79]." Self-severity, in marked contrast to the self-indulgence of his children, allows Elya the discipline to transcend his fury at his children and to spare them the pain of seeing him die. Elya is "a dependable man—a man who took thought for others [p. 85]" and therefore deserves Sammler's final prayer.

Sammler, it seems, prays quite often and in this Shula is her father's daughter for she

> performed acts originating far beyond, in the past, of unconscious ancestral origin. He was aware how true this was of himself. Especially in religious matters. She was a praying nut, but he, after all, was given to praying, too, often addressed God. (p. 200)

Sammler's prayer over the body of Elya Gruner asserts the power of the Jewish covenant with the qualifications that modern life imposes, an important caveat. It will be recalled that Elya had performed abortions for the Mafia. Sammler concedes that Elya, like other rich men, might have "been corrupt," making him like the black, Shula, and Sammler a kind of criminal [p. 76]. Nevertheless, Sammler commends the soul of Elya Gruner to God because Elya "through all the confusion and degraded clowning of this life through which we are speeding—he did meet the terms of his contract. The terms which, in his inmost heart, each man knows [p. 313]." Despite the worldly-wise qualifications and the somber and precise diction, Sammler's prayer echoes in essence the ethical code that Morris Bober expressed in more homely terms. The contract is of course the Law, which emphasizes man's responsibility to man.

What makes the expression of such highmindedness significant and serious is the explicit recognition that dealing humanly and humanely with one's fellowman is extremely difficult. Little wonder that on Elya Gruner's "lips bitterness and an expression of obedience were combined [p. 313]." He may be bitter but in his obedience to an ancient code he transcends the situational amorality around him. Elya, like Sammler, Margotte, and Shula, gains moral strength through his commitment to past values. It might be extravagant to suggest that Shula's finding of Elya's money is an elaborate parody of the biblical Isaac "mistakenly" by-passing Esau to bestow his legacy on Jacob. Nevertheless if Sammler is the spiritual Patriarch for Lal, Margotte, and Shula, Elya shoulders the material patriarchal burden for the Sammlers and others as well as for his own family.

Just as Elya represents the older generation of assimilated immigrants, other central Jewish experiences are embodied in characters other than Sammler. At no point in the novel is there any mention or description that would indicate that Sammler spent time in a concentration camp, although the impression remains that Sammler's wartime Poland was a vast death camp. But the camp experience is specifically excluded from Sammler's background. Given the plenitude of Jewish experience in the novel, this omission shows Bellow's reluctance to focus directly on this most central of Jewish survivor experiences.

Bellow does, however, refer to the concentration-camp past in the novel. He limits his depiction to the pre-1939 concentration-camp experience, which he presents through the eyes of a refugee-figure, an absurd yet sympathetic survivor-clown. Walter Bruch suffered terrible degradation at Buchenwald but was released before Nazi technology was geared up for the final solution. His *galgen* humor includes mock masses and funerals, imitations of Nazi mass meetings, and other travesties. Walter is like Wallant's Goberman and Singer's Yasha Kotik, an American equivalent of the blackly humorous characters in the German postwar fiction of Günter Grass and Jakov Lind.

Walter comes to Sammler to confess. Sammler attempts to absolve him from his guilt over a ludicrous but humiliating fetish: Walter achieves sexual climax by rubbing himself against a briefcase as he looks at the dark, plump arms of Puerto Rican women. Despite his comic Krafft-Ebing degradation and his buffoonery, Walter is quite gifted. He has a rich singing voice. "By profession he was a baritone and musicologist," although when he spoke "he gobbled, he quacked, grunted, swallowed syllables [pp. 56–57]." Sammler is sympathetic to Walter because of his talent and because, although Walter is driven by his fetish, at the same time he has "a highly idealistic and refined relationship with some lady. Classical! Capable of sympathy, of sacrifice, of love. Even of fidelity, in his own Cynara-Dowson fashion [p. 60]." The nineteenth-century reference is deliberately anachronistic as is Walter's "old nineteenth-century Krafft-Ebing trouble [p. 60]."

Sammler is severe with Walter when he reminisces about the horrors of Buchenwald. Walter's memories are of the degrading fecal experiences that have been noted in the writings of Wallant, Singer, and in other Holocaust literature:

> And then a man fell into the latrine trench. No one was allowed to help him, and he was drowned there while the other prisoners were squatting helpless on the planks. Yes, suffocated in the feces! . . . Yes, I know, I wasn't there for the worst part, Uncle Sammler. And you were in the middle of the whole war. But I was sitting there with diarrhea and pain. My guts! Bare *arschloch*." (p. 58)

Sammler rejects Walter's recital, silently, as "all that dreadful, comical, inconsequent, senseless stuff [p. 58]." Burial by feces is the grotesque equivalent of Sammler's burial in a mass grave. Walter's "comic" recital yields the Nazis a posthumous victory by reducing man to the subhuman, by making death grotesque, comic, and banal, thus stripping the creature of his humanity.

Walter, Sammler tells us, still "loved playing corpse [p. 58]." To Sammler such reductivism represents acquiescence to the Nazi evil. Walter is thus a comic counterpart of the all too grotesquely real Rumkowski. At the end of his confession "Walter wept because he felt he had lost his life. Would it have been possible to tell him that he hadn't? [p. 61]." Clearly Sammler is fond of Walter and finds his "rollicking, guttural Dada routine" contagious [p. 64]. However, Sammler must reject Walter's consistently comic approach. Walter, a parodist who scoffs at the very idea that Sammler prays, belittles

Sammler's hard-won faith: " 'Uncle Sammler, I have my arms.
You have prayers?' He gave a belly laugh [p. 63]." For Sammler, man's relationship to God and questions of life and death
are hardly joking matters. Walter is charming but his responses are as outdated as his obsession.

Walter, despite his absurdities, is a real artist. Fittingly,
he is the first person to mention Eisen, the artist manqué.
Eisen, after surviving the battle of Stalingrad, was

> thrown from a moving train, apparently because he was a
> Jew. He had frozen his feet; his toes were amputated. "Oh,
> they were drunk," said Eisen . . . "Good fellows—
> tovarischni. But you know what Russians are when they
> have had a few glasses of vodka." (p. 24)

Eisen's "good humour" and his comic reductivism cause
Sammler to characterize him as "an amiable madman" and
more seriously as "an insane mind and a frightening soul."
Appropriately this iron man is taught welding in Israel. He is
now an aspiring artist in iron, an immigrant who had "heard
the frantic music of America and wanted to get into the act [p.
155]." Eisen comes in pursuit of the American dream armed
with "art." According to Sammler, in Eisen's art everyone is
depicted like a pretty corpse, Sammler himself "like a kewpie
doll from the catacombs [p. 65]." Eisen has no significant past
to draw on for perspective or stability. His past embodies
mindless brutality; he only has the facile theory that rational-
izes violent, simplistic solutions. Unlike Bruch, who retains
much of his European cultural identity, Eisen immediately
adopts the most vulgar of current American fashions, which
make him "stiff, cramped under the arms and between the
legs. . . . The madman wore a magenta shirt with a per-
simmon-colored necktie as thick as an ox tongue [p. 167]."
Clothes may not make the man, as in the case of David Levinsky, but Eisen's garish garments offer insight into what he
finds appealing in American life.

Important as outer appearance in this novel with its plethora of immigrant characters are the surviving fragments of languages other than English. Bellow is extremely careful in mat-

ters of diction, accent, and levels of speech. In this most "Jewish" of his novels there are none of the "Yinglish" passages that Moses Herzog found so offensive in the speech of Valentine Gersbach: "Valentine loved to use Yiddish expressions, to misuse them, rather. Herzog's Yiddish background was genteel. He heard with instinctive snobbery Valentine's butcher's, teamster's, commoner's accent."[9] Although Artur Sammler is Bellow's first foreign-born protagonist, he is not linguistically a typical Jewish immigrant. Bellow, in part to stress Sammler's cosmopolitanism and in part to avoid comic dialect problems, has been careful to make Sammler's speech "Polish Oxonian." Such a combination is quite proper for an Anglophile who spent twenty years between the wars in London and has lived in the United States for well over twenty years.

Yet there is enough of Eastern Europe and Yiddish in Sammler's speech to cause a New York policeman to call him "Abe" instead of Artur when he talks to him on the telephone. There are those deviations from normal English word order and misplaced modifiers that Bellow uses so subtly and skillfully. When Sammler speaks of H. G. Wells he says "he seemed also to enjoy conversation with me. . . . Everything he said I found eventually in written form [p. 30]." When the firemen come in response to the burst water pipes Sammler notes with irony "water, they had brought [p. 246]." Speaking of Elya he says "my nephew wished always to agree [p. 312]." Sammler is a listener rather than a talker. Just as he hides what he is thinking, his unuttered speech is racier than the formal, foreign-tinged, careful speech that characterizes his utterances. The difference may be illustrated in Sammler's internal and external references to H. G. Wells. Aloud Sammler always speaks with respect, but he thinks about Wells as "a horny man of labyrinthine extraordinary sensuality . . . a little lower-class Limey . . . an aging man of declining ability and appeal [p. 28]." The combination of street slang and elegant diction is distinctly Bellovian and indicative of the care expended on matters of language, accent, and cadence.

Sammler recognizes the power of language. Shula at-

tempts to mollify her father's anger by speaking Polish—
"severe, he denied her permission to speak that language. She
was trying to invoke her terrible times of hiding—the convent,
the hospital, the contagious ward when the German searching
party came [p. 195]."

The magazine version of the novel offers evidence of Bellow's attention to matters of language. In the important encounter with Walter Bruch the magazine version has Walter
saying, with reference to his leather briefcase, " 'I paid thirty-
eight fifty for it at Wilt Luggage on Fifth Avenue.' "[10] The
novel only changes the word order: " 'I paid for it thirty-eight
fifty at Wilt Luggage' [p. 59]." The change enriches Walter's
speech with a slight but recognizable middle-European cadence. It has been noted that I. B. Singer's changes signify a
partial Americanization of Jewish speech forms and contents.
Bellow's revisions, on the other hand, emphasize and clarify
the Jewish content of his novel.

Bellow adds Jewish specificity to the novel. The magazine
has Sammler muse that "if the war had lasted a few months
more he would have died like the others."[11] The novel adds
the phrase "not a Jew would have avoided death [p. 273]."
The magazine version says only "his experiences were respected. The war."[12] The novel adds "Holocaust. Suffering [p.
77]." To Sammler's solo aria to Lal, Shula, and Margotte the
novel adds a passage from Job that does not exist in the magazine version. To be sure these additions are rhetorical, if not
didactic, and appropriate to Bellow's "unapologetic venture
into the realm of ideas."[13] Thus Bellow chooses a postsexual
reflective hero whose most important reflections have to do
with his experience of unprecedented evil and the possible
wisdom that he, with such moral and intellectual equipment
as he possesses, may be able to extract from it and transmit to
others. Through Sammler's distance and wisdom, Bellow has
become a witness through the imagination to the Holocaust.

Artur Sammler exemplifies those aspects of Diaspora Man
that Daniel Bell stresses in the previously cited "Parable of
Alienation." The positively alienated Jew sees "as if with a
double set of glasses. . . . the nature of the tragedy of our

time." Bellow's hero also sees the irony and even the comedy of our time. Sammler, because of his experience of suffering and his knowledge, inevitably, and perhaps deliberately, assumes the "role of prophet" as well as that of *tsadik*. It involves "the acceptance of the Jewish tradition—its compulsion to community—and the use of its ethical precepts as a prism to refract the codes and conduct of the world."[14] Bell's original example was the Polish Jewish martyr Zygielbojm. The fictional Polish Jewish Artur Sammler, his perspective enriched by time and fruitful speculation, is Zygielbojm's fitting imaginary descendant and an effective incarnation of his creator's post-Holocaust sensibility.

Nine

Cohen's Ultimate Diasporan

Bellow, I. B. Singer, Malamud, and others include philosophical and theological concepts, traditional Jewish motifs and myths as parts of the fictional worlds of their immigrants and immigrant-survivors, although the fictional works are products of secular novelistic imaginations. In their employment of such materials, these contemporary Jewish writers resemble Yiddish writers who at the end of the nineteenth century drew their fictional worlds from a tradition that they knew was doomed and that no longer afforded intellectual sustenance. Irving Howe expresses the paradox "that faith abandoned could still be a far more imperious presence than new creeds adopted." Comparing the Yiddish writers to Thomas Hardy and George Eliot, he states "that the greatest influence on the work of such writers is the rich entanglement of images, symbols, language, and ceremonies associated with a discarded belief."[1] The impetus to preserve ceremonies, symbols, and moral teachings of Eastern European Jewry, albeit fictionally, is greatly intensified by the tragedy of modern Jewish history. The earlier world of the classic Yiddish writers was eroded by modernity, by industrialization and new ideas; it was not brutally and deliberately destroyed. Modern, secular Jewish writers enrich their secular immigrant characters with vestiges of Jewish tradition, law, and lore, not for local color like earlier immigrant novelists, but to commemorate the significant past and to demonstrate the moral relevance of such vestiges to contemporary life.

In Arthur Cohen's *In the Days of Simon Stern*, the specifics of Jewish history, tradition, theology, philosophy, and myth, used subtly by Bellow and Malamud, directly by Schaeffer, and naturally by I. B. Singer, are the most important matter of the novel.[2] Cohen's encyclopedic novel is an unabashed aggada that shatters the limits of realistic fiction with its deliberate and sometimes obscure anachronisms, its legends, excerpts from doctoral dissertations, talmudic commentary, declarations of conscience, cabalistic references, and modern detective agency reports. The work contains letters, courtroom scenes, a play, meditations, and four versions of the creation myth, and it ends with two epilogues and an appendix. If Wallant's *The Pawnbroker* fails because of its lack of *dianoia*, Cohen's far more ambitious attempt may be said to sink beneath the weight of its abstractions. In a word, Cohen's novel, like his characters, is unassimilated.

The ironic but deliberate gnosticism and anachronism of the novel are nowhere more apparent than in its narrative strategy. The work is contemporary, allegedly written in the late fifties and early sixties by a blind scribe, Nathan Gaza, who is himself a survivor of the Nazi death-camp experience. Nathan's blindness is the result of his Holocaust experience. Cohen, like Bellow and Wallant, uses metaphors of impaired physical sight and superior moral and intellectual insight to set his survivor apart from others. It is characteristic of the extremity of his approach that, unlike Wallant's bespectacled Nazerman and Bellow's one-eyed Sammler, Cohen's Nathan is totally blind.

The associations and allusions surrounding Nathan go beyond allusions to Samson and the Philistines and intimations of Tiresias. Nathan is admittedly writing a hagiography of a modern Messiah, Simon Stern, and as befits the writer of a worshipful biography, Nathan cuts his quills, mixes ink, and bathes away his impurities. There are few works in English that make so little concession to an audience ignorant of the particulars of orthodoxy, traditional Judaism, and Jewish history. Even Nathan's name is full of Jewish specificity. The original Nathan of Gaza (ca. 1634–1680) was a cabalist and a learned man who was the *disciplus primus* of Sabatai Zevi (ca. 1626–1676), the "false" Messiah who converted to Islam in 1666. Despite the apostasy, Nathan and others remained faithful to Sabatai Zevi. But the parallel between ancient and modern messiahs and disciples appears more allusive than analogous, since Simon Stern does not declare himself to be the Messiah. He uses his considerable earthly power and money to form the Society for the Rescue and Resurrection of Jewish Survivors of the Holocaust. Simon is more of a Joseph figure than he is a reincarnated failed messiah. In microcosm Simon experiences twentieth-century Diasporal life, especially the life of the Jewish American immigrant. The microcosmic aspect is underlined by Simon's extreme physical smallness, which sets him apart, just as Sammler's height differentiates him from others. Cohen's theme of Jewish difference and estrangement from the rest of the world is sounded early in the novel. Ruth, Simon's mother, leaves the small world of the *shtetl* and depends on the good will of other Jews to protect her on her solitary trip to Warsaw. She "believed as do we all that there is a monstrous divide which separates Jews from the others of this world [p. 8]." Years later, halfway through World War II, when over two million Jews had been slaughtered, Simon makes a declaration in Ratner's lower East Side restaurant. He will devote himself and his huge fortune to the rescue of a "remnant whose strength shall be in mutual love and helpfulness and disdainful removal and estrangement from others [p. 198]."

To accomplish his high purpose, Simon builds on New York's lower East Side a Solomonic fortress based on an ancient plan. This survivors' compound is elaborately disguised so as to appear old and in disrepair, like its surroundings. Simon does not want the outside world to know about the inner workings of his community. Perhaps this suggests that even in free America the idiosyncratic differences that separate Jews from others are not to be ostentatiously displayed. Perhaps also the elitism of "disdainful removal" needs to be disguised so as not to provoke and offend in a democratic society.

Ultimately, even after Simon's compound is destroyed by

evil from within and without, even when he leaves his beloved "downtown" for the second time in his life and ven-
tures uptown to Central Park, and even after he becomes a
wanderer in the large world, his final insight is that "everything is embedded in particularity" and difference [p. 451].
The Israeli experience of Jewish hegemony does not enter into
this work, which is concerned with the survival by selective
isolation of a minority within a larger political unit. The novel
examines the European Jewish experience but focuses upon
America, especially the idea of America as a haven even for
those who wish to remain apart from society.

All of the major characters except Simon himself are immigrants. He, however, is an embodiment of the Eastern European immigrant past through his parents, whose traditional
nineteenth-century origins are rendered with loving detail at
the beginning of the novel. Cohen conveys much of the Jewish
European experience: Eastern, Western, Spanish Marrano, secular and sacred, assimilated and traditional, Hasidic and revolutionary. Nathan Gaza's religiously orthodox family emigrated early in the twentieth century from Hungary to
Palestine, thereby traversing both Sephardic and Eastern European traditionalisms. Another survivor, doctor of philosophy
Fisher Klay, personifies the aristocratic Viennese Jewish intellectual; he has earned a law degree and written a dissertation
on Spinoza. Rabbi Lazare Steinmann is an idealistic supporter
of lost causes and a characteristically Jewish mixture of piety
and progressive politics. Steinmann chose Kerensky over the
Bolsheviks, Trotsky over Lenin, territorialism over Zionism,
among others. Steinmann evaluates himself as follows: "In all
things pragmatic I have been wrong. But I don't think I have
ever been morally wrong [p. 250]." Gaza, Klay, and Steinmann
represent three approaches to Jewish Diasporal life; all three
eventually find a haven in America. Klay and Steinmann are
themselves the idealistic sons of crassly mercantile and unsympathetic fathers—Klay's father was murdered by being
"literally choked to death on his money [p. 186]." But Simon
Stern, in the American mold, is able to achieve financial suc-

cess in the new world without the corrupting exploitation that accompanied such success in the old.

Simon exemplifies the American Horatio Alger myth of monetary success achieved through hard work. Unlike other successful immigrants, Simon does not assimilate to American ways. He remains orthodox, adheres to *shtetl* ways, continues to study the Talmud, does not become another David Levinsky. Nor does he move from the lower East Side. Simon's father enjoys his son's prodigious wealth not by retiring to the suburbs but by devoting all his time to the study of the Torah. Simon, at the same time, is too preoccupied with money and too careless with American technology. Thus, the refurbished tenement that Simon buys for his parents is inadequately wired for the many electrical appliances that his mother purchases with abandon. Simon's lack of attention causes his parents to perish in the fire, a bitterly ironic microcosm of the Holocaust. For Simon, at this same time (1940), is innocently selling scrap metal to the Japanese. Perhaps Cohen is pointing to the ignorance and materialism of the American Jewish community in the face of the destruction of European Jewry. Cohen is also reiterating a common theme in immigrant-survivor literature. The encounter of European Jew with American technology has far more serious consequences in Cohen's book, however, than in the novels of Roth, Wallant, and Bellow.

Simon appears to learn something from the tragedy. Despite his isolation from many aspects of American life, he is able to come to terms with strange if representative Americans—private detectives, Jewish criminals, anti-Semitic bankers, building inspectors, FBI agents—all playing their mythic, clichéd parts, but doing so on Simon's East Side turf. At the climax of the novel, Simon's negotiations with Jewish gangsters for the purchase of arms end in the destruction of his Solomonic compound. But Simon is American after all and has learned about technology, perhaps from the television series "Mission Impossible." Attached to the biblically erected compound is a secret courtroom modeled after the inner sanctum of the Temple in Jerusalem. The courtroom is reached through a candy store where "the buttons behind the jars of chocolate raisins concealed a dial panel which governed the electrical system [p. 427]." One may acknowledge Cohen's courage and ingenuity and yet recognize that the work is not entirely successful.

Just as Simon is technically a nonimmigrant, who nevertheless encapsulates the American immigrant experience, he is also technically a nonsurvivor, who, in microcosm and at considerable remove, undergoes the survivor experience. According to Nathan, after the death of his parents for which he holds himself responsible, Simon is "the first survivor of the fire, the first to come back from the pit [p. 229]." Perhaps because Simon feels the weight of survivor guilt, or perhaps because Simon offers himself to God with complete faith untinged by doubt, his claim to survivor status seems metaphorically and fictionally valid. It is buttressed by his commitment to the survival of the Jewish East Side. Cohen, like other American writers, does not focus directly on the concentration-camp experience. Instead the novel concentrates on specific experiences that illustrate how people were able to endure.

Like the actual immigrants Levinsky, Broder, and Sammler, this metaphoric immigrant, Simon Stern, is homeless at the end of the novel. He leaves his beloved (if changed) East Side to wander in the world as part of the traditional penance of the holy and pious. Simon, as messiah, is comfortable in his homelessness. Klay and Steinmann, modern Jewish intellectuals, interact somewhat with others outside the survivors' compound and are also comfortable in the wider world. Only Nathan, who is the most traditional and the most overtly disabled, appears to need the security and isolation of the rebuilt compound. However, Nathan's need is more for scholarly isolation, so that he can write the hagiography of Simon Stern, than for a specific home. Nathan's blindness effectively separates him from the American milieu.

Also, like other fictional immigrants and despite his American birth, Simon speaks idiosyncratic "Yinglish." Like

Henry Roth's David Schearl, Simon's mother tongue is Yiddish. Peculiarities in the speech of the real immigrants are ignored, but the characteristics of Simon's speech are noted. Nathan describes Simon's English as spoken "in that gestural cadence immediately recognizable as Yiddish in origin [p. 76]." Klay, who was an adult when he came to America, responds to the familiarity of Simon's English, which he recognizes as "the acquired tongue coated with the deprecatory sadness of natal Yiddish [p. 184]." Simon will neither Americanize his life style nor his diction. Those who desert the lower East Side for "uptown" and suburbia are deprecated for giving up "oi veh and Gewalt for 'so what else is new?' [p. 103]." David Schearl's preference (in Call It Sleep) for his aunt's Yiddish over her vulgarized English is recalled here without, it must be added, Roth's dialectical and linguistic virtuosity. Cohen has Simon speak on a number of language levels. When he acts as an entertainer in a Jewish night club, this downtown messiah says " 'Gentiles didn't exist without Jews. There would be no gentiles—goyim to you, but I'm speaking gentiles because there are eleven slumming gentiles with us this evening and I want they should understand what it's all about' [p. 176]." Simon is also capable of expressing himself elegantly, pompously, and with metaphysical complexity. Cohen is much less rigorous and careful than Henry Roth, Bellow, and Malamud about language, but he does convey the unassimilated quality of Simon's speech.

Biblical and mythic allusions are also unassimilated. Thus the legendary figure of Elijah, whose presence is sensed in Malamud's humble matchmakers and messengers, appears in propria persona in Cohen's novel. It is typical of Cohen's method that he endows Simon's midnight visitor with the traditional characteristics of Elijah well known to readers of Jewish folk tales, and yet he never identifies him by name. Elijah, the traveler and wanderer, is also a heavenly messenger and the precursor of the Messiah, an "inveterate visitor" who is always "showing up unannounced, unexpected, dropping in and having a chat [p. 116]." Elijah tells Simon a parable, "The Legend of the Last Jew on Earth," a tale that combines the past of the Spanish Inquisition with a future in which all the world has been converted to Catholicism and the experience of difference is no longer tolerated. Simon's encounter with the mythical Elijah in a dreamlike sequence is followed by Simon's historical encounter with the real Chaim Weizman. Weizman, the father of Zionism, is called by Simon the "Elijah of the Jews," that is, one who had a message for all Jews.

The story of Job is also presented overtly. The villainous, sadistic, Jew-hating half-Jew Janos Baltar is first seen in the Edenic confines of the Rothschild chateau in France where a group of survivors is awaiting transport to America and Israel. Appropriately Baltar is first seen in the garden of the chateau "slithering across the grass . . . like a man become serpent [p. 276]." Janos is rehearsing for his own version of the play of Job. Baltar plays the devil and narrates Job's story as well. He makes fitting references to the story of Isaac and allusions to other instances that support his characterization of a willful, vain, and demanding God, one who constantly requires sacrifice and suffering. Baltar spells out the implied "moral" by reminding his wretched audience that their lost sons, daughters, and parents, unlike Job's, can never be restored.

Perhaps the most telling example of the explicit didacticism of Cohen's work is his treatment of the same talmudic source that Bellow employs in *Mr. Sammler's Planet.* Both works refer to the ambiguous debate in the talmudic academies about whether it would have been better had man not been created. By a close vote the sages agree that it would have been better had man not been born, but that once born there is no choice but to try to live according to "the will of God." In Bellow's novel, it will be recalled, the reference is made without attribution. In Cohen's work, not only is the Talmud cited, but Simon comments on the controversy, calling it daring. In typical talmudic fashion Simon first draws a further conclusion from the passage, then disagrees with that conclusion (p. 293). His tone is aggressively didactic.

Cohen's novel may be said to exhort, preach, threaten, and, above all, urge retention and transmission of the Jewish past. The work is not always lively and interesting, but its aspirations are high. Nathan Gaza, like a Hebrew prophet, sets forth the continuing and ongoing war of the survivor as a war "of explication, the inculpation of the innocent and the exculpation of the guilty, the torment of broken hearts, moans in the night, visits to the cemetery of remembrance [p. 277]." Similarly portentous is Cohen's employment of the theme of Diasporal salvation, of the Jewish moral function in an unredeemed world. Daniel Bell's exploration of alienation moves along similar lines. But the universalism expressed by Bell in 1949 and exemplified in Malamud's oft-quoted statement "All men are Jews," is rejected by Cohen and by contemporary Jewish American writers such as Hugh Nissenson and Cynthia Ozick. Expressed by Simon Stern is an assumption of moral authority and an insistence on the survival of Jewish particularity:

> The task of Jews is not alone that we should not forget, nor should we cause them to remember, but that we should never be forgotten. And to avoid that fatal decree, the ignominious insult of being forgotten after more than three millennia of our walking upon this earth, we must stay with what we have struggled to become—endurers who say over and over again what must be. (pp. 445–46)

The critic for the *Times Literary Supplement* found in Cohen's novel "a certain air of contemptuous isolation from those experiences of life that do not happen to be Jewish."[3] The element of contempt may be arguable but the isolation and moral authority are not. Cynthia Ozick, far more sympathetic than the English critic, points out how the work grapples with the idea of America as perhaps "a ruined and bungled" haven "not just as refuge for the historically maimed but for the Messiah."[4] But the novel projects something considerably more militant than the idea of America as haven. Simon Stern builds a fortress that is deliberately disguised to resemble its surroundings. The purpose of the fortress is to maintain Jewish separation and isolation from a possibly corrupting and diluting American environment. The work offers obvious contrasts to earlier immigrant fiction, which presented assimilation and acculturation as necessary corollaries to American affluence. In Cohen's novel, American affluence is used to create a modern Jewish ghetto. Paradoxically the idea is fundamentally American, for running counter to the prevailing idea of assimilation and the "melting pot" is the also prevalent image of America as a setting for religious particularists and social experimenters. The Puritan concept of "a city on a hill," with its emphasis on separation from a hostile or indifferent environment, has been repeated by Mormons, Shakers, and other religious sects as well as by nonreligious Socialists and other Utopians.

The concept of a fortified ghetto is not one that would appeal to all immigrant-survivor protagonists despite their determination to maintain and transmit aspects of their Jewish heritage. Bellow's Sammler and Gruner, Wallant's Nazerman, and Malamud's Bober are *tsadikim* whose Diasporal role includes interaction with the non-Jewish world. I. B. Singer's survivors (and those of Ozick), however, would be at ease in Cohen's modern ghetto. So would Schaeffer's Anya.

In *In the Days of Simon Stern* the secret ghetto is allowed to exist under the wary and occasionally clumsy surveillance of the FBI and CIA. American society, as has been acknowledged by novelists of immigrant life from Cahan to Cohen, tolerates considerable variation in ways of living. In his most recent novel Cohen changes his emphasis somewhat to picture America as a source of open Jewish spiritual renewal. *A Hero in His Time* concerns itself with a Soviet Jewish musicologist who comes to America as part of an official Soviet-American cultural mission.[5] Technically the novel does not fall within the boundaries of this study because the hero does not remain in America, but his encounter with older Jewish immigrants in the United States is germane. In America Yuri Isaacovsky encounters a *tsadik* whom he remembered from Kiev as a "retired rabbi" who deliberately "did not look religious. He was shrewd enough to wear a cap instead of a broad-brimmed black hat, and he kept his little twisted tassels of hair shirt virtually invisible to all but the meticulous and foreknowing [p. 81]." In America the *rebe* was "dressed in white stockings, silver buckled shoes, a long black silk coat . . . fur hat with the velvet crown." The *tsadik* asks Yuri whether he intends to return to the Soviet Union "and continue to sweat out your life's blood or live a full Jew's life outside the furnace. . . . consider whether it is worth the price to return or to remain behind and learn to become a full Jew [pp. 194–97]." The immigrant novel has come full circle. In *The Rise of David Levinsky* David's mentor, the pious Reb Sender, is horrified at the idea of David's going to America for "one becomes a Gentile there." The contemporary *tsadik* urges the Russian Jew to stay in America to live openly as a committed Jew.

Commitment for Cohen involves religious observance. All the principal figures in *In the Days of Simon Stern* are observant, practicing Jews. Even the elegant assimilated Dr. Fisher Klay every morning says the "*Shema Yisrael* with prolongation and complete attention followed by a reading of Psalms or Job or Ecclesiastes—whichever book of the Scripture seemed right to his daily intention [p. 248]." Not all of the immigrant-survivors of recent fiction are as orthodox or as theological as Cohen's protagonists or those of Ozick. Yet those Jewish prayers and practices that earlier fictional immigrants discarded along with their *shtetl* clothing are preserved internally and meaningfully by the modern appearing heroes of Bellow, Singer, and Malamud. No longer represented anachronistically by minor figures such as Reb Sender, Reb Yidel Pankower, and Reb Feldman, traditional Jewish values and practices are incorporated into the daily lives of major figures such as Sammler, Bober, Tamar, Broder, and, of course, Anya.

The inclusion of religious elements in Jewish American fiction does not always coincide with a central focus on the Holocaust experience. Cohen's *Simon Stern* is the most concentrated and conscious example of what may be a much more general phenomenon. It is one of the works discussed by Earl Rovit in a mammoth review of some forty-eight current novels. Rovit draws the following conclusions:

> Fifteen or twenty years ago, it made very good sense to talk about contemporary fictional characters in terms of *rebels* and *victims*; those labels smell very musty today. Then, there was a very active industry in search of the Faust or the Christ archetype. . . . Today if I had to speculate about a replacement for the rebels and the victims, I would suggest the *survivor*—an equally ancient fictional possibility whose lineage goes back to that crafty hero of many wiles, Odysseus, and whose archetype is probably the Wandering Jew. . . . It's also possible that such a development might prove receptive to a religious sensibility that has been sorely lacking in our recent fiction.[6]

To Rovit's ancient Greek Odysseus, this discussion counters equally ancient survivors—Joseph, Noah, Lot—who survive not primarily because of craft and wile but because of moral strength. Further, these survivors save not only themselves but endure to preserve a people and a tradition. Rovit's archetype of the Christian idea of the Wandering Jew, whose punishment consists of homelessness, is countered by the Jewish idea of a meaningful Diasporan life as lived by the modern Elijahs, *tsadikim*, and secular *rebes* and sages who are part of the post-Holocaust fictional world of the immigrant-survivor.

Part III

Conclusion

Ten

Characteristics
of the
Immigrant Survivor

It remains to be seen whether Earl Rovit's prediction about the future of the fictional survivor is pertinent to the particular future of the Jewish immigrant-survivor. What has been demonstrated is that the works discussed in my study represent a recognizable subgenre of Jewish American literature and that the immigrant-survivor is a recognizable persona and an effective embodiment of post-Holocaust consciousness. For the American writer the immigrant-survivor is the means to approach the subject of the Holocaust with essential distance and perspective. Unlike the European survivor, the immigrant-survivor is placed in America. Unlike the exile, the immigrant-survivor is presented as having spent considerable time in America. Even for Schaeffer's Anya, vivid memories of her ordeal are tempered by twenty-five years of living in America. Only the immigrant I. B. Singer sets his novel in a time close to the event, the 1950s. That the novel itself is a product of the seventies indicates Singer's sensitivity about his distance from both European and American experiences.

Although the immigrant-survivor is in America, he or she cannot be said to be of America as was the pre-Holocaust immigrant. The pressure to conform and assimilate, so much a part of the early immigrant novel, is not significant in the later novels. The survivor is indifferent to economic and social success in America. Even Cohen's variation of the Horatio Alger myth is not the story of the "rise" of Simon Stern. Like Nazerman, Stern needs money to maintain his isolation from American society. Stern's commitment to isolation, unlike

Nazerman's, is collective rather than personal. Other immigrant-survivors are either failures in conventional terms (Malamud's protagonists) or indifferent to material and social success. The strength of the immigrant-survivor is demonstrated not by his pursuit of American success, but by the moral power derived from his experience of suffering and the succor he receives from Jewish traditional sources.

Recent fictional immigrants tend to remain isolated from the society around them. Unlike Henry Roth's David Schearl, who becomes part of New York's lively street scene, or even Cahan's lonely Levinsky, who can sincerely join other new Americans in singing "My Country 'Tis of Thee," Malamud's characters—Bober and Alpine; Salzman and Leo; Fidelman and Susskind; Bok—tend to be isolates and loners. Singer's Broder in his various surrogate haylofts, Nazerman in his pawnshop or his private room in his sister's house, Sammler grinding his coffee alone in his room in Margotte's apartment, all are demonstrating their separation from their environment and from friends and family. Most extreme in this regard is Simon Stern, whose compound is elaborately designed to foster "disdainful removal and estrangement from others" and whose own private quarters in the compound are virtually inaccessible. What is especially distinguishing is that the isolation is ultimately mildly softened by the most qualified communion. Sammler delivers his testament to three other immigrant-survivors but withholds it from the American-born characters. Nazerman reaches out to the survivor Tessie and extends his own isolation to include his nephew. Singer's characters interact with other Yiddish-speaking Jews. Schaeffer's Anya chooses to live in a dangerous and unfashionable part of the city with "more people from the camps" because it reminds her of the neighborhoods "that haunted us after the war in Europe [p. 475]." Simon Stern rebuilds his fortress but although "its windows are somewhat larger and more light is allowed to penetrate its inner space" its inhabitants return to the compound at the end of the day just as European Jews returned to their ghettos. In America the immigrant-survivor is free to choose isolation and separation.

Having lost the European world in the Holocaust, the survivor does not attempt to establish a permanent home in America. Instead he inhabits temporary havens and is always prepared to move on. Even Simon Stern modifies his allegiance to the lower East Side and at the end of the work is as much a wanderer as is Broder or Sammler. Nazerman and Broder respond somewhat positively to the American rural landscape, but Sammler and Stern are most at home in an urban milieu. Indifference to place is characteristic of the new immigrant. He is both homeless and at ease wherever he is for he has learned to carry his "homeland" with him in ceremony, thought, memory, and language. Unlike the earlier fictional immigrant, the post-Holocaust immigrant is not eager to lose vestiges of Yiddish and other fragments of the past.

Visible and invisible signs differentiate the immigrant-survivor from others in his fictional world. Among the most striking of the former are the stigmata that constitute a semiology of the Holocaust. Sammler's false eye and smoked glasses, Nazerman's distorted body and peculiar spectacles, Tamar Broder's German bullet, Anya's headaches, and Nathan Gaza's blindness are physical evidence of previous lives that were destroyed and aborted. These manifestations of experienced horror are not only handicaps: for failed conventional sight the survivor substitutes bitterly won insight. Tamar Broder wants to keep her German bullet to remind her of her experience. Marked physical signs make it impossible for the survivor to forget even if forgetting seems desirable. On a different level Sammler's excessive height, Stern's excessive smallness, Anya's unusual good looks are further signs of overt difference. These signs of difference also contrast with the outward conformity that is characteristic of the earlier immigrant.

The earlier immigrant discarded ritual as easily as he discarded earlocks and *shtetl* clothing. That the new immigrant novel demonstrates a change in attitude toward Jewish tradition is seen in the evolution of the *tsadik* figure. In the earlier novels religious observances were practiced and transmitted by minor and anachronistic figures such as Cahan's Reb

Sender (who stayed behind in Europe), Henry Roth's Reb Yidel, and Rosenfeld's Reb Feldman. In Malamud's fiction some *tsadik* figures are anachronistic and observant, like Pinye Salzman, others are secular like Bober and Susskind. All are at least dual-protagonists who transmit wisdom and morality to their younger co-heroes. In Singer's *Enemies* the protagonist has the knowledge but not the moral power to be a preserver and transmitter of values. But in Reb Nissen, who exemplifies the older tradition, and in Tamar Broder, who represents secular Jewish ethical values, Singer has created true *tsadikim.* Wallant's Nazerman is a reluctant and cynical teacher to Jesus Ortiz, but he becomes a *tsadik* figure when he reaches out to his nephew. Anya's saintlike father and mother guide her from beyond the grave and she herself is a mythic heroine. Artur Sammler is an urbane *tsadik* who passes on a testament of wisdom and power. Among Cohen's neoorthodox characters, the *tsadik* figure is Simon Stern; but Nathan, Fisher Klay, and Steinmann also act as teachers, preservers, and transmitters of values. The *tsadik* figure is often the central figure in the recent novels.

Represented in post-Holocaust immigrant fiction are other traditional figures such as Elijah, who share some of the qualities of the *tsadik.* There are also frequent allusions and references to biblical archetypes. The figure of Job is evoked as the archetype of the suffering Holocaust survivor (Sammler, Nazerman, Tamar Broder) and of other sufferers, especially in Malamud's works (Bok, Bober, Manischevitz). The figure of the patriarch Joseph is reflected in immigrant figures such as Simon Stern and Elya Gruner. These modern representatives of biblical and traditional archetypes freely use biblical, talmudic, and other Jewish sources, usually without attribution, as in the writings of Bellow, Malamud, Singer, and sometimes Cohen. References to the traditional and historic Jewish past are part of the central character's consciousness and need no explication or apologia. The recent Jewish historical past, which is so much a part of the protagonist's consciousness, is presented more overtly and directly.

Present-day interest in the Holocaust, in actual survivors,

and in the offspring of survivors is relevant to the discussion of fictional survivors as well. In his review of Dorothy Rabinowitz's *New Lives: Survivors of the Holocaust Living in America* (1977), Leon Wieseltier says of Holocaust survivors that "they had become not, as some in America have said, twice-born, but more precisely, people of whom their descendants would say with despair that they had been twice-dead."[1] Early immigrant fiction typically emphasized the rebirth experience: Cahan likens the immigrant's arrival to a "second birth." Second-generation novels such as Henry Roth's *Call it Sleep* and Michael Gold's *Jews Without Money* (1930) end in rebirth experiences. America for the earlier immigrant was the place to begin a new life. The immigrant-survivor, even when he appears to be experiencing rebirth as in Wallant's *The Pawnbroker*, is more accurately once again surviving death.

Wallant's Nazerman survives the death of his symbolic son, Jesus Ortiz, just as he has survived the deaths of his own children. His final act in the novel is to join another survivor in an act of ritual mourning. Artur Sammler survives the death of his younger relative Elya Gruner, and his final act is a prayer for the dead, a kaddish. Singer's Herman Broder survives the death of Masha, who is herself memorialized in the conventional Jewish manner—a child is named for her. Schaeffer's Anya survives the annihilation of her family, her friends, her benefactors. Even in America she survives a holdup in her store, as do Bober and Nazerman. Simon Stern, who has survived his parents' death by fire, also survives the destruction of his community by fire and the death of Janos Baltar.

Even in America, where he has found a haven, the immigrant-survivor may encounter death by murder, suicide, and fire, instead of the new life that beckoned so convincingly in earlier immigrant fiction. So pervasive is the sense of unexpected and unnatural death that in *Mr. Sammler's Planet* Gruner, who dies in a hospital, dies of a violent and medically unpredictable aneurysm. One can be "walking along strong, beautiful, full of beans, when it explodes inside [p. 96]." Unexpected, arbitrary, violent death is a possibility even in

America. But each of the novels makes clear that even though the immigrant-survivor cannot begin a new life in America, the manner of death is not dehumanized, anonymous, and bestial as it was during the Holocaust. In America the dying are attended by doctors, the dead are buried, mourned, and memorialized. The elderly Sammler and the middle-aged Anya look forward to a death as dignified as that of Elya Gruner and as unlike the brutal deaths that dominate their memories. The dead are always present to immigrant-survivors, in dreams and in recollection of those slaughtered in Europe, in the deaths of those around them in America, in the survivors' commemoration of past and present deaths.

The Holocaust past pervades the memory of the immigrant-survivor. Whether in grim nightmare, like Nazerman's; with deliberate or involuntary memory, like Singer's characters; with systematic and dogged recollection, like Anya; in archaic imitation, like Nathan Gaza; or in ever-present fragments, like Sammler, the survivor contains and is committed to his past. In contrast to the shtetl past, which was rendered chronologically and sequentially in The Rise of David Levinsky and other first-generation novels, the past of the immigrant-survivor is usually presented in fragments.

In Anya the narrator's efforts to order her past are compromised by her internal disorder. The immigrant-survivor's past and present are discontinuous and he is disconnected from others, especially those who are not themselves survivors. With the temporal and spatial distance that the American Diaspora provides, the survivor, involuntarily or deliberately, confronts his past and searches for viable connections between past and present. The search may result in increased isolation as in the novels of Singer and Schaeffer, but usually the survivor moves toward significant, if limited, communion.

Despite considerable efforts of mind, the events of the Holocaust past remain as they were, untransformed and inexplicable. The pawnbroker does not assimilate his dreams of past horror, and Anya's numerous attempts at understanding are futile. Even in the anatomical novels with their intellectually sophisticated personae, the Holocaust is apprehended rather than comprehended in the consciousness of the survivors. Singer's characters lament that the full truth cannot be known, let alone understood; Bellow's Sammler abjures premature understanding and conveys his wisdom in "short views" with numerous qualifications. Cohen's garrulous philosophers ponder many topics but not the meaning of the Holocaust. Each questions his own survival and, at the same time, searches for what is worth preserving in the destroyed past. The pawnbroker rediscovers the power of love, while Anya creates and transmits a glowing past from the ashes. In the anatomical novels survivors and *tsadikim*, who may themselves be survivors, rescue traditional Jewish values and transmit them in nontraditional forms. The wisdom thus preserved (in the writings of Malamud, Singer, Bellow, and Cohen) carries demonstrated intellectual weight and the authority derived from the experience of tragedy.

The immigrant-survivor protagonist in the American setting allows the Jewish American writer to write about the Holocaust with authority and with rectitude. Distance makes it possible for the American writer to omit, or only touch peripherally on, *l'univers concentrationnaire*, which is the central experience in European Holocaust literature. Lawrence Langer has written eloquently about the problem of authenticity and the tension between historical event and imaginative truth. Langer accordingly limits his examples to works written by survivors or others who in some way experienced the European tragedy. Two gifted writers who were themselves in Auschwitz, Elie Wiesel and Tadeusz Borowski, are representative. Out of humiliation, pain, rage, and at immeasurable emotional cost, they selected and ordered even these unspeakable events and created memorable works of art. Over and over these writers and others express their disbelief at what they are experiencing and seeing with their own eyes. In the immigrant-survivor novels, Nathan Gaza's blindness, Sol Nazerman's and Artur Sammler's poor sight are symbolic rejections of the unbelievable sights they have seen, as well as signs of their suffering and of their superior insight. The causeless, meaningless, and unexpected cruelty, the sadistic treatment of children, the atrocities committed by creatures who appear to be human beings—all are factual and not diseased fantasy or nightmare. The central preoccupation of those writers who were themselves eyewitnesses is conveying the truth of their testimony.

The world of the death camps and the crematoria and all the systemized horror of the "final solution" are historical evils of the greatest magnitude. In Aristotelian terms they are what has happened rather than what may happen. What were unimaginable historic particulars before the Holocaust remain "unspeakable" and do not comport easily within the probabilities and universals of conventional literature. Wallant's novel is weakened because the unbelievable is embedded in a conventional realistic form, while the strength of Schaeffer's fictional mode is in the ironic correspondence and fateful contrast of monstrous historic reality and literary fantasy.

Many and varied are the ways in which history is made part of the fictional world of the more anatomical works. Malamud transforms the particulars of the Beilis case so that the reader makes the metaphoric but not analogous connection between Russian anti-Semitism and Nazi genocide. Singer, Bellow, and Cohen create a community of survivors and emphasize the effects of highly selective experience. Singer and Cohen depict the events and effects of the Holocaust against a background of Jewish history and thought. Bellow uses Sammler's highly developed mind and Western civilization as background and context. The events of the Holocaust remain aberrant and disproportionate even in the context of Cohen's history of Jewish suffering and despite Singer's pessimistic personae. Within the diverse and digressive anatomical form, despite the bizarre and lurid foreground that Sammler, Bellow, and Cohen provide, the European tragedy is perceived as a disparate atrocity. The Holocaust past as rendered in the flexible and comprehensive anatomical novel retains the intensity of its extremity.

The immigrant-survivor novel includes religious as well as philosophical speculation. Not all the works are suffused with references to traditional Judaism as are *In the Days of*

Simon Stern and *Enemies*. Nevertheless, in *Mr. Sammler's Planet*, *The Fixer*, and *Anya* a religious sensibility is exercised or, at the least, commemorated. Bellow, Malamud, and Schaeffer may not include overt reference to the Jewish past or tradition in their subsequent fiction. However, along with Cohen and Singer in the works discussed here, they have performed traditional roles. For it is enjoined by Jewish custom, law, and religion that the dead should live in the memory of those who come after them. The frequently aggadalike form of the immigrant-survivor novel is well within the collective-historical tradition; it is an analogue to the Passover Haggadah, which requires the active participation of all in the act of remembering a central experience of Jewish history. Through their intermingling of historical and religious themes, secular, modern Jewish American writers are thus dramatizing a post-Holocaust consciousness in an ancient, ritualistic, and traditional manner.

In the Haggadah and elsewhere the act of remembering is considered an act of survival. Knowingly or unknowingly Malamud, Bellow, Singer, Schaeffer, Cohen, and others are heeding the words of the Baal Shem Tov (ca. 1700–1760), the founder of Hasidism, who admonished from the Polish Diaspora that "forgetfulness leads to exile while remembrance is the secret of redemption."[2]

Notes

1: The New Immigrant Novel

1. *After the Tradition* (New York: E. P. Dutton, 1969), p. 163.
2. "Zion as Main Street," in *Waiting for the End* (New York: Stein & Day, 1964), p. 70.
3. *The Jewish Writer in America* (New York: Oxford University Press, 1971), p. 226.
4. Ibid., pp. 11–12. Guttmann devotes a chapter in his book "to the conversion of apostates and the recovery of a sense of peoplehood" ("One's Own People," pp. 93–133). Of the writers he mentions, only Bernard Malamud is of major interest to this study. I disagree with Guttmann that Malamud "sometimes sounds like the contemporary of Philip Roth" or that he has "dramatized the commitment to peoplehood" ambiguously, but I agree with Guttmann that Malamud is "in his heart of hearts . . . a believer in peoplehood [p. 120]."
5. Ibid., p. 227.
6. Fiedler, *Waiting*, p. 89.
7. Ibid., p. 70.
8. Granville Hicks, "Literary Horizons," *Saturday Review* (10 September 1966): 37–39.
9. *Anatomy of Criticism* (New York: Atheneum, 1968), p. 365.
10. Elie Wiesel, *Souls on Fire* (New York: Vintage, 1972), p. 260.

2: Backgrounds: Literary and Nonliterary

1. "Jewishness and the Younger Intellectuals," *Commentary* 31 (April 1961): 351.
2. "In Search of Kafka and Other Answers," *New York Times Book Review* (15 February 1976): 6–7.
3. *New Lives* (New York: Alfred A. Knopf, 1976), p. 191.
4. Ibid., p. 193.
5. Maurice D. A. Atkin, "United States of America," *Encyclopedia Judaica* (Jerusalem: Keter, 1972).
6. Moses Rischin, *The Promised City* (Cambridge: Harvard University Press, 1962), chaps. 6, 7; Irving Howe, *World of Our Fathers* (New York: Harcourt Brace Jovanovich, 1976), pp. 50–63.

192 NOTES

7. Rischin, *Promised City*, p. 33.

8. This is the date of the publication of the Yiddish original. The English version was published by Vanguard Press in 1969.

9. German exile literature has been recognized since the 1930s. Guy Stern, who has written widely on the genre, traces its development in "Exile Literature," *Colloquia Germanica* (1971–72): 167–78. Robert Edgar Cazden, *German Exile Literature in America 1933–1950* (Chicago: American Library Association, 1970); Robert Boyers, ed., *The Legacy of the German Refugee Intellectuals* (New York: Schocken, 1972).

10. Jacob Glatstein, Israel Knox, and Samuel Margoshes, *Anthology of Holocaust Literature* (New York: Atheneum, 1973) gives some idea of the scope of Yiddish literature on the Holocaust written in the 1940s, as does I. Howe and E. Greenberg's *A Treasury of Yiddish Stories* (New York: Schocken, 1973) and *A Treasury of Yiddish Poetry* (New York: Holt, Rinehart & Winston, 1969). A comprehensive bibliography of belletristic work in Yiddish and English on the Holocaust is published annually in *The Jewish Book Annual*.

11. "The Wandering Jew," *New Republic* (10 February 1941): 186.

12. Bell's article, "A Parable of Alienation," first appeared in *Jewish Frontier* (November 1946) and has been reprinted many times. The citation in this study comes from *Mid-Century*, ed. Harold Ribalow (New York: Beechhurst Press, 1955), pp. 133–51.

13. Terrence Des Pres, *The Survivor* (New York: Oxford University Press, 1976), pp. 172–77. Among survivor accounts of the experience of the mass grave are Krystyna Zywulska, *I Came Back* (London: Dennis Dobson, 1951); Reska Weiss, *Journey through Hell* (London: Valentine Mitchell, 1961); A. Kuznetsov, *Babi Yar* (New York: Farrar, Strauss, & Giroux, 1970). The Eichmann trial included testimony from others who survived this experience and some of this testimony is part of an Israeli documentary film entitled *The Eighty-First Blow*.

14. *The Tents of Jacob* (Englewood Cliffs, N.J.: Prentice-Hall, 1971), p. 25.

15. Ibid., pp. 24, 26, and 30.

16. Ibid., p. 46.

17. Haim Hillel Ben Sasson, "Galut," *Encyclopedia Judaica* (Jerusalem: Keter, 1972).

18. "Kabbalah," *Encyclopedia Judaica* (Jerusalem: Keter, 1971).

19. N. M. Nahmad, *A Portion in Paradise and Other Jewish Folk Tales* (New York: Schocken, 1970), p. 24.

20. Harold Fisch, *The Dual Image* (London: World Jewish Library, 1971), pp. 23–24, 55–57.

21. "The Stranger and the Victim," *Commentary* 8 (August 1949): 148.

22. " 'O Workers Revolution . . . The True Messiah': The Jew as Author and Subject in the American Radical Novel," *American Jewish Archives* 2 (October 1959): 157–75.

23. Allen Guttmann, *The Jewish Writer in America* (New York: Oxford University Press, 1971), p. 34.

24. (Reprinted New York: Harper & Row, 1960), p. 3. All further references to this novel appear in the text.

25. "David Levinsky: The Jew as American Millionaire," first appeared in *Commentary* 14 (August 1950). The citations in this study come from Rosen-

feld, *An Age of Enormity* (Cleveland: World Publishing, 1962), pp. 273–81, 278.

26. Ibid., "Levinsky," p. 280.

27. Ibid.

28. As quoted by Theodore M. Pollock, "The Solitary Clarinetist" (Ph.D. diss. Columbia University, 1959), p. 266. Pollock's citation for this quotation is the *New York World*, 4 June 1922.

29. Cahan's more positive immigrant characters are depicted in *Yekl and the Imported Bridegroom and Other Stories of the New York Ghetto* (1896; reprinted New York: Dover, 1970). In *The Rise of David Levinsky*, Dora Margolis, the Tevkin family, and others act as foils to Levinsky.

30. The National Origins Quota System was enacted through passage of the Johnson Act of 1924. The legislation restricted immigration to 2 percent of the 1890 census and established national quotas that allowed five-sixths of the annual immigration total to be allotted to Western and Northern Europe and one-sixth to Southern and Eastern Europe.

31. Rideout, "The True Messiah," p. 167.

32. "Stranger and Victim," pp. 148–49.

33. Walter Allen, "Afterword," *Call It Sleep*, by Henry Roth (1934; reprinted New York: Avon, 1964), p. 445. All subsequent references to Roth's novel will be to this edition and will appear in the body of the text.

34. Jane Howard, "The Belated Success of Henry Roth," *Life* (8 January 1965): 76.

35. Bonnie Lyons, "An Interview with Henry Roth," *Shenandoah* 25, No. 1 (Fall 1973): 66, 70.

36. "The Surveyor," *The New Yorker* (6 August 1966): 22–30.

37. Abraham Chapman, ed., *Jewish American Literature* (New York: New American Library, 1974), p. xxvii.

38. "Another Jewish Problem Novel," *Menorah Journal* 16, No. 4 (April 1929): 378.

39. "Stranger and Victim," pp. 154–56.

40. "A Parable of Alienation," p. 137.

41. Ibid.

42. Ibid., p. 150.

43. (New York: Dial Press, 1946). All further references to this work appear in the text.

3: Survivor Literature

1. Haim Hillel Ben Sasson, "History," *Encyclopedia Judaica* (Jerusalem: Keter, 1972); Lucy Dawidowicz, *The War Against the Jews* (New York: Holt, Reinhart & Winston, 1975), p. 403.

2. Robert Alter paraphrases Kazin in "Confronting the Holocaust," in *After the Tradition* (New York: E. P. Dutton, 1969), p. 163.

3. A. Alvarez, *Beyond All This Fiddle* (New York: Random House, 1969; London: Allen Lane, 1968); T. W. Adorno, "Engagement," in *Noten zur Literatur* (Frankfurt on Main: Suhrkamp Verlag, 1965), 3: 125–27; George Steiner, *Language and Silence* (New York: Atheneum, 1966).

4. *Persecution and Resistance under the Nazis*, The Weiner Library Cata-

logue Series No. 1 (London: Vallentine, Mitchell, 1960). A more recent bibliography, *The Holocaust and After: Sources and Literature in English* (1973), edited by Jacob Robinson, is part of a twelve-volume bibliographical series published jointly by the Yad Vashem Martyrs' and Heroes' Memorial Authority in Jerusalem and the YIVO Institute for Jewish Research in New York.

5. Of the eighty-four Yiddish books that the *Jewish Book Annual* lists for the period between April 1975 and May 1976, thirty-five can be considered examples of survivor literature. The Yiddish writer Chaim Grade designates Hebrew as the "holy tongue" and Yiddish as the "martyrs' tongue." In Hebrew and in Yiddish the terms for both holy tongue and martyrs' tongue are phonetically similar as *loshn-koydesh* and *loshn-kedoyshim*.

6. (New Haven and London: Yale University Press, 1975).

7. (New York: Oxford University Press, 1976).

8. Langer, *The Holocaust* p. xxi.

9. Ibid., p. 20.

10. Ibid., p. 266.

11. "A Kind of Survivor," in *Language and Silence*, pp. 143–44.

12. Langer, p. xii.

13. Ibid., pp. 270, 271.

14. Ibid., p. 265.

15. *In the Days of Simon Stern* (New York: Random House, 1973), p. 196.

16. "The New York Intellectuals," in *Decline of the New* (New York: Harcourt Brace Jovanovich, 1970), p. 244.

17. "The Meaning of Terror," in *An Age of Enormity* (Cleveland: World Publishing Co., 1962), p. 209.

18. Introduction, *Great Jewish Short Stories* (New York: Dell Publishing Co., 1963), p. 14.

19. "The Holocaust and the American-Jewish Novelist," *Midstream* (October 1974): 57.

20. Ibid., p. 58.

21. "America Toward Yavneh," *Judaism* 19 (1970): 282.

22. In *The Pagan Rabbi and Other Stories* (New York: Alfred A. Knopf, 1971), pp. 40–100.

23. John Winthrop, "A Model of Christian Charity" (1630), in *American Literature: The Makers and the Making; Book A* (New York: St. Martin's Press, 1974), p. 25.

24. "Genesis: The American Jewish Novel Through the Twenties," in *Jewish American Literature*, ed. Abraham Chapman (New York: New American Library, 1974), p. 570.

4: Malamud's Secular Saints and Comic Jobs

1. *The Holocaust and the Literary Imagination* (New Haven and London: Yale University Press, 1975).

2. Robert Alter, "Bernard Malamud: Jewishness as Metaphor," in *After the Tradition* (New York: E. P. Dutton, 1969), pp. 116–30; Theodore Solotaroff, "Bernard Malamud's Fiction: The Old Life and the New," *Commentary* 33 (March 1962): 197–204.

3. *The Assistant* (New York: Farrar, Strauss & Cudahy, 1957), p. 184. All

subsequent citations from the novel will be designated by page number in the text.

4. Sandy Cohen, *Bernard Malamud and the Trial by Love*, Melville Studies in American Culture, ed. Robert B. Pearsall (Amsterdam: Rodopi N.V., 1974), p. 38.

5. Edith Hersch, "Hillel," *Encyclopedia Judaica* (Jerusalem: Keter, 1972).

6. Leslie Fiedler, "Malamud: The Commonplace as Absurd," in *No! In Thunder* (Boston: Beacon Press, 1960), p. 107; Max F. Schulz, *Radical Sophistication* (Athens: Ohio University Press, 1969), p. 61.

7. All citations are from the paperback edition (New York: Pocket Book, 1972) and will appear in the text designated as MB. The collection was first published by Farrar, Strauss in 1958.

8. *Bernard Malamud* (New York: Twayne, 1966), p. 123.

9. All citations are from the paperback edition (New York: Pocket Book, 1963) and will appear in the text designated as IF.

10. Haskel Frankel, "An Interview with Bernard Malamud," *Saturday Review* (10 September 1966): 39.

11. All references to *The Fixer* (New York: Dell Publishing Co., 1966) will appear in the text.

12. "Fantasist of the Ordinary," *Commentary* 24 (July 1957): 90.

13. "Bernard Malamud," *New Statesman* (30 March 1962): 452.

14. Sheldon Grebstein, "Bernard Malamud and the Jewish Movement," in *Contemporary Jewish American Literature*, ed. Irving Malin (Bloomington: Indiana University Press, 1973), pp. 202–203.

15. Alfred Kazin, "Bernard Malamud: The Magic and the Dread," in *Contemporaries* (Boston: Little, Brown, 1962), p. 204; Ihab Hassan, "The Qualified Encounter," in *Radical Innocence: Studies in the Contemporary American Novel* (Princeton, N.J.: Princeton University Press, 1961), p. 168.

16. *The Tenants* (New York: Farrar, Strauss & Giroux, 1971), p. 230.

17. *Tradition*, p. 117.

18. "Bernard Malamud: The Magic and the Dread," p. 206, in *Contemporaries* (Boston: Little Brown, 1962).

19. "Fantasist of the Ordinary," p. 90.

20. Langer, *The Holocaust*, pp. 88, 33. Some European literature of the Holocaust contains comic elements. Langer analyzes the "black humor" of Jakov Lind in a chapter fittingly entitled "Blessed Are the Lunatics" (pp. 205–49). Romain Gary, in *The Dance of Ghengis Cohen*, has a comic dybbuk haunt the Nazi guard who was his tormentor and murderer. I. B. Singer, Bellow, Wallant, and Cohen incorporate these grotesque comic elements in their fictions. Malamud's work manifests similar "comic" grotesqueries in *The Fixer* and in *The Tenants*.

21. Langer, *The Holocaust*, pp. 45–46.

22. Leslie and Joyce Field, "An Interview with Bernard Malamud," in *Bernard Malamud: Twentieth-Century Views; A Collection of Critical Essays* (Englewood Cliffs, N.J.: Prentice-Hall, 1975), p. 11.

23. *The Holocaust*, p. 61.

24. In *Peretz*, trans. and ed. Sol Liptzin (New York: YIVO, 1947), p. 378.

25. In one of Sholem Aleichem's most serious works, *Tevye's Daughters*, Tevye relates several misfortunes (one daughter's marriage to a gentile, another daughter's suicide) in a dramatic monologue to a silent Sholem Aleichem. Considerable time has elapsed between the events and the telling.

Tevye's monologue is a way of distancing tragic events and turning them into art.

5: Wallant's Reborn Immigrant and Redeemed Survivor

1. (New York: Harcourt Brace Jovanovich, 1960). All references to this novel will be included in the text.
2. (New York: Manor Books, 1962). All citations will be included in the text.
3. *The Holocaust and the Literary Imagination* (New Haven and London: Yale University Press, 1975), p. 51.
4. (London: Victor Gollancz, Ltd., 1964).

6: Schaeffer's Romantic Survivor

1. I am indebted to Susan Fromberg Schaeffer for her letter of June 14, 1979, which contained information about the genesis and the sources for *Anya*.
2. (New York: Macmillan, 1974). All further references to this work appear in the text.
3. Northrop Frye, *Anatomy of Criticism* (1957; reprinted New York: Atheneum, 1968), p. 33.
4. See note 1.
5. *The War Against the Jews* (New York: Holt, Rinehart & Winston, 1975), pp. 287–288.
6. Ibid. Ringelblum is quoted by Dawidowicz on p. 259.
7. Frye, *Anatomy*, p. 39.

7: Singer's Diasporan Survivor

1. *Enemies, A Love Story* (1972; reprinted Greenwich, Conn.: Fawcett, Crest, 1973). All further references to this work appear in the text.
2. *The Passover Haggadah*, ed. Nahum N. Glatzer (1953; rev. ed. New York: Schocken, 1969), p. 5.
3. Author's Note to *A Crown of Feathers* (1973; reprinted Greenwich, Conn.: Fawcett, Crest, 1974), p. 9.
4. *Language and Silence* (New York: Atheneum, 1966), p. 151.
5. Jeffrey H. Tigay, "Adultery," *Encyclopedia Judaica* (Jerusalem: Keter, 1972).
6. Ben-Zion Schereschewsky, "Bigamy and Polygamy," *Encyclopedia Judaica* (Jerusalem: Keter, 1972).
7. *The Holocaust and the Literary Imagination* (New Haven and London: Yale University Press, 1975), p. 211.
8. *Forverts* (24 June 1969): 2. Translations are mine.
9. Cyrena N. Podrom, "Isaac Bashevis Singer: An Interview and a Bio-

graphical Sketch," *Wisconsin Studies in Contemporary Literature* 10 (Winter 1969): 2.

10. Ibid., p. 24.

11. Irving Howe, at a conference entitled "Yiddish Literature in Translation" (Waldorf Astoria, 16 February 1975), told of Saul Bellow's problems in translating Sholem Aleichem's *On Account of a Hat* and Isaac Bashevis Singer's *Gimpel the Fool.* Bellow commented on the leisurely, digressive pace of Yiddish story-telling, a pace which encourages digression, extrapolation, and commentary. Needless to say, Bellow's translations of both stories are masterful. It should be added that Bellow's work also shows considerable evidence of the purposeful digressiveness he notes in Yiddish literature.

12. *Forverts*, p. 2.

8: Bellow's Wordly *Tsadik*

1. (New York: Viking Press, 1970). All further references from the Viking Compass paperback edition of 1973 appear in the text.

2. Jane Howard, "Mr. Bellow Considers His Planet," *Life* (3 April 1970): 59.

3. *A Rhetoric of Irony* (Chicago: University of Chicago Press, 1974), p. 237.

4. *Mr. Sammler's Planet* appeared in the *Atlantic* (November 1969): 95–150; (December 1969): 99–142.

5. *Eichmann in Jerusalem* (New York: Viking, 1965).

6. (New York: Holt, Rinehart, & Winston, 1975), p. 422.

7. "Dictator of the Lodz Ghetto: The Strange History of Mordechai Chaim Rumkowski," *Commentary* (February 1949): 122. Leslie Epstein's novel, *King of the Jews* (New York: Coward, McCann and Geoghegan, 1979), is based on Rumkowski's life as lord of the Lodz ghetto. Not surprisingly more works about Rumkowski are in the offing.

8. Erubin, 13b, *The Babylonian Talmud*, translated into English with notes, glossary, and indices, ed. Rabbi Dr. I. Epstein (London: Soncino, 1938).

9. *Herzog* (New York: Fawcett, Crest, 1961), p. 78.

10. *Atlantic* (November 1969): 138.

11. Ibid. (December 1969): 150.

12. Ibid. (November 1969): 119.

13. Howard, "Mr. Bellow."

14. "A Parable of Alienation," *Jewish Frontier* (November 1946): 137, 150.

9: Cohen's Ultimate Diasporan

1. Y. L. Peretz, *Selected Stories*, eds. and trans. I. Howe and E. Greenberg (New York: Schocken, 1974), p. 10.

2. (New York: Random House, 1973). All further references to this novel appear in the text.

3. "Hebrewing Up," *Times Literary Supplement* (15 March 1974): 269.

4. "In the Days of Simon Stern," *New York Times Book Review* (3 June 1973): 6.

5. (New York: Random House, 1976). All further references to the novel appear in the text.

6. "Some Shapes in Recent American Fiction," *Contemporary Literature* 15 (Spring 1974): 560.

10: Characteristics of the Immigrant-Survivor

1. "In a Universe of Ghosts," *New York Review of Books* (25 November 1976): 22.

2. *The Besht on Pirkey Avoth*, eds. Isaiah Aryeh and Joshua Dvorkes, trans. Charles Wengrov (Jerusalem: Feldheim Publishers, 1974), p. 69.

Selected Bibliography

Primary Sources

Aichinger, Ilse. *Herod's Children*. New York: Atheneum, 1963.

Amichai, Yehuda. *Not of This Time, Not of This Place*. New York: Harper & Row, 1968.

Antin, Mary. *The Promised Land*. 1912; reprinted New York: Houghton Mifflin, 1969.

Bellow, Saul. *Herzog*. New York: Fawcett, Crest, 1961.

———. *Mr. Sammler's Planet*. New York: Viking, 1970.

Borowski, Tadeusz. *This Way for the Gas, Ladies and Gentlemen*. Translated by Barbara Vedder. New York: Penguin Books, 1976.

Bryks, Rachmil. *Kiddush Hashem*. Translated by S. Morris Engel. New York: Behrman House, 1977.

Cahan, Abraham. *The Rise of David Levinsky*. 1917; reprinted New York: Harper & Row, 1960.

Cohen, Arthur. *In the Days of Simon Stern*. New York: Random House, 1973.

———. *A Hero in His Time*. New York: Random House, 1976.

Elman, Richard. *The 28th Day of Elul*. New York: Scribner, 1967.

———. *The Reckoning: The Daily Ledgers of Newman Yagodah Advokat and Factor*. New York: Scribner, 1969.

———. *Lilo's Diary*. New York: Scribner, 1969.

Friedlander, A. H. *Out of the Whirlwind: A Reader of Holocaust Literature*. New York: Doubleday, 1968.

Fuks, Ladislav. *Mr. Theodore Mundstock*. New York: Orion, Grossmann, 1968.

Gary, Romain. *The Dance of Genghis Cohn*. Cleveland: World Publishing, 1968.

Glatstein, Jacob et al. *Anthology of Holocaust Literature*. New York: Atheneum, 1973.

Howe, Irving, and Greenberg, Eliezer; eds. *A Treasury of Yiddish Poetry*. New York: Holt, Rinehart & Winston, 1969.

————. *A Treasury of Yiddish Stories.* New York: Schocken, 1973.

Karmel-Wolfe, Henia. *The Baders of Jacob Street.* New York: Lippincott, 1969.

Kosinski, Jerzy. *The Painted Bird.* New York: Pocket Books, 1966.

Levi, Primo. *Survival in Auschwitz.* New York: Collier Books, 1961.

Lind, Yakov. *Soul of Wood and Other Stories.* New York: Grove Press, 1965.

Lustig, Arnöst. *Night and Hope.* New York: E. P. Dutton, 1962.

Malamud, Bernard. *The Assistant.* New York: Farrar, Strauss & Cudahy, 1957.

————. *Idiots First.* New York: Farrar, Strauss & Cudahy, 1963.

————. *The Fixer.* New York: Farrar, Strauss & Cudahy, 1966.

————. *The Tenants.* New York: Farrar, Strauss & Cudahy, 1971.

————. *The Magic Barrel.* 1958; reprinted New York: Pocket Books, 1972.

Neugeboren, Jay. *An Orphan's Tale.* New York: Holt, Rinehart & Winston, 1976.

Nissenson, Hugh. *My Own Ground.* New York: Farrar, Strauss & Giroux, 1976.

Ornitz, Samuel. *Haunch, Paunch, and Jowl.* New York: Boni & Liveright, 1923.

Ozick, Cynthia. *The Pagan Rabbi and Other Stories.* New York: Alfred A. Knopf, 1971.

————. *Bloodshed.* New York: Alfred A. Knopf, 1976.

Potok, Chaim. *The Chosen.* New York: Fawcett, Crest, 1967.

————. *In the Beginning.* New York: Alfred A. Knopf, 1975.

Rawicz, Piotr. *Blood from the Sky.* New York: Harcourt Brace & World, 1964.

Rosen, Norma. *Touching Evil.* New York: Curtis Books, 1969.

Rosenfeld, Isaac. *Passage from Home.* New York: Dial Press, 1946.

Roth, Henry. *Call It Sleep.* 1934; reprinted New York: Avon Books, 1964.

————. "The Surveyor." *The New Yorker* (6 August 1966): 22–30.

Roth, Philip. "Eli, the Fanatic." In *Goodbye, Columbus and Five Short Stories.* 1959; reprinted New York: Bantam, 1974, pp. 179–216.

————. *The Ghost Writer.* New York: Farrar, Strauss & Giroux, 1979.

Schaeffer, Susan Fromberg. *Anya.* New York: MacMillan, 1974.

Schwarz-Bart, André. *The Last of the Just.* New York: Atheneum, 1960.

Singer, Isaac Bashevis. *The Seance and Other Stories.* New York: Farrar, Strauss & Giroux, 1968.

———. *Enemies, A Love Story.* 1972; reprinted Greenwich, Conn.: Fawcett, Crest, 1973.

———. *A Crown of Feathers and Other Stories.* 1973; reprinted New York: Fawcett, Crest, 1974.

Singer, Israel Joshua. *The Family Carnovsky.* New York: Vanguard Press, 1969.

Stern, Daniel. *Who Shall Live, Who Shall Die.* New York: Crown Publishers, 1963.

Wallant, Edward Lewis. *The Human Season.* New York: Harcourt Brace Jovanovich, 1960.

———. *The Pawnbroker.* New York: Manor Books, 1962.

Yezierska, Anzia. *Hungry Hearts.* 1920; reprinted New York: Arno Press, 1975.

Secondary Sources

Adorno, T. W. "Engagement." In *Noten zur Literatur.* Frankfurt on Main: Suhrkamp Verlag, 1965, pp. 127–29.

Alter, Robert. *After the Tradition: Essays on Modern Jewish Writing.* New York: E. P. Dutton, 1969.

Alvarez, A. *Beyond All This Fiddle.* New York: Random House, 1969.

Angoff, Charles. "Jewish-American Imaginative Writings in the Last Twenty-five Years." *Jewish Book Annual* 25 (1967): 129–39.

Arendt, Hannah. *Eichmann in Jerusalem: A Report on the Banality of Evil.* New York: Viking, 1965.

Atkin, Maurice D. A. "United States of America." *Encyclopedia Judaica.* Jerusalem: Keter, 1972.

Auden, W. H. "The Wandering Jew." *New Republic* (10 February 1941): 185–86.

Baal Shem Tov. *The Besht on Pirkey Avoth.* Edited by Isiah Aryeh and Joshua Dvorkes. Translated by Charles Wengrov. Jerusalem: Feldheim Publishers, 1974.

Babylonian Talmud. Erubin, 13b. Translated into English with notes, glossary, and indices. Edited by Rabbi Dr. I. Epstein. London: Soncino, 1938.

Baumbach, Jonathan. *The Landscape of Nightmare: Studies in the Contemporary Novel.* New York: New York University Press, 1965.

Beck, Evelyn Torton. "The Many Faces of Eve: Women, Yiddish, and I. B. Singer." *Working Papers in Yiddish and East European Studies.* No. 16. New York: YIVO, 1975.

Bell, Daniel. "A Parable of Alienation." In *Mid-Century: An Anthology of Jewish Life and Culture in our Times*, Edited by Harold Ribalow. New York: Beechhurst Press, 1955, pp. 133–151.

Bell, Pearl K. "An Orphan's Tale." Rev. of *An Orphan's Tale* by Jay Neugeboren. *New York Times Book Review* (15 August 1976): 12–13.

Bellow, Saul. Introduction. *Great Jewish Short Stories*. New York: Dell Publishing Co., 1963.

Ben Sasson, Haim Hillel. "History." *Encyclopedia Judaica* (1972).

Bloom, Solomon. "Dictator of the Lodz Ghetto: The Strange History of Mordechai Chaim Rumkowski." *Commentary* (February 1949): 111–22.

Booth, Wayne C. *The Rhetoric of Fiction*. Chicago: University of Chicago Press, 1961.

————. *A Rhetoric of Irony*. Chicago: University of Chicago Press, 1974.

Bourjaily, Vance. "Cool Book on a Warm Topic." Rev. of *The Professor of Desire* by Philip Roth. *New York Times Book Review* (18 September 1976): 50.

Boyers, Robert, ed. *The Legacy of the German Refugee Intellectuals*. New York: Schocken, 1972.

Buchen, Irving. *Isaac Bashevis Singer and the Eternal Past*. New York: New York University Press, 1968.

Cahan, Abraham. *Bleter fun mayn lebn*. 5 vols. New York: Forverts Association, 1926–31.

Cazden, Robert Edgar. *German Exile Literature in America 1933–1950*. Chicago: American Library Association, 1970.

Chapman, Abraham, ed. *Jewish American Literature: An Anthology*. New York: New American Library, 1974.

Cohen, Sandy. *Bernard Malamud and the Trial by Love*. Rodop: N.V., 1974. Melville Studies in American Culture. Edited by Robert B. Pearsall.

Cohen, Sarah B. *Saul Bellow's Enigmatic Laughter*. Champaign-Urbana: University of Illinois Press, 1974.

Dawidowicz, Lucy S. *The War Against the Jews: 1933–1945*. New York: Holt, Rinehart & Winston, 1975.

————, ed. *A Holocaust Reader*. New York: Behrman House, 1976.

Des Pres, Terrence. *The Survivor: An Anatomy of Life in the Death Camps*. New York: Oxford University Press, 1976.

Ducharme, Robert. *Art and Idea in the Novels of Bernard Malamud: Toward the Fixer*. The Hague: Mouton, 1974.

Eckardt, Alice L. "The Holocaust: Christian and Jewish Responses." *Journal of the American Academy of Religion* (September 1974): 453–69.

Fiedler, Leslie A. *The Jew in the American Novel.* New York: Herzl Press, 1959.

———. *No! In Thunder—Essays on Myth and Literature.* Boston: Beacon Press, 1960.

———. *Waiting for the End.* New York: Stein & Day, 1964.

Field, Leslie A., and Field, Joyce W., eds. *Bernard Malamud and the Critics.* New York: New York University Press, 1970.

———. *Bernard Malamud: Twentieth-Century Views: A Collection of Critical Essays.* Englewood Cliffs, N.J.: Prentice-Hall, 1975.

Fine, David M. "Attitudes Toward Acculturation in the English Fiction of the Jewish Immigrant 1900–1917." *American Jewish Historical Quarterly* 62, 1 (1973): 45–56.

Fisch, Harold. *The Dual Image: The Figure of the Jew in English and American Literature.* London: World Jewish Library, 1971.

Frankel, Haskel. "Interview with Bernard Malamud." *Saturday Review* (10 September 1966): 39–40.

Freedman, Morris. "The Jewish Artist as Young American." *Chicago Jewish Forum* 10, 2 (Winter 1952): 212–14.

Frye, Northrop. *Anatomy of Criticism: Four Essays.* 1957; reprinted New York: Atheneum, 1968.

Fuchs, Daniel. "Saul Bellow and the Modern Tradition." *Contemporary Literature* 15 (Winter 1974): 67–89.

Grebstein, Sheldon N. "Bernard Malamud and the Jewish Movement." In *Contemporary American-Jewish Literature—Critical Essays.* Edited by Irving Malin. Bloomington: Indiana University Press, 1973.

Gregory, Horace. "East Side World." *Nation* (27 February 1935): 140.

Guttman, Allen. *The Jewish Writer in America: Assimilation and the Crisis in Identity.* New York: Oxford University Press, 1971.

Hassan, Ihab. "The Qualified Encounter: Three Novels by Buechner, Malamud, and Ellison." In *Radical Innocence: Studies in the Contemporary American Novel.* Princeton, N.J.: Princeton University Press, 1961, pp. 153–79.

"Hebrewing Up." Rev. of *In the Days of Simon Stern* by Arthur Cohen. *Times Literary Supplement* (15 March 1974): 269.

Hersch, Edith. "Hillel." *Encyclopedia Judaica.* Jerusalem: Keter, 1972.

Hicks, Granville. "Literary Horizons." *Saturday Review* (10 September 1966): 37–39.

Howard, Jane. "The Belated Success of Henry Roth." *Life* (8 January 1965): 76.

——. "Mr. Bellow Considers His Planet." *Life* (3 April 1970): 59.

Howe, Irving. "The Stranger and the Victim: The Two Jewish Stereotypes of American Fiction." *Commentary* 8 (August 1949): 147–56.

——. *Decline of the New*. New York: Harcourt Brace Jovanovich, 1970.

——. Introduction. *Selected Stories*, by Y. L. Peretz. New York: Schocken, 1974.

——. *World of Our Fathers*. New York: Harcourt Brace Jovanovich, 1976.

Hoyt, Charles Alva. "The Sudden Hunger: An Essay on the Novels of Edward Lewis Wallant." In *Minor American Novelists*. Edited by Charles Alva Hoyt. Carbondale: Southern Illinois University Press, 1970, pp. 118–37.

Kazin, Alfred. "Fantasist of the Ordinary." *Commentary* 24 (July 1957): 89–92.

——. *Contemporaries*. Boston: Little, Brown, 1962.

——. "Living with the Holocaust." *Midstream* 16 (June–July 1970): 3–7.

Kermode, Frank. "Bernard Malamud." *New Statesman* (30 March 1962): 452–53.

Klein, Marcus. *After Alienation: American Novels in Mid-Century*. Cleveland: Meridian, 1965.

Lamont, Rosette C. "Bellow Observed: A Serial Portrait." *Mosaic* (Fall 1974): 247–62.

Langer, Lawrence. *The Holocaust and the Literary Imagination*. New Haven and London: Yale University Press, 1975.

Liebman, Charles. *The Ambivalent American Jew*. Philadelphia: Jewish Publication Society of America, 1973.

Liptzin, Sol, trans. and ed. *Peretz*. New York: YIVO, 1947.

Lorch, Thomas M. "The Novels of Edward Lewis Wallant." *Chicago Review* 19, 2 (1967): 78–91.

Lyons, Bonnie. "The Symbolic Structure of Henry Roth's *Call It Sleep*." *Contemporary Literature* 13 (Spring 1972): 186–203.

——. "An Interview with Henry Roth." *Shenandoah*, 25, 1 (Fall 1973): 48–71.

Macy, John. "The Story of a Failure." Rev. of *The Rise of David Levinsky* by Abraham Cahan. *The Dial* (22 November 1917): 521–23.

Malamud, Bernard. "Theme and Content and the New Novel." *New York Times Book Review* (26 March 1967): 28–29.

Mandel, Ruth B. "Bernard Malamud's *The Assistant* and *A New Life*: Ironic Affirmation." *Critique* 7 (Winter 1964–65): 110–21.

Mashberg, Michael. "American and Jewish Refugees." *Midstream* (November 1970): 74–78.

Mellard, James M. "Malamud's Novels: Four Versions of Pastoral." *Critique* 9 (1967): 5–19.

Mudrick, Marvin. "Who Killed Herzog? or, Three American Novelists." *University of Denver Quarterly* 1 (Spring 1966): 61–97.

Nahmad, N. M. *A Portion in Paradise and Other Jewish Folk Tales.* New York: Schocken, 1970.

Ozick, Cynthia. "America Toward Yavneh." *Judaism* 19 (1970), 264–82.

———. "In the Days of Simon Stern." Rev. of *In the Days of Simon Stern* by Arthur Cohen. *New York Times Book Review* (3 June 1973): 6.

———. "Hanging the Ghetto Dog." *New York Times Book Review* (21 March 1976): 47.

The Passover Haggadah. Edited by Nahum N. Glatzer. 1953; rev. ed. New York: Schocken, 1969.

Patai, Raphael. *The Tents of Jacob: The Diaspora—Yesterday and Today.* Englewood Cliffs, N.J.: Prentice-Hall, 1971.

Pavel, Ernst. "Fiction of the Holocaust." *Midstream* 16 (June–July 1970): 14–26.

Peretz, Y. L. "Escaping Jewishness." Translated by Sol Liptzin. In *Peretz.* Edited by Sol Liptzin. New York: YIVO, 1947.

Persecution and Resistance Under the Nazis: A Bibliography. The Weiner Library Catalogue Series, No. 1. London: Valentine, Mitchell, 1960.

Podrom, Cyrena N. "Isaac Bashevis Singer: An Interview and a Biographical Sketch." *Wisconsin Studies in Contemporary Literature* 10 (Winter 1969): 1–38; 10 (Summer 1969): 323, 332–51.

Poliakoff, Leon. *Harvest of Hate.* Syracuse, N.Y.: Syracuse University Press, 1954.

Pollock, Theodore M. "The Solitary Clarinetist." Ph.D. dissertation, Columbia University, 1959.

Rabinowitz, Dorothy. *New Lives: Survivors of the Holocaust Living in America.* New York: Alfred A. Knopf, 1976.

Rahv, Philip. Introduction. *A Malamud Reader.* New York: Farrar, Strauss & Giroux, 1967.

Richman, Sidney. *Bernard Malamud.* New York: Twayne, 1966.

Rideout, Walter B. *The Radical Novel in the United States 1900–1954.* Cambridge: Harvard University Press, 1956.

―――. " 'O Workers' Revolution . . . The True Messiah': The Jew as Author and Subject in the American Radical Novel." *American Jewish Archives* 2 (October 1959): 157–75.

Rischin, Moses. *The Promised City: New York's Jews 1870–1914.* Cambridge: Harvard University Press, 1962.

Roback, A. A. "Sarcasm and Repartee in Yiddish Speech." *Jewish Frontier* (April 1951): 19–25.

Robinson, Jacob, ed. *The Holocaust and After: Sources and Literature in English.* Ass't by Mrs. Philip Friedman. Jerusalem: Yad Vashem and YIVO, Israel Universities Press, 1973.

Rosen, Norma. "The Holocaust and the American-Jewish Novelist." *Midstream* (October 1974): 54–62.

Rosenfeld, Isaac. *An Age of Enormity: Life and Writing in the Forties and Fifties.* Cleveland: World Publishing Co., 1962. ["David Levinsky: The Jew as American Millionaire," pp. 273–81; "Terror Beyond Evil," pp. 197–99; "The Meaning of Terror," pp. 206–209.]

Roth, Philip. "Writing American Fiction." *Commentary* (March 1961): 223–33.

―――. "Jewishness and the Younger Intellectuals." *Commentary* (April 1961): 350–51.

―――. "Writing About Jews." *Commentary* (December 1963): 446–52.

―――. "In Search of Kafka and Other Answers." *New York Times Book Review* (15 February 1976): 6–7.

Rovit, Earl. "A Miracle of Moral Animation." *Shenandoah* 16 (Winter 1965), 59–62.

―――. "Some Shapes in Recent American Fiction." *Contemporary Literature* 15 (Spring 1974): 539–61.

Rubin, Louis. "The Experience of Difference: Southerners and Jews." In *The Curious Death of the Novel: Essays in American Literature.* Baton Rouge: Louisiana State University Press, 1967, pp. 262–81.

Schereschevsky, Ben-Zion. "Bigamy and Polygamy." *Encyclopedia Judaica.* Jerusalem: Keter, 1972.

Scholem, Gershom. "Kabbalah." *Encyclopedia Judaica.* Jerusalem: Keter, 1972.

Schulz, Max F. *Radical Sophistication: Studies in Contemporary Jewish American Novelists.* Athens: Ohio University Press, 1969.

Sherman, Bernard. *The Invention of the Jew: Jewish-American Education Novels 1916–1964*. New York: T. Yoseloff, 1969.

Siegel, Ben. "Victims in Motion: Bernard Malamud's Sad and Bitter Clowns." *Northwest Review* 5 (1962): 69–80.

Solotaroff, Theodore. "Bernard Malamud's Fiction: The Old Life and The New." *Commentary* 33 (March 1962): 197–204.

Stern, Daniel. "Bernard Malamud and the Art of Fiction: An Interview." *Paris Review* 65 (Spring 1975): 40–64.

Stern, Guy. "Exile Literature: Sub-Division or Misnomer." *Colloquia Germanica* (1971–72): 167–78.

———. "Über das Fortleben des Exilromans in der sechziger Jahren." In *Revolte und Experiment: Die Literatur der sechziger Jahre in Ost und West*. Edited by Wolfgang Paulsen. Heidelberg: Lothar Steihm Verlag, 1971, pp. 165–85.

Tigay, Jeffrey. "Adultery." *Encyclopedia Judaica*. Jerusalem: Keter, 1972.

Trilling, Lionel. "Another Jewish Problem Novel." *Menorah Journal* 16, 4 (April 1929): 378.

Vortriede, Werner. "Vorlaufige Gedanken zu einer Typologie der Exilliteratur." *Akzente* 6 (1968), 556–75.

Wershba, Joseph. "Not Horror, but Sadness." *New York Post Magazine* (14 September 1958): M2.

Wiesel, Elie. *Souls on Fire*. New York: Vintage, 1972.

Wieseltier, Leon. "In a Universe of Ghosts." Rev. of *New Lives: Survivors of the Holocaust Living in America* by Dorothy Rabinowitz. *New York Review of Books* (25 November 1976): 20–23.

Index

death and rebirth, themes of, 16, 49,
184–86. See also *Anya, Call It
Sleep, Days of Simon Stern, In
the, Enemies, A Love Story,
Human Season, The, Mr.
Sammler's Planet, Pawnbroker,
The,* and *Rise of David Levinsky,
The*
"Defender of the Faith" (Philip Roth),
12
Des Pres, Terrence, 6–7, 87. See also
Survivor, The
Diaspora, 16, 19, 176
Doctorow, E. L. See *Ragtime*
Dostoyevski, Fëdor, 65, 66, 146

Ecclesiastes, 145, 154
Eckhart, Meister, 154
Eichmann, Adolf, 13, 46, 147–51
Eichmann in Jerusalem (Arendt), 148
Eliade, Mircea, 16
Elijah, 68, 79, 173–74, 178, 184
"Eli the Fanatic" (Philip Roth), 46–47
Eliot, George, 167
Ellison, Ralph, 68
Enemies, A Love Story (Singer), 5–6,
7–9, 43, 47–51, 74, 78–80, 87–88,
93, 96–97, 98, 102–3, 104, 109,,
110, 111, 113–35, 152, 155,
167–68, 172, 176, 177, 181–89;
original Yiddish version, 7,
131–35, 165
America: as home, 48–49, 78,
114–17, 119–20, 130–31, 181–83;
185–86; nature in, 115–16, 183;
as wasteland, 74, 79, 125–26, 131
authorial distance in, 5–6, 7–8,
48–51, 74, 78, 79–80, 87–88, 104,
111, 117–18, 125, 132–34,
137–38, 181, 186, 187
characters of: age of, 9; "comic survivor figure," 59, 93–94, 126–28,
161, 195n; as immigrant-
survivors, 5–6, 48–49, 74, 78–79,
87–88, 115, 116, 117–18, 119,
121, 125, 128, 130–31, 181–87
death and rebirth, themes of, 43, 49,
110, 115, 124–25, 129, 185–86
Europe in, 109, 113–14, 117, 155
evil world, theme of, 115, 116–17,
119, 126, 129–30

homelessness and isolation, themes
of, 78, 109, 110, 114–17, 120,
126, 131, 172, 176, 182, 186
Jewish past and, 5–9, 47–51, 78–80,
87–88, 109, 110, 114, 115, 119,
120–21, 122–23, 124–26, 130–31,
133, 135, 167–68, 176, 177,
183–84, 188–89
language in, 7, 9, 78, 96–97,
127–28, 131–33, 134–35, 183
literature and history in, 8, 49–51,
78–79, 87–88, 98, 102, 104,
117–18, 125, 152, 168, 184,
186–88, 189
Yiddish literature and, 130, 132,
167
"Envy; or Yiddish in America"
(Ozick), 46
Epstein, Leslie. See *King of the Jews*
"Epstein" (Philip Roth), 12
exile literature, 7, 15

Family Carnovsky, The [*Di mis-
hpokhe Karnofski*] (Israel Joshua
Singer), 15
Faulkner, William, 68
Fiedler, Leslie, 4, 5, 48, 78
"First Seven Years, The" (Malamud).
See *Magic Barrel, The*
Fixer, The (Malamud), 6, 49, 50–51,
53–54, 58, 64–66, 70–72, 74, 77,
79, 87–88, 182, 184, 188, 195n
Focus (Miller) 29–30
Frank, Anne, 12
Friedman, Bruce Jay, 9. See also *Stern*
Fuks, Ladislav. See *Mr. Theodore
Mundstock*
Frye, Northrop, 7–8

Gary, Romain. See *Dance of Genghis
Cohen, The*
Gentlemen's Agreement (Hobson),
29–30
Ghost Writer, The (Philip Roth), 12
Glatstein, Jacob, 40
Gold, Michael. See *Jews Without
Money*
goles, 17
Goodbye Columbus (Philip Roth), 4
Grade, Chaim, 40, 194n

About the Author

Dorothy Seidman Bilik was born in New York City. A graduate of Brooklyn College, she received her master's degree from the University of Cincinnati and her doctorate from the University of Maryland, where she is assistant professor in the department of Germanic and Slavic Languages and Literature. Bilik teaches Yiddish language and literature, Holocaust literature, and Eastern European Yiddish culture, engaged, as she describes it, in an attempt "to explore and even preserve and transmit a vanished culture." She is at work on a study of Moshe Kulbak, a Soviet-Yiddish writer.